D1545765

DAFYDD AP GWILYM AND THE EUROPEAN CONTEXT

Dafydd ap Gwilym
and the
European Context

HELEN FULTON

UNIVERSITY OF WALES PRESS
CARDIFF
1989

British Library Cataloguing in Publication Data

Fulton, Helen, *1952–*

    Dafydd ap Gwilym and the European Context.
    1. Poetry in Welsh.   Dafydd ap Gwilym —
    Critical studies
    I. Title
    891.6′611

    ISBN 0-7083-1030-3

Typeset in Wales by Megaron, Cardiff
Printed in Great Britain by The Bath Press, Avon

To
Gareth and Declan

Acknowledgements

I am particularly indebted to Stephen Knight, Rachel Bromwich and R. Geraint Gruffydd, who each contributed a great deal of time and expert advice.

Special thanks are also due to Max Walkley, Pat Watson, Georgina Bitcon and Ann Parry Owen, who checked my translations, though the final responsibility for inaccuracies or inelegancies is entirely mine.

Finally I would like to thank Susan Jenkins for her editorial skill and patience, and my family for their moral support.

Contents

Introduction

THE poetry of Dafydd ap Gwilym is usually approached either as a closed set of themes and stylistic devices or in the wider context of Dafydd's European influences. The purpose of this book is to show that these two approaches can, and should, be developed together in order to understand the full significance of Dafydd's verse.

It is my intention to discuss the traditions of courtly and popular poetry which have particular relevance for a study of Dafydd's work, and then to examine his poems in the light of this literary context as well as his own social context. We shall see from this study that Dafydd's literary inheritance from Europe came to him already assimilated into the native poetic tradition, and that his function as a court-poet was instrumental in shaping his verse.

The early tradition of critical scholarship, with its implications of a non-native inspiration for Dafydd's poetry, was examined very thoroughly by Theodor Chotzen,[1] who summarized the theories of origin so far proposed by early scholars. These were the Italian, Classical, Provençal, Medieval Latin, and Celtic theories, and Chotzen himself favoured the last.[2] According to this theory Dafydd's poetry reflects two literary currents, the poetic tradition of the *bardd teulu*, whose poetry scarcely survives before Dafydd's time, and an ultimately Continental influence which passed through the great Welsh monasteries to Dafydd and his contemporaries.

Since the time of Chotzen's seminal work on European influences, the publication of Thomas Parry's edition of Dafydd's poems, *Gwaith Dafydd ap Gwilym* (Gwasg Prifysgol Cymru, 1952) has had a profound effect on the study of Dafydd's literary inheritances.[3] Chotzen based his researches on the early edition by Owen Jones, William Owen Pughe and Edward Williams, *Barddoniaeth Dafydd ap*

Gwilym (London, 1789), containing about two hundred and fifty poems. Parry's edition of an authentic canon of about one hundred and fifty poems laid an essential foundation for further research.

More recently, the whole question of Dafydd's sources and the possible influences on his work has been taken up by Rachel Bromwich, who has combined Chotzen's work with the researches of later Welsh scholars in order to show the difficulties involved in tracing Dafydd's sources of inspiration, and also the range of literary traditions and conventions on which he draws. It is apparent from Dr Bromwich's research that the native Welsh tradition deserves more attention than it has previously attracted from scholars concerned with Dafydd's literary heritage.

Dr Bromwich's findings, which have been published in three important works,[4] may be summarized as follows:

1. The *gogynfeirdd* inheritance provides a substantial native tradition of praise-poetry on which Dafydd draws.
2. In terms of the contemporary social and historical situation, opportunities for borrowing from Continental literary traditions would have been available to Dafydd.
3. Support for his likelihood of borrowing can be found in certain poems which use Continental motifs or *topoi*, or which are in the form of identifiable European genres such as the dream-vision or fabliau.
4. Reference to Ovid and to Ovidian themes also suggests Dafydd's familiarity with secular Latin literary traditions.
5. The importance of nature themes in early Celtic literature allowed foreign conventions on similar topics to be more readily assimilated into Dafydd's poetry.
6. With regard to foreign borrowings, a similar pattern can be seen in medieval Irish literature, where *fin' amors* themes occur in Irish court-poetry and popular French motifs occur in later Irish folk-poetry, representing two waves of borrowing. This pattern is also found in Middle English verse such as the Harley Lyrics.
7. In addition to the influence of Welsh court-poetry and foreign borrowings, there is some evidence, particularly in the Grammar of Einion Offeiriad and in the later *canu rhydd*, of a thriving popular poetic tradition in Wales on which Dafydd also drew. His poetry shares themes with this popular tradition, as well as verbal parallels with poems quoted in the Grammar.

8. However, this early popular tradition may itself have been influenced by the French popular conventions of the *reverdie* and the personification of birds.
9. It is therefore likely that Continental influence reached Dafydd in the form of court-poetry as well as popular song, probably through different channels of a sub-literary kind. This is supported by the evidence of Irish poetry which also consists of courtly and popular types, both of which show traces of French *fin' amors* motifs.
10. Finally, the role played by the Welsh *clêr*, and their links with the *clerici vagantes*, must be considered as another way of transmitting *fin' amors* material in a non-courtly form.

The result of Dr Bromwich's researches is to bring into prominence the significance of popular tradition, both Welsh and European, in relation to Dafydd's poetry. The importance of popular motifs, and Dafydd's evident familiarity with a range of international popular literary conventions imply that the channels through which Dafydd received foreign borrowings were of a non-literary and non-bardic kind, and that his connection with European courtly love-poets is even more tenuous and indirect than has previously been assumed.

In the courtly love-lyrics of European poets, with their emphasis on a moral and ideological code of love, and in the formal eulogies of the *gogynfeirdd* which are restricted in terms of form and function, popular motifs such as the nature opening may be used with conscious effect but without becoming the major theme of the court-poem. The inheritors of the troubadour tradition, the trouvères and the Italian poets of the *dolce stil nuovo*, went further in excluding popular motifs almost entirely in order to concentrate and purify the essence of *fin' amors*. As a result, this restricted type of courtly love-poetry remained crystallized in time and form, with no possibility of further growth, to be gradually superseded by the more dynamic conventions of popular song which utilized narrative rather than philosophical argument.

The vital force of medieval poetry had its basis in popular rather than courtly conventions. Learned and court-poets, such as Walther von der Vogelweide in Germany and Colin Muset in France, who assimilated elements from popular literature into their court-poems, were able to achieve a more flexible interpretation of courtly love akin to that of medieval romance. In this process of assimilation, popular motifs were raised in status to the point where they were no longer considered inappropriate in a formal love-poem. The same process took place in the medieval Latin love-lyric, where seasonal celebration and drinking-songs were composed in accordance with classical poetic standards.

In Wales, Dafydd was among the inheritors of a relatively inflexible and limited poetic tradition which was enlivened and transformed by the assimilation of originally popular material into the structure of bardic poetry. This development from *gogynfeirdd* to *cywydd* poets, with a movement away from abstract concepts of love and virtue to a less formal and rigid interpretation of love, parallels the European poetic movement and the subsequent elevation of popular and oral traditions to an acceptable source of bardic imagery and diction.

It is therefore more accurate to envisage Dafydd as part of a native literary continuum which is homologous to, as well as influenced by, that of France, rather than as the end-product of a long line of Continental influence. Such influence manifestly reached Dafydd, but at a popular rather than courtly level. Those vestiges of *fin' amors* which appear in his work are far removed from troubadour poetry, having been processed through northern French romance and popular poetry, while his own native tradition of praise-poetry is at least equally influential in determining his stance towards the women of his love-poems. His poetry can best be regarded as a blending of extended courtly love conventions from Europe into a base of native *gogynfeirdd* tradition, with a leavening of popular material both oral and literary.

The assimilation of popular and courtly traditions, which characterized Dafydd's poetry as much as French lyric and romance, took place as a result of the emergence of a specific kind of audience in France and Wales. This audience, comprising remnants of an older aristocracy and a new nobility of wealthy townspeople and royal servants, responded to a literature which justified their social position and excluded those who were considered inferior. The conventions of troubadour poetry, though specific to southern France and the rise of the knights, carried with them a guarantee of nobility that provided an attractive basis for northern French poetry and romance, while the conventions of popular poetry were immediately accessible to non-aristocratic audiences. Such a combination acted powerfully to reassure the new nobility of its social status, and could be turned, in the form of satire, against the lower bourgeoisie to discourage their upward mobility.

In order to demonstrate the centrality of Dafydd's position as a representative of courtly literature in northern Europe, I will first establish the uniqueness of *fin' amors* as a troubadour manifestation and the elements which remained pervasive throughout later courtly lyrics. I will then discuss the growing significance of popular material in medieval poetry from the evidence of vernacular and Latin secular poetry, before examining the native tradition of court-poetry in Wales before Dafydd's time. Finally, I will look at the whole canon of Dafydd's verse in the light of the native courtly tradition, the conventions of extended courtly love, and his integration of influences from popular verse into the bardic tradition.

CHAPTER I

Court-poetry and the Provençal Courtly Love-lyric

COURT-POETRY of Europe during the Middle Ages must be seen not only as a great literary flourishing of lyric themes and techniques, but also as a response to certain social and cultural conditions. Many of the conventions of court-poetry, including the whole structure of themes known as courtly love, relate to social institutions peculiar to the aristocratic society of a particular place and time. As court-poetry developed over the centuries and was disseminated among the countries of Europe, most of these conventions lost their original social reference and became mere stylizations or idealizations, symbols of a type of society—chivalric, courtly, aristocratic, feudal—which was fast disappearing. Thus although we may find a continuum of courtly conventions from the twelfth-century troubadour lyrics to fifteenth-century English lyrics, there is a vast difference in the relevance of these poetic conventions to the society in which they were composed.

The nature of medieval society in Europe, particularly France, has been analysed and discussed by many historians. The most significant development from the point of view of medieval poetry was the creation of a powerful ruling aristocracy out of the early feudal system. Robert S. Hoyt traces the evolution of feudal states in tenth-century France, including the powerful Capetian dynasty in the royal domain of Paris and Orleans:

> The rest of France was divided into feudal principalities, ruled by lords who were for all practical purposes independent, although most of them were royal vassals. A few were the descendants of Carolingian counts who had converted their offices into hereditary titles and their counties into hereditary fiefs; others were magnates who had risen to local predominance and had gained recognition from the king and

1

from the lesser lords of the region. All of them fulfilled the same functions in their provinces as the king in the royal domain: maintaining a precarious semblance of order, protecting their subjects and vassals from external attack, and enforcing obedience from them.[1]

The function of the feudal system (which was not uniform throughout Europe but was subject to many regional variations) was therefore to provide protection and sustenance for people living in what were predominantly agricultural communities, subject to vagaries of nature and warfare.

During the eleventh century, however, the old feudal hierarchy had to adjust to economic changes and the growth of larger towns and villages. In such a climate of economic growth, and an ever-widening gap between the material status of the nobility and that of the peasants, the concerns and values of the ruling aristocracy became an important key to the conventions found in court-poetry. More significantly, the changing economic and political climate encouraged the emergence of the knights into the ruling class.

The original distinction between a nobleman and a knight was one of class and economy; knights were aristocratic warriors attached to fortresses commanded by noblemen, and formed only a small part of the total aristocracy. However, Georges Duby has shown that, during the twelfth century, knights began to build their own 'fortified houses' and thus vie with the ruling noblemen for manorial status.[2] This distinction within the aristocracy was therefore gradually eliminated until it came to be accepted that knights were also noble and possessed the same power to command as the rest of the aristocracy: knights who were once supported by noblemen in their castles came to acquire estates and property of their own which were passed on to their heirs. In this way, an exclusive ruling nobility, organized in regional centres, based on wealth, and maintained by judicious and selective marriage, arose out of the original feudal hierarchy of king, nobleman and knight. In addition a religious element entered the secular ceremony of bestowing knighthood, formalizing the Church's recognition of knighthood as a service to God as well as a necessary part of secular society.

This new class of knights and the court-centred society to which it belonged provided both the themes and the audiences for a new type of literature which drew on the accepted conventions of noble behaviour, presenting them in an idealized, 'romantic' way. The new literature has been described by R.W. Southern:

The portrayal of knightly character in verse and song, in sermons and educational manuals, impressed a unity of social ideals on the Latin world. The themes of Charlemagne and King Arthur, of the Crusade and the formation of the Christian ruler, were all sustained by and developed round the character of the knight. From very humble origins the word 'knight' became charged with an emotional significance, which outlived the social environment of its birth. The literature in which the ideal of knighthood was set forth had probably little influence on the art of government or the practical life of society at large; its impact was on the individual in his social conduct, in the refinement of his emotions and manners.[3]

This romantic, courtly tradition, as opposed to the earlier epic tradition epitomized by the *Chanson de Roland* and other *chansons de gestes*, was interpreted in a variety of ways by poets and story-tellers of the eleventh and twelfth centuries, notably Chrétien de Troyes. Geoffrey of Monmouth's Latin prose cycle, *Historia Regum Britanniae*, introduced the 'matter of Britain' to European story-tellers, making available many of the elements of the Arthurian legends previously found only in Latin and early Welsh sources. The emphasis here was on the mystical and supernatural events surrounding the figure of Arthur and his knights, an aspect also found in the Welsh Arthurian tales such as *Culhwch ac Olwen* and *Owein*. Later English romances such as *King Horn* and *Floris and Blancheflour* relied on a brisk plot movement and minimal character delineation and conveyed ideals of chivalry and virtue which were already declining in European society.

Without doubt, the major contribution of French writers to the genre of romantic literature was their development of the theme of love. The works of Chrétien de Troyes in the twelfth century did much to disseminate certain ideas about love as an ennobling force, an idealized relationship between a knight and his lady which inspired both to reach extremes of noble behaviour. But it was in the genre of lyric-poetry, in the work of the twelfth-century troubadours of Provence, that the concept of courtly love as a manifestation of courtly behaviour received its most powerful generating impulse.

Many writers and critics have offered interpretations of the social and literary importance of the theme of courtly love.[4] Clearly, most of the medieval literary examples of romantic love are 'courtly' in the sense that they involve members of the aristocracy and the values of a noble society. So the term 'courtly love' can have a broad application referring to the theme of love in romantic courtly literature in general, or a much more specific application with regard to the lyrics of the troubadours. In courtly love literature in general, the theme of love can be used as a medium through which other important social preoccupations such as the nature of chivalry, the functions of knighthood, and the connection between secular and spiritual intentions can be examined. In the case of the troubadour love-lyrics, however, the theme is much more individual and subjective, voicing the concerns and preoccupations of a particular section of society, young knights in pursuit of social advancement.

Two interpretations of courtly love, labelled by Roger Boase as 'Courtly Experience' and 'Stylistic Convention',[5] offer broad and non-specific definitions of courtly love. The first of these interpretations emphasizes the universal possibility of the phenomenon of courtly love. Consequently, medieval court-poets are not considered to be startlingly innovative but merely the presenters of poetic formats and a technical vocabulary able to rationalize those ideas about love already expressed in different literatures and societies. So for Peter Dronke, 'the feelings and conceptions of *amour courtois* are universally possible, possible in any time or place and on any level of society'.[6]

The second interpretation understands courtly love as a purely literary format comprising a set of established themes and images from which poets could draw their material. Paul Zumthor's theory of medieval poetry depends on the isolation of certain *types*, or literary devices, which are transferable from one context to another.[7] He discusses the medieval concept of *courtoisie* and its importance firstly as a set of social structures and secondly as a form of literary expression. Zumthor is arguing for the uniformity of the poetic expression of the ideals of courtly love; for the existence, reflected first of all in twelfth-century poetry, of a common vocabulary and set of idioms which were translated into other languages and societies of Europe.

These broad-based interpretations of courtly love, represented by Dronke and Zumthor, stress the importance of the social concept of *courtoisie* in producing a generalized courtly love literature, but minimize the contributions of particular societies and individual poets. Roger Boase, on the other hand, takes a narrower view and applies the label 'courtly love' only to 'the complex of ideas and sentiments implicit in the troubadour movement'.[8] This means that, while certain attitudes towards love and certain modes of expression may be universally possible, for Boase the concept of courtly love is confined to twelfth-century Provence. He further defines courtly love as 'a comprehensive cultural phenomenon: a literary movement, an ideology, an ethical system, a style of life, and an expression of the play element in culture, which arose in an aristocratic Christian environment exposed to Hispano-Arabic influences'.[9] In his terms, therefore, the entire courtly love ethic was first formulated and given literary expression by Provençal society and its poets, with later interpretations by poets of other societies providing different versions of the original courtly love ethic.

The critical dichotomy between broad and narrow understandings of courtly love needs to be maintained and not argued away, since both views have validity. Though the impulses behind courtly love literature may be universally possible, nevertheless each society has to re-invent the concept in accordance with its own values and requirements. This is how the court-poets of Europe, including Dafydd ap Gwilym and his contemporaries, came to produce poems which have affinities with, and yet are so different from, the work of the troubadours. The conventions and motifs of *fin' amors* were culture-specific for twelfth-century Provence, but the concept of courtly love in its broader sense was transferable to any other medieval western society where a similar social climate prevailed— namely, the existence of an emergent aristocracy whose rise to power was ratified through courtly lyric and romance.

It is convenient, then, to have separate terms to distinguish the different types of courtly love, the general and the specific. I shall be using 'courtly love' to mean the characteristic set of literary conventions associated with the genre, and *fin' amors* to mean the concept of courtly love as expressed by the troubadours in particular. An examination of troubadour poetry and its preoccupying issues will clarify the function of *fin' amors* and its role in justifying the pursuit of power by young men of birth and ambition.

Fin' amors, in its original Provençal form, is characterized by a set of key terms and motifs, and by an intrinsic element of conflict. Both these features are directly related to the audience of knights to whom the poems are addressed. The language of the lyrics is based on an assumption of feudal organization, so that the main topic—the love relationship—is described in terms of the feudal relationship between lord and vassal. The element of conflict, which appears in a number of forms, reflects the struggle of the knights to enter the ruling class and to be accepted by the old nobility.

Certain themes and forms, essential to the whole nature of the poetry, are used by nearly all the troubadours although these are also subject to individual emphases and interpretations. Central to the whole movement, from Guilhem IX of Aquitaine onwards, are the key concepts of *joi* and *amors*, explored experimentally at first by the twelfth-century troubadours, and with increasing confidence by the later poets. Discussing Guilhem's poetry, L.T. Topsfield says:

> Guilhem sees the conflict between *Jois*, or the impulse to find one's own individual happiness, and *Amors*, the power which demands submission to a social code of courtly behaviour. This conflict, which is resolved in the poetry of Raimon de Miraval with the triumph of *Amors*, becomes a major theme in troubadour poetry of the twelfth century.[10]

The troubadours understand *joi* as the peak of *fin' amors*, both physically and emotionally, and it can even be used synonymously for *fin' amors* itself.

Another pair of abstract qualities which are crucial to an understanding of the troubadour love-lyric is *mezura* and *jovens*. The first means literally 'moderation' and implies a particular combination of self-control, discretion, and mastery of behavioural codes, by which desire and passion can be assimilated into a rational way of life. This concept was particularly important to Marcabru's understanding of *fin' amors* and characterizes the poetry of later troubadours, such as Peire d'Alvernhe, who sought a rational explanation of earthly love.

The term *jovens*, strictly speaking 'youth' or 'youthfulness', acquired a special significance for the troubadours, representing the sum total of virtues and obligations demanded of a true courtly lover. Topsfield considers Bernart de Ventadorn to represent 'the spirit of *jovens*'.[11] Georges Duby has described the social position of the aristocratic *iuvenes* in the literal sense of the word, calling them 'a mob of young men let loose, in search of glory, profit and female prey, by the great noble houses in order to relieve the pressure on their expanding power'.[12] He suggests that the courtly love-lyrics of the second half of the twelfth century represent the voice of this section of society, and that the abstract concept of *jovens* is a poetic transformation of the existing ideals and requirements of the aristocratic youth.

Finally, the combined qualities of *pretz e valor* make an important contribution to the troubadour concept of the true courtly lover. Topsfield translates the first as 'prestige and reputation' and the second as 'personal courtly virtue',[13] while Lazar defines them further in relation to other courtly virtues:

> Lorsqu'on est *cortes* et *jovens* et que l'on garde scrupuleusement la *mezura* en toute chose, on se voit attribuer *pretz e valor*. Ce ne sont point des vertus qui engendrent la *cortezia* mais qui sont plutôt les effets de celle-ci, ses marques de distinction.[14]

These pairs of interdependent abstract ideals and virtues—*joi* and *amors*, *mezura* and *jovens*, *pretz* and *valor*—are important links between the metaphor of the love relationship, and the reality of the knight's position in society. These qualities not only define and identify a true courtly lover, possessor of *cortezia*, they are also the hallmarks of a true chivalric knight, possessor of *courtoisie*. The opposition between *joi* and *amors* reflects the tension between a knight's pursuit of individual success, and his need to submit to a higher social order. *Mezura* is the quality by which the spirit of *jovens* is restrained and brought within the confines of chivalry. *Pretz e valor* are courtly virtues which can operate within the arena of love or on the battle field.

Troubadour poetry can therefore be seen in a particular perspective, embodying a set of ideals and abstract concepts which nevertheless had some reality within a courtly chivalric society. The poets had to balance individual expression of sentiment against the social expectations of their audience, a compromise which leads modern critics to question the 'sincerity' of the lyrics. As Maurice Valency points out:

> The knight who sang in the love-song may never have quite existed as an individual, but as a social being his existence was of great significance to his time. The love-song portrayed the behaviour of an ideal character in a situation which evidently had the utmost reality for the society to which it was addressed . . .
>
> The troubadour *chanson* is the song of the suppliant knight, but the troubadour was not necessarily a suppliant knight; he was a song-writer in the guise of a suppliant knight. What the song expressed was therefore not the details of his private life, but his emotions projected through the medium of the archetypal lover, whom he conceived in accordance with the normal expectation of the audience for which he worked.[15]

What we find, therefore, in troubadour poetry, is an abstraction, an idealization, of the social reality of the knight and chivalry, expressed through the concepts of the courtly lover and *cortezia*. The 'courtliness' of courtly love has a literal frame of reference, in that it evolved in the courts of the nobility of southern France, and its poetry was usually addressed to, or in praise of, noblewomen at court. The social function of this court-poetry becomes clearer in the context of the impact made by the penetration of the knighthood into the old nobility. This new class of noblemen, based on merit rather than birth, brought with it a new set of ideals, expressed in terms of love since most of the knights at court were young and unmarried. Troubadour poetry reflects the ideology of the knights and their relationship to the existing aristocracy.

When we turn to the poems themselves, we can see that the pursuit of love is envisaged as part of a totality of chivalric activities, juxtaposed to references to Crusades, battles, political events, and social ethics. Love as a social reality is given poetic interpretation through the use of the feudal relationships between a knight and his lord: the figure of the beloved, the *domna*, takes on the role of the overlord, and the poet plays the part of her loyal knight. The whole nature of *fin' amors* depends on this unequal relationship between the lover and the beloved. Moreover, the pursuit of spiritual ennoblement through love is not only a striving to be worthy of the beloved, but also an analogy of the knight's duty to serve God. From both these levels, secular and religious, unresolvable conflicts arise to test the lover.

The reciprocal notions of service and reward epitomize the love relationship: the lover vows to serve his lady faithfully, while she is obliged to offer in return a reward in the form of her physical presence. Bernart de Ventadorn expresses the idea of courtly love service and total submission to his *domna* in 'Non es meravelha':

> Bona domna, re no.us deman
> mas que.m prendatz per servidor,
> qu'e.us servirai com bo senhor,
> cossi que del gazardo m'an.
> ve.us m'al vostre comandamen,
> francs cors umils, gais e cortes!
> ors ni leos non etz vos ges,
> que.m aucizatz, s'a vos me ren.[16]

(Noble lady, I ask nothing of you except that you take me as your servant, for I will serve you as I would a noble lord, however it may be as regards reward. Behold me at your command, noble and indulgent one, lively and courtly. You are not at all a bear or lion, that you would kill me if I surrender myself to you.)

For Bernart, Amors is the allegorical representation of his beloved, and he addresses Amors as the source of all his joy and pain. Other troubadours may turn their pleas into complaints or even rejection if their hope of reward is too rigorously denied, but they are seldom able to throw off entirely the chains of love.

The simultaneous joy and pain experienced by the lover as mutually dependent products of *amors* give rise to the set of motifs and images most often associated with courtly love-poetry. The sufferings of the lover—sleeplessness, pain, grief—and the opposite and concurrent emotions of joy, hope and fulfilment, are expressed in literal terms and also through a range of conventional metaphors and figures. Thus Guilhem IX, for example, describes his love in terms of bondage, implying the recurring notion of love as a two-edged weapon with the power to wound as well as to inflame:

> Farai chansoneta nueva
> Ans que vent ni gel ni plueva;
> Ma dona m'assai' e.m prueva,
> Quossi de qual guiza l'am;
> E ja per plag que m'en mueva
> No.m solvera de son liam.
>
> Qu'ans mi rent a lieys e.m liure,
> Qu'en sa carta.m pot escriure.
> E no m'en tengatz per yure
> S'ieu ma bona dompna am,
> Quar senes lieys non puesc viure,
> Tant ai pres de s'amor gran fam.
> (Hill and Bergin, no.5, 11.1–12)

(I'm going to compose a new little song, before wind and snow may sweep down; my lady tries and tests me on the way in which I love her; and yet whatever quarrel she may pick with me, I would not set myself free from her chain.

On the contrary, I yield and deliver myself up to her, so that she may write me into her charter. And do not take me for a madman if I love my noble lady, for without her I could not live, I have developed such a great hunger for her love.)

The poem opens with the common formula 'Farai chansoneta', indicating it is for public hearing. The poet addresses his audience directly, presenting himself as love's slave, whose very existence depends on his lady. Though his captor torments him, he has no desire to escape.

The metaphors of imprisonment and starvation caused by love are commonplaces of courtly love-poetry, and indicate an awareness of composing within certain conventions. Bernart de Ventadorn says, for example:

> Per bona fe e ses enjan
> am la plus bel' e la melhor.
> del cor sospir e dels olhs plor,
> car tan l'am eu, per que i ai dan.
> eu que.n posc mais, s'Amors me pren
> e las charcers en que m'a mes,
> no pot claus obrir mas merces,
> e de merce no.i trop nien?
> (Hill and Bergin, no.27, 11.17–24)

(In good faith and without deceit, I love the most beautiful and the best, my heart sighs and my eyes weep, for I love her so much, because of which I am in pain. But what can I do, if Love takes me, and that prison in which it has put me cannot be opened by any key except mercy, and of mercy I find none in her?)

Having stated the inherent paradox of love in the first half stanza, the poet presents himself as a helpless victim and the personified figure of Love as his gaoler. His only release is through his lady's *merce*, another key term indicating one of the conventional virtues sought by the poets in their mistresses, but rarely obtained. The references to mercy have a dual significance, suggesting a connection with religious worship and prayers for God's mercy, and also the secular pleas for patronage voiced by both poets and knights to their lords.

The kind of reward sought by the troubadours when they entreat their ladies to show them mercy is invariably of a physical nature, and allusions to different kinds of sensual experience occur sporadically throughout the troubadour lyrics, for example:

> Quan la candela. m fetz vezer
> Voz baizan rizen, a! cal ser!
> (Raimbaut d'Aurenga)

(When the candle lets me see you, kissing and laughing, oh! what an evening!)

> C'ab sol lo bel semblan que.m fai
> can pot ni aizes lo.lh cossen,
> ai tan de joi que sol no.m sen,
> c'aissi.m torn e.m volv'e.m vire.
> (Bernart de Ventadorn)

(For only from the beautiful expression she shows me, when she can or when opportunity allows it, I have so much joy that I cannot even know what I feel, for thus do I turn and spin and reel.)

> E no.n puesc trobar mezina
> Si non au vostre reclam
> Ab atraich d'amor doussana
> Dinz vergier o sotz cortina
> Ab dezirada compahna.
> (Jaufre Rudel)[17]

(And I can find no cure for it except from your call, with its attraction of sweet love, within the orchard or beneath a curtain with my longed-for companion.)

Lazar maintains that *fin' amors* is ultimately an adulterous love, with physical consummation as its specific aim,[18] but in fact few of the troubadours express this intention explicitly, and some clearly reject it altogether. The conflict between the joy and pain caused by love is actually symptomatic of a more fundamental paradox of courtly love, the difficulty of reconciling physical desire with the cerebral interpretation of love as the source of all virtues.[19] The quest for spiritual ennoblement through devoted love-service is incompatible with the desire for physical possession, and yet the two are inextricably bound together. The search for some kind of resolution or compromise for this situation is a preoccupation of most of the troubadours.

The early troubadours tended to keep the impulses towards spiritual ennoblement and towards physical fulfilment clearly apart. Guilhem IX actually composes two different kinds of poem, the ribald burlesques such as 'Farai un vers pos mi sonelh', and the more serious love-poems such as 'Farai chansoneta nueva'.[20] Guilhem thus compartmentalizes the two sides of love, the carnal and the spiritual, as being more or less mutually exclusive, though equally acceptable.

In searching for a similar kind of dichotomy, Jaufre Rudel made a major contribution to the ideology of courtly love through his concept of *amors de lonh*, or 'love from afar'. Geographical distance between a poet and his mistress rationalizes the emotional conflicts inherent in courtly love: the separation causes longing and suffering but at the same time produces joy because it preserves the fine quality of *amors* and prevents it from descending to mere lust. Jaufre's desire for physical union can therefore be safely expressed without undermining the value of his love:

> Amors de terra lonhdana,
> Per vos totz lo cors mi dol;
> E no.n puesc trobar mezina

Si non au vostre reclam
Ab atraich d'amor doussana
Dinz vergier o sotz cortina
Ab dezirada companha . . .

De dezir mos cors no fina
Vas selha ren qu'ieu pus am;
E cre que volers m'enguana
Si cobezeza la.m tol;
Que pus es ponhens qu'espina
La dolors que ab joi sana;
Don ja non vuelh qu'om m'en planha.
(Hill and Bergin, no.22, 11.8–14 and 22-8)

(Love of a distant land, for you my whole heart grieves; and I can find
no cure for it except from your call, with its attraction of sweet love,
within the orchard or beneath a curtain with my longed-for companion
. . . My heart does not cease from desire for the one whom I love the
most; and I believe my wish deceives me and deceiving robs me of her;
for that grief which is cured by joy is sharper than a thorn; because of
that, I never wish that I should be pitied for it.)

The double-sided nature of *fin' amors*, causing both joy and pain, is
still an inevitable part of *amors de lonh*: though the poet suffers pain
he is not to be pitied, for it is because of this cruel separation that he
experiences the exquisite sensations of *amors* and *dezir*. Through
amors he can strive to achieve *joi*, his own personal summit of bliss as
opposed to the conventional feelings shared by all love-poets; and the
distance between him and his beloved will prevent his desire from
becoming realized as *cobezeza* or 'lust', and therefore maintain his
love at an appropriately idealistic level. Topsfield interprets the
poem, 'Quan lo rius de la fontana', in a similar way, emphasizing
Jaufre's fear of the strength of his love:

Jaufre . . . fears that physical desire growing to *cupiditas* may remove
from him the joy of the 'distant' aspiring love, represented by *dezir*,
that he feels. . . This grief and the *Jois* which can assuage it are
synonymous with 'distant' love. . . a love which controls indiscriminate
physical desire and . . . is preferable to the wish for immediate physical
possession.[21]

The early troubadours are concerned with *amors* as a source of joy
and virtue, but through their imagery and diction *amors* is personified
in terms of conflict, pain, and suffering. *Amors de lonh* offers a means
of balancing the pursuit of love in its purest spiritual form against the
desire for physical consummation, but it also has the effect of
intensifying the polarization between joy and torment.

Other troubadours offer similarly individual interpretations of *amors* in an attempt to find a personal joy untainted by suffering or dissatisfaction. These attempts result in a bias towards either the spiritual or the physical aspect of love, since a perfect synthesis of the two aspects is impossible. Those poets who pursue love with the expectation of physical reward must try and rationalize the clash between this expectation and the idealized concept of *fin' amors* as the source of all virtue.

Bernart de Ventadorn, composing slightly later than Jaufre Rudel in the latter half of the twelfth century, justifies his moral and spiritual interpretation of courtly love by making a distinction between *fin' amors coraus* (fine true love), and *amors comunaus* (common love): that is, between the courtly love of the nobility and the base love of the common people. Unlike Marcabru, a contemporary of Jaufre's who considered *fin' amors* in terms of its moral implications, Bernart defines the concept entirely within a social context, openly acknowledging the *service* demanded by courtly love and his own allegiance to its demands and conventions:

> Chantars no pot gaire valer,
> si d'ins dal cor no mou lo chans;
> ni chans no pot dal cor mover,
> si no i es fin' amors coraus.
> per so es mos chantars cabaus
> qu'en joi d'amor ai et enten
> la boch' e.ls olhs e.l cor e.l sen . . .
>
> . . . Amor blasmen per no-saber,
> fola gens; mas leis no.n es dans,
> c'amors no.n pot ges dechazer,
> si non es amors comunaus.
> aisso non es amors; aitaus
> no.n a mas lo nom e.l parven,
> que re non ama si no pren! . . .
>
> . . . En agradar et en voler
> es l'amors de dos fis amans.
> nula res no i pot pro tener,
> si.lh voluntatz non es egaus.
> e cel es be fols naturaus
> que de so que vol, la repren
> e.lh lauza so que no.lh es gen.
>
> (Hill and Bergin, no.28, ll.1–7, 15–21, 29–35)

(Singing can scarcely be worth anything unless the song originates from within the heart; and the song cannot originate from the heart unless there is in it a heartfelt pure love. In view of this, my singing is superior, since I have joy of love and towards it I direct my mouth and eyes, my heart and mind . . .

Love is criticized by ignorant foolish people; but that does no harm to it, for love cannot decay at all, unless it is a vulgar love, and that is no love at all; it has nothing except the name and the appearance, since it only loves on condition of receiving something in return . . .

In accord and willingness is the love of two noble lovers. There can be nothing advantageous from it unless the desire is equal. And he is indeed a natural fool who blames it [love] for the fact that it has desire, and recommends to it what is not noble.)

The poem opens conventionally with a discussion of the poet's song, proceeds to its definition of *fin' amors*, and concludes by applying this definition to the poet's own relationship with his beloved, in which he is the conventional courtly lover devoted to the service of his lady. In his service to love, Bernart uses 'la boch' e.ls olhs e.l cor e.l sen' (mouth and eyes and heart and mind), thereby defining his approach to love as both sensual and emotional, that is, essentially worldly rather than spiritual or abstract. His love-poetry is that of a participator, not a spectator like Marcabru, and this lack of detachment allows him to appreciate and welcome *amors* by means of conventional and emotive terms such as *ver, enjans, fos, faus, voler, voluntatz, fols, lauza*. The opposite sides of love, joy and despair, are felt all the more keenly by Bernart since he experiences both on a sensual rather than spiritual plane, on which love is not an idealized aspiration towards inner bliss but a realistic longing for *fin' amors*, with two faithful lovers sharing and returning love equally.

Nevertheless, these attempts by the early troubadours to recognize a duality of impulses within the courtly love ideal do not succeed in being completely clear-cut and unambiguous. The conflict is inevitably present. In the poetry of Guilhem IX, verbal echoes between the burlesque poems and the sensuous love-poems imply a relationship between the two genres, a suggestion that each contains elements of the other. Moreover, the courtly love-poems themselves, while concentrating on the inner joy produced by love, contain an explicit awareness of the importance of physical contact in contributing to that joy.

A similar realization of the intrusion of physical desire into the courtly love ideal causes Jaufre Rudel to reject completely the kind of

amors which seeks physical fulfilment and to aspire instead to the *fin'
amors* based on *joi* and *valor*:

> Amor no vueill ni dezir,
> Tan sap d'engan ab mentir;
> Per aiso vos ho vueill dir
> C'anc d'Amor no.m puec jauzir.
> Tan l'en vueill mal e l'azir
> Can m'en membra.m fai languir.
> Fols fui per Amor servir,
> Mas vengut em al partir.[22]

(I do not want or desire love, it knows so much of deceit by lying; for I
want to tell you this, that I can never rejoice in love. So much do I wish
it harm, and hate it since remembering it makes me weaken. I was
foolish in serving love, but we have come to the end.)

With the fervour of the proselytizer, Jaufre attempts to suppress by
force the physical aspect of love and to embrace entirely the idealized
abstract notion of *fin' amors*.

For Bernart de Ventadorn too, *fin' amors* was the fine, true love
which brought moral and spiritual satisfaction and the inevitable and
necessary physical desire which accompanied it often clashed with his
pursuit of pure love. In his poem 'Per melhs cobrir' he shows how
unable he is to accept the two sides of love as mutually dependent:

> A mo talen volh mal, tan la dezire,
> e pretz m'en mais, car eu fui tan auzatz
> qu'en tan aut loc auzei m'amor assire,
> per qu'eu m'en sui conhdes et ensenhatz.
> e can la vei, sui tan fort envezatz:
> vejaire m'es que.l cors al cel me salha.
>
> Dins en mo cor me corrotz e.m azire,
> car eu sec tan las mias volontatz. –
> mas negus om no deu aital re dire,
> c'om no sap ges com s'es aventuratz.
> que farai doncs dels bels semblans privatz?
> falhirai lor? mais volh que.l mons me falha![23]

(I hate my inclination, so much do I desire her, and I value myself more
for it since I was so bold that I set my love in such a high place, because
of which I am amiable and well-bred. And when I see her, I am so
completely overwhelmed: it seems to me that my heart jumps to the
sky. Within my heart I am grieved and angry, because I follow my
desires so much. But no man ought to say such a thing, for a man does
not know at all what will befall him. What shall I do then about the fair

and intimate glances? Shall I be false to them? I would rather that the world be false to me!)

Both Topsfield and Wilhelm see a similarity between Bernart and Ovid in his interpretation of *amors* and his use of imagery such as the wounds, loss of reason, and even death, caused by love.[24] C.B. West agrees that 'the conventional descriptions of lovers' symptoms' may be traced to Ovidian influence but draws a definite line between Ovidian love and courtly love:

> Fundamentally, however, the attitude of the courtly lover is probably more in harmony with contemporary religious feeling than with the spirit of Ovid. The cynical advice of the *Ars Amatoria* reveals a conception of love so far removed from the seriousness of amour courtois, which both requires and confers nobility of heart and mind, that it is difficult to believe that the actual doctrine of courtly love owes much to Ovid.[25]

It is possible to see a similarity between Ovid and Bernart in 'the interplay of sacred and profane values (the constant shifting of the woman from angelic divinity dispensing grace to a superior earthly lord-lady bestowing favours to a Satanic denier of the "natural" functions of life)'.[26] But while Ovid could reconcile the fulfilment of physical desire with the spiritual demands of pagan deities, the Christian troubadours display considerable ambivalence towards the accepted conventions of courtly love and the inevitable opposition of religious teaching. This conflict between the religious and the worldly is another aspect of the fundamental paradox of courtly love, the inability to pursue it at both a spiritual and a physical level, and most of the troubadours attempt to come to terms with the spiritual conflict in some way. Jaufre Rudel and Bernart de Ventadorn were able to rationalize the problem through their understanding of *amors* and *joi*, while others such as Marcabru and, later, Peire Cardenal, solved the dilemma by detaching themselves from love and trying to define it for others.

The insoluble conflict within the very concept of courtly love is given new direction by Marcabru, whose distinction between *fin' amors* and *fals' amors*, echoed by other troubadours, is based on a Christian understanding of love. He evades the conflict by distancing himself from the quest for love, commenting on its conventions and its realities through metaphor and satire rather than from personal involvement. His stand is that of the Church, supporting *bon' amors* as a love between two social equals which is acceptable in the eyes of the Church, and condemning *amars* as the base physical lust of adulterers. But he also recognizes *amors fina* as the true refined love between two lovers of noble birth, a concept shared by Bernart de Ventadorn.[27]

This is Marcabru's alternative to a code of courtly behaviour which he condemns as lustful and adulterous. He parodies the sufferings of a courtly lover with biting wit and mocks those who commit adultery in the name of courtly love:

> Drudari' es trassaillida
> E creis Putia s'onor,
> E.il moillerat l'ant sazida
> E so.is fait dompnejador;
> Tant m'es bel quand us s'en vana
> Cum de can quant prist farina.[28]

(Love is violated and the domain of Prostitution increases, for the married men have taken possession of it and made themselves wooers; when one of them boasts of it I am as pleased as I would be with a dog who kneaded dough.)

Satire and parody are not the only means by which Marcabru demonstrates his faith in a love based on Christian morality. In 'Pois la fuoilla revirola' he contrasts the harmony of the natural world, achieved through the pursuit of a true and noble love, with the confusion and deceit of human society governed by lust and pride. His *pastorela*, 'L'autrier jost' una sebissa' deviates from the normal pattern of the genre to show the virtuous peasant girl, representing a chaste and morally acceptable love, repulsing the advances of the knight who seeks a shallow and carnal love through deceit and flattery.

Through metaphor and allegory, Marcabru is able to deliver moral statements concerning men's behaviour, in particular the folly of pursuing adulterous love at the expense of virtues such as *mezura* and *jovens*. He laments the disintegration of love into mere carnal lust, and seeks to replace it with an idealized perfect love, *amors fina* or *fin' amors*, an ideal similar to that of Jaufre Rudel and Bernart de Ventadorn. This perfect love, based on *mezura*, excludes the possibility of physical consummation and is monitored by God rather than by man.

In his poem 'Pus mos coratges s'es clarzitz',[29] Marcabru's appeal to *fin' amors* is couched in the form of a prayer, and his use of terms familiar to courtly love-poetry, such as *bontat, merce, pres, confortat,* bears a distinctly Christian overtone. While Bernart de Ventadorn equated love with his lady, addressing one as the other, Marcabru equates love with God, or at least with Christian doctrine, a difference which underlines the attitudes of the two poets, one firmly rooted in the temporal social world, and the other aspiring to spiritual purification in a Christian sense.

Because of this aspiration, and his general preoccupation with moral philosophy, Marcabru is frequently concerned with virtues and vices in the abstract, compared with the application of these in specific situations explored by other troubadours. Many of his poems contain warnings or advice regarding the kind of behaviour to which men should aspire, while others are introspective assessments of his own struggles to practise what he preaches. In both kinds of poems, the courtly virtues which form the basis of courtly love, and the vices which threaten it, are examined in isolation from love itself.

Though Marcabru can distance himself from the implications of his teachings by the barriers of satire, allegory or direct instruction to others, he nevertheless confesses to fears of his own weakness. These fears are overcome by his faith in the rationality and self-control which God has given him so that he can avoid the traps of foolishness, deceit, and lust which endanger all men.

The conflict between the spiritual and physical aspects of love is therefore reduced to a minimum in Marcabru's poetry, since he equates the spiritual ennoblement of the lover with the Christian pursuit of spiritual salvation. *Amors* must be followed as a religion, devoid of any sensual temptations which will destroy the structure of moral virtues upon which *amors* is based. Marcabru's solution to the conflict is perhaps the most drastic: he denies that any conflict exists and interprets love as a one-dimensional set of Christian virtues.

Two other troubadours who adopt a similar approach in stressing the validity of Christian morals are Peire d'Alvernhe, a contemporary of Marcabru's in the mid twelfth century, and Peire Cardenal, composing a generation later at the beginning of the thirteenth century. Unlike Marcabru, Peire d'Alvernhe experiences the joy and despair of love, but within limits controlled by *mezura*, the virtue so essential to Marcabru. He avoids the exaggerated imagery of the sufferings of love and believes that true love, by its nature, must ultimately lead to happiness. But he also recognizes the difficulty of reconciling secular conventions with Christian doctrine, and his religious lyrics reveal a turning away from the worldly pleasures of courtly love in favour of God's forgiveness and ultimate salvation. In contrast to Marcabru, therefore, he associates love with the temporal world rather than with the pursuit of a Christian morality, and makes a conscious choice between them. In his poem 'En estiu, qan crida.l iais', he uses the metaphor of imprisonment, conventionally used to describe the power of courtly love, to convey the conflicting demands of love and religion:

> Pres ai estat en caslar,
> ab so que no.i aus estar,
> e pero non puosc mudar
> de mos enemics no.l gar;
> ja non serai assaillitz,
> q'en auta roch' es bastitz.
>
> Si.l portiers me vol iurar
> c'autre non i lais intrar,
> segur poirai gerreiar;
> mas al sagramen passar
> tem que serai escarnitz,
> que mil vetz i sui faillitz.[30]

(I have been a prisoner in a castle, but I do not dare to remain in it, and yet I cannot help defending it against my enemies; I shall never be attacked, since it is built on a high rock.

If the gatekeeper would swear to me that he will not let anyone else enter it, I could wage war securely; but if the oath is broken I fear that I will be ridiculed, since I have failed in this a thousand times.)

The symbolism here is profound and enigmatic: the castle may be a metaphor for both religion and love, and the gatekeeper may represent the strength of the poet's own faith in God which he must use to sustain him in the fight against temptations of earthly love. For Peire d'Alvernhe, there is no resolution to the conflict except by constant suppression of the sensual by the spiritual.

Peire Cardenal's work, written during the aftermath of the Albigensian Crusades, reflects the increasing disintegration of the courtly love ideal propagated by the earlier troubadours, and its lack of relevance and firm definition within the shifting social framework of southern France in the thirteenth century. The conflicting demands of love are no longer a live issue: moral and religious considerations such as those which preoccupied Marcabru and Peire d'Alvernhe have replaced the urge to define and to realize the ideal of *fin' amors*.

The poetry of Peire Cardenal is wide-ranging in its subjects and forms, condemning corrupt churchmen and noblemen as well as courtly lovers. In one poem he constructs an allegory in which the world is a city of madmen and the wisdom of God is their lost reason; in another, he rejects the ideal of courtly love by negating all the usual images and conventions of the troubadours and contrasting these with positive statements about man's duty to act with reason and truth:

> Ar mi posc eu lauzar d'amor,
> Queno.m tol manjar ni dormir,
> Ni.n sent freidura ni calor,
> Ni no.n badalh ni no.n sospir
>   Ni.n vauc de noit a ratge,
> Ni.n sui conques ni.n sui cochatz,
> Ni.n sui dolens ni.n sui iratz,
>   Ni non logui messatge
> Ni.n sui trahitz ni enganatz,
> Que partitz m'en sui ab mos datz . . .
>
> Mais deu hom amar vensedor,
> No fai vencut, qui.l ver vol dir;
> Quar lo vencens porta la flor,
> E.l vencut vai hom sebelir;
>   E qui vens son coratge
> De las desleials voluntatz,
> Don mou lo faitz desmezuratz
>   E li autre outratge,
> D'aquel vencer es plus honratz
> Que si vencia cent ciutatz.[31]

(Now I can speak well of love since it does not deprive me of food or sleep, nor make me feel cold or hot, nor do I yawn or sigh because of it, or roam at night from passion, nor am I defeated or tormented, nor am I wretched or angry, nor do I hire a messenger, nor am I betrayed or deceived, since I have got out of it [the game] with my dice [as well] . . .

But a man ought to love the one who can conquer, not the one who is conquered, to tell the truth; for the conqueror wears the wreath, and the conquered goes to be buried; and he who conquers his heart, against the unworthy desires which move him to unrestrained deeds and other outrages, will become from that more honoured than if he had conquered a hundred cities.)

Peire Cardenal here combines a subjective statement in the first person with a more general directive urging his listeners to acquire and cultivate self-discipline. The virtues originally associated with courtly love have become transferred to a more widely applicable set of moral standards related to orthodox Christian doctrine.

Not all the later troubadours interpret the ethics surrounding courtly love as a pursuit of spiritual perfection in the religious sense. Guiraut de Bornelh and Arnaut Daniel, composing around the turn of the twelfth century, follow Jaufre Rudel and Bernart de Ventadorn in accepting love in its secular courtly form and trying to find in it an earthly joy which yet will not endanger eternal salvation.

These poets attempt an entire assimilation of the temporal and spiritual aspects of love by equating their pursuit of an earthly mistress with the worship of the Virgin Mary, and terms such as *merce, pechat, ador*, are used with conscious ambiguity. God controls the lover's destiny, and it is to God that appeals for help are directed. Earthly love is distanced to avoid the temptations offered by physical nearness, and there is an implicit analogy with the Crusades conducted by knights in far-off lands, fighting for the love of God. Thus some attempt is made by the poet to keep a spiritual perspective while pursuing an undeniably earthly course, but the conflict remains in the poetry as consciously irreconcilable.

This vying of the two ethical codes is evident in the poetry of Guiraut de Bornelh, regarded by his contemporaries as 'maystre deis trobadors'. Many of the chief conventions of the troubadour lyric before its decline in the next century are summed up in his poems: *bona domna* is his sovereign lady to whom he has sworn allegiance, *fin' amors* is the earthly deity to whose laws he and his mistress are subject, whether this means joy or despair.

This earthly love is entirely separate from the love of God and the quest for spiritual salvation; Guiraut resolves the conflict by failing to acknowledge it explicitly. But in an *alba* (dawn-song) in which the companion keeping watch on the stairs urges the knight to arise and leave his lady, Guiraut implies that God's intervention, represented by the coming of dawn, is an unwelcome spiritual reminder of the temporal nature of his love. There is a strong contrast between the companion's true worship of God in the first stanza, and the knight's rejection of God's creations in favour of earthly love:

> Reis glorios, verais lums e clartartz,
> Deus poderos, Senher, si a vos platz,
> Al meu companh siatz fizels ajuda;
> Qu' eu non lo vi, pois la noitz fon venguda;
>
> Et ades sera l'alba . . .
> Bel dos companh, tan soi en ric sojorn
> Qu'eu no volgra mais fos alba ni jorn,
> Car la gensor que anc nasques de maire

> Tenc e abras, per qu'eu non prezi gaire
> Lo fol gelos ni l'alba.[32]

(Glorious king, true light and brilliance, powerful God, Lord if it pleases you, may you be a faithful help to my companion, for I have not seen him since night has fallen; and soon it will be dawn . . .

Fair sweet companion, I am engaged in such a precious pastime that I would wish dawn or day might never be, for the most noble lady who was ever born of mother I hold and embrace, so that I scarcely have regard for the jealous fool, nor the dawn.)

With Arnaut Daniel, one of the last troubadours to be composing before the Albigensian Crusade, we find what is perhaps the most successful resolution of the ideological conflict of courtly love. While the earlier troubadours begged for God's favour to help them in their pursuit of earthly love, Arnaut explicitly involves God in his courtships with a bold mingling of secular and religious imagery which presupposes God's approval and support:

> Dieus lo chauzitz,
> Per cui foron assoutas
> Las faillidas que fetz Longis lo cecs,
> Voilla, si.l platz, q'ieu e midonz jassam
> En la chambra on amdui nos mandem
> Uns rics convens don tan gran joi atendi.[33]

(May God the indulgent, by whom were absolved the faults committed by blind Longinus, be willing, if it pleases him, that I and my lady may lie together in that room where we may both swear a precious covenant from which I hope for such great joy.)

Arnaut offers masses and burns candles to God to pray for success in love, anticipating that his joy will be doubled in Paradise if he and his beloved enter there together. Thus *fin' amors* is seen as the complement rather than the rival to spiritual joy, and is ultimately sanctified by God as a valid pursuit which does not threaten spiritual salvation.

In contrast to the earlier troubadours, there is no opposition in Arnaut's poetry between a true and perfect *fin' amors* and a base unworthy *amars*. His love is explicitly physical but is also an emotional bond between himself and his lady, the sharing of a secret between true lovers. Arnaut believes that love is maintained by reason as much as passion, and it is his reason which forces him to keep his love a secret, though his heart would declare it openly. Love still brings conflicts and difficulties therefore, but Arnaut has a confidence in the essential goodness of *fin' amors*, and in his own ability to cope with its reversals, which finds expression in most of his poetry.

I have been discussing the 'courtliness' of Provençal poetry with regard to its key terms and motifs, its conventions arising from the kind of society in which it flourished, and the conflicts which were fundamental to its concept of courtly love. The parodies of Marcabru and the irony of Peire Cardenal, as much as the subjective search for a tenable passion by Bernart de Ventadorn and Arnaut Daniel, indicate the actual existence of a particular mode of courtly behaviour which regulated the relationships between noblemen and ladies in an aristocratic society. The sentiments expressed by the troubadours are their own realization of this courtly code in emotional rather than social terms: they use their own experiences of courtly love, whether real or created, to codify and analyse the conventions associated with it. They share many key words of an abstract and connotative kind— words such as *amors, joi, platz, jovens, cortezia, mezura*—and these are further refined and polished by each troubadour, seeking his own understanding of their meaning. Thus Jaufre Rudel understood two kinds of *joi*: the lesser *joi* of lust and the greater, more lasting *joi* of ideal love; Marcabru modified the pursuit of *amors* to become the quest for *fin' amors*, a rationalization of the search for satisfaction in love which will restore social and individual harmony to the quest; and Bernart de Ventadorn experienced love as a spiritual force based on reason or *mezura*.

The troubadours were therefore giving a range of interpretations to ideas which were highly conventional in both social and literary terms. Their *cansos* represent only one genre among several practised by Provençal poets, so that the love-poetry itself is part of a conventional range of topics. Marcabru expressed his ideas about love in the form of the *pastorela* and *tenso*, or debate-poem, as well as by using allegorical figures and metaphor for a moralizing purpose. Among Guiraut de Bornelh's work, we find the *tenso* and *alba* forms, as well as a *sirventes* in which he reflects on the wickedness of a world which once offered so much richness and moral worth.[34] Bertran de Born also composed several *sirventes*, poems dealing with social or moral subjects external to the poet's own personal life, and a *planh*, or lament, on the death of Henry, eldest son of Henry II and Eleanor of Aquitaine.[35] This diversity of poetic material common to all the troubadours points to the official and public nature of their work: their love-poems formed part of a general commentary on religious, political, and social aspects of courtly society, presented in a subjective and emotive manner.

The pre-existence of many troubadour themes and genres in popular song and in Latin poetry emphasizes the function of the troubadours as court-poets, refining and adapting earlier themes for a specifically courtly audience. It seems likely that the *pastourelle*, first given a courtly form as the Provençal *pastorela*, has its origins in popular poetry.[36] Raby disputes the views of Brinkmann and Faral, who tried to prove that the *pastourelle* was an aristocratic genre imitated by popular poets, and supports the theory of popular origin.[37]

This theory has been set out most thoroughly by William Powell Jones, who maintains that the Old French and Provençal pastourelles and goliardic Latin poetry represent three different manifestations of the same theme at about the same time. There is probably a common source in which this theme is the prominent feature, but the nature of this source is still unknown. He concludes, 'The Old French pastourelle has no essential element of plot or setting which does not occur in the folk-songs, whereas the popular pieces contain a variety of character and incident which cannot be found in the courtly poems. The rise of the artistic genre out of the [folk] theme seems highly probable'.[38] Alfred Jeanroy states that the *pastourelle* as an aristocratic genre originated in the south of France before being passed on, in a slightly different form, to the north, and that 'en Provence, la pastourelle avait perdu, dès les plus anciens temps, toute trace de son origine populaire'.[39]

Another genre shared by both courtly and popular poetry is the *aube*, Provençal *alba*, or dawn-song. The immense collection of dawn-songs from both eastern and western countries, compiled by Arthur T. Hatto, indicates the importance of this genre in the literatures of many cultures. Its origin is essentially popular, since the theme of dawn meetings and partings is associated with social rituals such as the greeting of spring, wooing customs, and wedding ceremonies. The courtly treatment of the theme by Provençal poets resulted in a particular type of poem, the *alba*, whose characteristic features include the use of dialogue and a refrain, and the figure of the watchman. The *alba* then influenced the composition of dawn-songs in other vernacular languages of Europe, particularly the *aube* in northern France.

It seems most likely that popular and courtly dawn-songs existed side by side but, as with a great deal of vernacular popular poetry, the non-courtly versions belonged purely to oral tradition and were seldom preserved in writing. It is significant that the dawn-song theme persists in later popular poetry of France, appearing in examples from the fifteenth century and later, suggesting that the genre always enjoyed considerable popularity amongst the folk but only emerged towards the end of the medieval period when folk-poetry was more likely to be written down.

In his examination of French lyric-poetry, Jeanroy suggests that the *aube* may have developed from the type of woman's monologue common in popular poetry.[40] Among the variations which developed from the original theme, he finds two distinct elements which characterize the *aube*, 'le chant du veilleur' and 'les adieux des amants', and points out that the figure of 'le veilleur' belongs to a society that is feudal and chivalric: 'La présence du veilleur dans une aube populaire serait un contresens.' In other words, despite the popular origins of the form, its manifestation as an *aube* (and an *alba*) is entirely courtly.

The troubadours were the earliest European court-poets to make use of popular genres, re-casting them in the form of courtly songs such as the *pastorela* and *alba*. The ribald poems of Guilhem IX are another example of a popular convention, that of burlesque humour, being made directly accessible to courtly audiences, although clearly such poems were set in contrast to the courtly love *cansos*. This use of popular themes became more widespread among the court-poets of northern France and Germany, where survivals of an ancient native folk tradition were absorbed into the repertoire of courtly conventions.

In their style and range of themes, the troubadours offer a variety of individual interpretations of a set of highly conventional ideas which relate specifically to their own society. The fundamental principle of troubadour courtly love is its recognition of the need for conflict and paradox. The individual pursuit of perfect love is in conflict with the social demands of chivalry; the metaphor of the feudal relationship allows the pretence that the beloved is the dominant figure; pursuit of earthly love must be reconciled with the need for spiritual salvation; and a physical reward is desired though this is not in harmony with the ideal of love as virtuous and ennobling. Even on its simplest level, the imagery of courtly love consistently presents the opposing emotions of joy and pain which form the core of the entire convention.

This element of conflict has an important social significance which helps to attach the whole ideology of *fin' amors* to its particular historical situation. Erich Koehler defines the meaning of *fin' amors* in terms of a tension between the old and new nobilities of Provence:

> l'état de tension permanente entre la basse noblesse et la haute féodalité dans leur vie commune à la cour, et la nécessité historique de neutraliser par un idéal de classe commun les divergences qui règnent sur le plan existentiel entre les intérêts de ces deux groupes.[41]

In other words, by constructing an ideal of courtly love which was itself a definition of nobility, the old and new aristocracies could share the illusion that they were united by common values into a single ruling class. However, the internal conflicts present in the *fin' amors* ethic reveal the actual tensions which existed between the two groups and which the poetry was supposed to conceal.

Troubadour poetry therefore relates specifically to the status and concerns of the knighthood, and the paradox of courtly love represents the struggle of this lower nobility to achieve social advancement and power. The poets typically adopt the persona of a young knight swearing allegiance to a woman of higher status, and this poetic convention represents the social reality of young knights seeking advancement through marriage or through the influence of wealthy aristocratic patrons. The women in the poems, though apparently held in high esteem, are merely the passive vehicles by which the knights hope to achieve worldly success. The parodies and diatribes of Marcabru and Peire d'Alvernhe deplore such worldliness and support a commitment to spiritual rather than earthly ennoblement.

In its 'superstructure poétique' as well as its 'infrastructure sociale',[42] troubadour love-poetry is manifestly unique and non-universal. However, the element of conflict which is crucial to its whole framework, and the underlying assumption of social dichotomy and change, occur in other bodies of court-poetry where the functions of praise-poem and love-song are similarly dictated by the ambitions of a social class.

CHAPTER 2

Medieval Latin Secular Poetry

T HE court-poetry of the Provençal troubadours is characteristic
of a particular social structure, specifically that of a feudal
aristocracy in twelfth-century Europe. Other feudal aristocracies of
Europe in the same period embraced the ideals of *fin' amors* with
equal fervour, adapting the concept to their own definitions of
knighthood and nobility. By composing songs on the theme of
courtly love, the court-poets of northern France, Germany and Italy
were reaffirming the élitism of the ruling class and providing a
literature which, by definition, was addressed only to those who
belonged to courtly society.

Medieval lyrics composed in Latin rather than the vernacular
languages of Europe offer a different, but nonetheless élitist,
viewpoint on the subject of love. The élitism is based on a specialized
kind of learning – philosophical, rhetorical and literary—available
only to those (exclusively male) who studied at monasteries and
universities as a preparation for entering into clerical orders.

Linguistically and technically, then, the lyrics composed by these
educated scholars are highly sophisticated and enveloped in a certain
mystique. In terms of theme and subject-matter, the poems go beyond
the range offered by vernacular courtly love-lyrics, bringing in
material from the rich world of popular song as well as from the
classical tradition. Their assimilation of classical and popular themes
and their juxtaposition of formal and comic modes give them a
significant role in the formation of the medieval lyric.

Religious and secular Latin poetry, like Latin and vernacular
lyrics, shared elements in common while also retaining their distinct
characteristics and individual patterns of development. Secular Latin
lyrics sprang from the same classical background as religious poetry,

27

but by the borrowing of themes from popular vernacular song, in particular themes of love and nature, a new type of learned poetry was created. Many of these early Latin lyrics pre-date the rise of the courtly tradition and are therefore composed in a simple style with no formal conventions of love; but they also express an intensity of emotion which prefigures the courtly tradition and which perhaps influenced the later court-poets.

The Latin lyrics made use of popular motifs, such as seasonal description, lament for the passing of the seasons, description of birds, pursuit of love, and humorous anecdotes, which also found their way into court-poetry, but they nevertheless remained learned and scholarly compositions which were not accessible to the masses. Popular material was transformed into a learned mode, which remained comparatively limited and exclusive in appeal because of its specialized skills. The themes of the Latin lyrics, often arising from vernacular folk-song and street entertainment, associate them with contemporary popular culture. But the language, poetic techniques, and classical inheritance of the lyrics show them to be the product of, and addressed to, an educated minority.

The classical inheritance which played an important part in the composition of secular Latin poetry in the medieval period depends particularly on Ovid, a poet whose work epitomizes the overlap between courtly and popular themes. Ovid's own compositions about love, particularly the *Amores*, the *Ars Amatoria* and the *Heroides*, were aimed at the Roman nobility and contain elements of parody and social satire. Many of his metaphors, motifs and situations involving the state of being in love were taken up by vernacular court-poets, particularly the troubadours, during the twelfth-century classical renaissance, and incorporated into their matrix of courtly love conventions. More than this, Peter Dronke recognizes expressions of *courtoisie* and *amour courtois* in Ovid's *Heroides* and *Amores*, such as the lover's plea for love without hope of reward, the notion of love as a source of virtue, the idea of love-service and of *amors de lonh*—all concepts which were taken up and expanded by the troubadours.[1] Some critics, such as Gaston Paris and C.S. Lewis, also propose an Ovidian origin for many elements of the courtly love phenomenon, while others again, for example Lazar and Boase, place less importance on Ovid's role in the formation of the medieval notion of courtly love.

The works of Ovid had more noticeable impact on popular medieval poetry, both in Latin and the vernacular, where the theme of love was expressed in more flexible, though none the less conventional, terms. E.K. Rand has pointed out that the influence of classical scholarship, far from declining during the thirteenth century, was still of seminal importance in the areas of rhetoric, grammar, and secular literature.[2] The *aetas Ovidiana* saw the spread of Ovidian themes and ideas into vernacular works, ranging from major poems such as the *Roman de la Rose* and Chaucer's *Canterbury Tales* to the lyric verse of France and Italy.

Though the didactic tone of the *Ars Amatoria* is not appropriate to lyric-poetry, the basic concept of love as an 'art', a skill with certain techniques to be mastered, underlies much vernacular literature. The love-poems of the *Amores* contain more specific metaphors and situations which could be used by medieval lyric-poets, such as the lover's jealousy, the wounds inflicted by love, the lover's total submission to his lady, and the inhibiting presence of stock characters such as the jealous husband, the door-keeper, and the old woman. Describing the poet's attitude in the *Amores*, L.P. Wilkinson says 'To sum up, his greatest desire is to have her love; failing that, to find her ever worthy of his love; at worst, to be allowed to love.'[3] This attitude is reflected by many vernacular poets composing in a non-courtly mode, where the lover's expectation of success and reward is often more confident than that of the courtly lover.

On the other hand, the erotic element in Ovid's poetry is given less prominence by poets of the medieval period. The joy of physical union as the ultimate goal of love-worship is often made explicit in troubadour poetry but the pursuit of love also has value for its own sake. In the *Amores* particularly, the relationship between the lover and his lady is seldom viewed as anything other than a sexual one which is equally advantageous to both parties. As in the courtly love-lyrics, marriage is an irrelevant issue; the lover is not pursuing a respectable courtship, but a diverting love-affair. In popular lyrics, however, marriage is often seen as a significant end-product of the pursuit of love, though not necessarily a satisfactory one.

Given the extent of Ovidian influence on vernacular poets of the medieval period, it is not surprising that Latin poetry of the same period reflects more noticeable borrowings. Both school poets and Latin lyricists imitated and adapted Ovidian expressions and images for their own purposes, along with those of other classical masters such as Virgil, Martial, and Juvenal. Despite the often erotic descriptions in Ovid's poetry, his work was considered suitable for study in cathedral schools and universities because of its moral and didactic content. This was not the prime function of his work, but it justified its use in the schools.

The Latin lyric-poets made use of their classical and rhetorical training to compose lyrics in the light-hearted mode of popular vernacular poetry, with its emphasis on nature and free-spirited love. For these poems, the eroticism of Ovid provided a recognized precedent and, despite the disapproval of the clergy, Ovid's sensual and confident approach to love was echoed by medieval poets in the depiction of scenes and encounters, in verbal echoes, or in direct quotations and references. Thus these Ovidian influences bring together two basic elements of Latin lyric-poetry, the formal classical training of its composers and the secular enjoyment of love which they uphold.

One of the earliest manuscript collections containing examples of secular Latin lyrics is that known as the Cambridge Songs, a diverse collection of poems, classical, religious and secular, copied in the monastery of St Augustine at Canterbury in the eleventh century, and now in the University Library at Cambridge.[4] It originally contained about a dozen love-poems, but these were partially destroyed after being copied as if they were not considered suitable for inclusion in the manuscript. The Cambridge Songs represent the beginnings of a renaissance in Latin poetry, when the lyrics of the Carolingian period (eighth and ninth centuries), which were largely imitations of classical models, were no longer understood by the noble audiences for whom they were intended, and Latin had to compete with vernacular poetry in theme and style.

As a result of this competition, Latin lyrics became less ornate and rhetorical in style, and used genres and motifs familiar from vernacular poetry. Some of the most famous of the Cambridge Songs are humorous narrative poems such as the 'Modus liebinc' and 'Mendosam quam cantilenam ago', which are akin to the vernacular fabliau tradition.[5] The surviving love-poems indicate borrowings from popular themes, as well as anticipating some of the motifs of court-poetry. For example, 'Levis exsurgit zephirus' (Strecker no. 40) is the lament by a young girl for the loss of her lover, a type of poem well known in the German vernacular tradition. As is common in courtly poems of lament, the poet's mood is related to the season, either harmoniously or contrastively. In this poem, the woman observes the coming of spring but cannot share the general mood of happiness and rebirth.

Another love-poem among the Cambridge Songs, 'Iam dulcis amica venito' (Strecker no.27) has affinities with two popular genres, the *pastourelle* and the German *Wechsel*, or lyrical dialogue. Here the man beseeches his lady to come to his rooms, promising every luxury of food and drink, and the lady replies:

> Non [me iuvat tantum con]vivium,
> qu[antum predulce c]olloquium,
> [nec rerum tantarum uber]tas
> [ut] clara fam[iliaritas.]

(A feast does not delight me so much as sweet conversation, nor an abundance of so many things as much as a bright intimacy.)

At the end of the poem, the poet uses natural imagery to suggest the coming of spring, with all its associations of regeneration and a time for wooing, and finishes with an urgent entreaty that the lady should not delay.

Although these two poems have borrowed their themes from popular poetry, their treatment of them is learned and classical. The latter poem particularly contains specific echoes of Virgil, Ovid, and the Song of Songs; in stanza 10 for example, the poet refers to his lady as 'soror electa', (chosen sister) and in the Song of Songs, the bridegroom says 'Vulnerasti cor meum, soror mea, sponsa' (*Song of Songs* 4:9). The lover's invitation to his lady to share food and drink with him is also echoed in an allegorical dialogue from the Song of Songs (4:12 to 5:1). This motif of the lovers' feast occurs regularly in vernacular poetry, particularly in association with a rustic or non-courtly environment.[6]

The Cambridge Songs mark an important stage in the development of the Latin lyric, showing the fusion of popular themes with learned techniques and language and the early flowering of an impulse towards lyrical composition. The poetry still emanates from the monasteries and cathedral schools of France and Italy, but finds an audience among educated classes of society as well as among the clergy. The Cambridge Songs are popular in many of their themes and motifs (particularly the humorous poems) but are also learned in their style and courtly rather than popular in their appeal. Some of the ways in which love is presented prefigure the courtly love conventions of the Provençal poets, for example, the link between nature and the poet's mood, the lover's plea for his love to be returned, and the association of love and pain, *sine te non potero vivere*; even phrases such as *dulcis amica* anticipate the *bona domna* of the troubadours. The evidence of the Cambridge Songs indicates one of the routes by which popular and classical material may have reached the vernacular court-poets of France.

The Latin poetry of the goliards, or *clerici vagantes*, most of it dating from the eleventh and twelfth centuries, exemplifies a greater interest in popular themes and genres from contemporary vernacular traditions. The exact nature and status of the goliards are difficult to define. Isolated references to 'Golias', fictional primate of the so-called 'goliardic' order, suggest a unified body of reprobate clerics, but this does not necessarily accord with the reality.[7]

It does seem certain that the growth of the universities during the twelfth and thirteenth centuries led to an over-supply of educated clerks who could not find livings as members of the religious or secular clergy and therefore had to fend for themselves. The Church had always disapproved of itinerant clergy, and the unemployed scholars came to be grouped with secular minstrels and wandering entertainers as a generally undesirable class of low social status. In 1231 the Church deprived the wandering scholars of their status as *clerici*, and without the protection of the Church or the law, the profession of 'goliard', if it can be so called, began to decline.

The collection of poems known as the *Carmina Burana* has long been regarded as a comprehensive selection of goliardic songs composed by Latin clerics and scholars during the twelfth and thirteenth centuries. The manuscript belongs to the Bavarian monastery of Benediktbeuern and dates from the end of the thirteenth century. Some of the poems are attributed to known poets such as Walter of Châtillon, but most of them are anonymous and appear to be largely of German origin, with evidence of some French and Italian influence.[8] It is tempting to view the *Carmina Burana* as the song-book of an amorphous group of cheerful students travelling from one university to another in search of knowledge, stopping off at taverns and congenial hostelries along the way. This is certainly the impression conveyed by early modern editors and translators of the poems, such as J.A. Symonds in his book *Wine, Women and Song*, whose witty, if misleading, title suggests an air of Victorian raffishness.

Another view of the goliards is as dissident and anti-social voices undermining the authority of the Church. Their anti-clerical satires, drinking-songs, and often erotic love-lyrics are used as evidence for a decadent and heretical way of life and set of attitudes. Helen Waddell distinguishes between the genuine scholars and a 'baser type, the unfrocked or runaway monk or clerk, and the type, not so base but just as irreclaimable, "the drunken M.A.", the scholar without influence or money to get him a benefice'.[9] In fact, the range of themes and genres in the *Carmina Burana* is eclectic and representative of voices both within and outside the established Church. Far from being anti-establishment, I would argue that the poems all represent the predictable concerns and attitudes of educated clerics either belonging to, or seeking to become part of, an élitist hierarchy.

The Latin secular lyric can be said to define the medieval churchman as part of an intellectual élite in the same way that the courtly love-lyric defines the knight. Like the institution of knighthood, the Church was a recognized means of social mobility within an otherwise rigidly-structured class system. Just as the knights sought entry to the ranks of the nobility, so too the clergy aspired to a material status and privileges appropriate to their learning. This pursuit of money led to various abuses in the Church system which attracted vociferous criticism from both clerics and laymen.

The satires and moralizing poems in the *Carmina Burana* are part of this widespread medieval tradition of anti-clerical satire. Chaucer, for example, frequently ridicules members of the clergy and satirizes their pretensions and materialism, as in his portrait of the friar in the General Prologue to the *Canterbury Tales*. The hypocrisy and greed of highly-placed members of the Church, their pursuit of material wealth, and the power of money to corrupt, are familiar anti-clerical themes found in the *Carmina Burana*.

Such satires may, in part, be voicing the dissatisfactions of the itinerant clerics who, initiated into the skills and learning of the Church, have none the less been deprived of the material rewards offered to the ordained clergy. They belong to the intellectual élite but are excluded from the corresponding social élite because of their lack of position in the hierarchy and its accompanying financial benefit. On the other hand, anti-clerical satires found a sympathetic audience among established members of the Church who deplored clerical abuses, and among the educated nobility.[10]

The drinking- and gambling-songs portray a socially decadent way of life, but are still indebted to the influence of church and school. Indeed, much of their impact as songs of amusement and humour depends on their witty parodies of more elevated forms of Latin scholarship, particularly religious works. Even the Church liturgy itself is commandeered for the purposes of humorous parody, as in the poem 'In taberna quando sumus' (Whicher, p.226), where the drinkers in the tavern imbibe round after round in the name of various groups of people—prisoners, the living, the faithful dead, boastful nuns—who are more properly associated with prayers during Church festivals.

The kind of humorous poem and drinking-song found in the *Carmina Burana* is also well illustrated in the vernacular, particularly French and German. The popular appeal of these songs was therefore widespread, and a reminder that the goliardic poets and *jongleurs* were not completely separate classes of composers, but in fact shared many themes and moods. However, the use they made of this shared material was rather different. While the *jongleurs* generally reassured their audiences that they participated in the popular culture of the majority, the goliardic poets referred to this same popular culture to reaffirm the élitism of the educated minority. By using the language and structures of the Church to describe socially decadent activities such as drinking and gambling, the Latin poets were not expressing subversive and dissenting ideals so much as drawing attention to their own membership of an intellectual élite, of which the established Church was the authoritative institution.

In the satires, moralizing poems, and drinking-songs, therefore, we find a uniformly scholarly approach to subjects ranging from the socially significant to the humorously profane. The full value of these songs, in terms of their wit and parody, could only be appreciated by those who shared a knowledge of classical and religious learning with the composers themselves. Such people would certainly include ordained members of the clergy and of monasteries, where many of the goliardic songs were doubtlessly performed; but they might also include men and women of noble birth who had some knowledge of Latin. The poems are therefore addressed to an exclusive and limited audience and do not represent an attack on Christian values. Instead they criticize the kind of inequalities and injustices within the Church system which have resulted in a great discrepancy in the material profits enjoyed by its various members. Being members of the intellectual élite is not enough for the goliardic poets, they aspire to the wealth and social status of those who listen to their songs.

The largest group of poems in the *Carmina Burana*, the love-lyrics, affirm the function of the secular Latin poets as entertainers of a noble and learned audience. Like the early troubadours, the goliards seek a love that is reciprocal and based on physical desire; unlike the troubadours, however, the Latin poets are concerned with the realities of love rather than its abstract concepts. The troubadours make of love a man-made ideal, circumscribed by the social conventions of *fin' amors* and pursued within the confines of a courtly society constructed on artificially created assumptions. Their definition of love as a manifestation of civilized, aristocratic society is in terms of conflict, basically the conflict between spiritual salvation and earthly desire. The goliards, on the other hand, often suggest that the immediate gratification of earthly love, however temporal and transient, is preferable to the long-term anticipation of eternal redemption. Paradoxically, then, the secular poets tend to be more concerned about the conflicting claims of the flesh and the spirit than the goliardic poets, who were trained as clerics, even if not officially ordained. W.P. Jones makes the same point:

> This goliardic freedom, however, often leads to a brutal treatment of the theme—a desire for quick possession stated with frank boldness. One tends to feel, as a consequence, that the clerk is characterized by sensuality, frivolity, and an overbrimming joy in pagan life, whereas the layman, who is in this case the troubadour and the minnesinger, is by comparison seen in a light of moral earnestness and sobriety.[11]

The goliards justify their pursuit of earthly love by placing it in a rural setting, where natural phenomena testify to abstract moral truths—the glory of God, the beauty of creation, the omnipresence of God, the evanescence of human life and emotion. This location of love in the woodland allows it to be seen in the context of the natural cycle of the world, ordained by God, and therefore containing the potential for spiritual as well as physical fulfilment. Such a context brings together the notion of the *locus amoenus* from classical tradition, and the association of love and the woodland from popular song.

The goliardic endorsement of the pursuit of earthly love finds parallels in vernacular love-poems, particularly those not located in a courtly context. This is not to say that the goliardic lyrics express only satisfaction and never conflict. Many of the formal Latin lyrics convey the despair of unrequited love as acutely as anything produced by the troubadours. The difference is that, whereas the troubadours were contemplating the ultimately irreconcilable opposition of social duty and individual fantasy, the goliardic poets are interpreting their ideal of love in terms of their classical background of philosophy and rhetoric.

By drawing on this background, the goliards were well able to compose love-poems of the same intensity as those of the court-poets, an intensity achieved not so much by the introspective analysis of the causes and effects of love, as by the use of techniques carried over from classical and religious Latin poetry. They do not interpret love from the point of view of *fin' amors*, that is, as a preoccupation involving specific social expectations and conventions. Nevertheless, they are aware of the power of such conventions in constructing images and rhetorical arguments. The author of 'Volo virum vivere viriliter' (Hilka and Schumann, no.178), for example, expressly rejects the courtly fantasy of subservience in love, and insists that he and his beloved are equally the servants of love. But in the last stanza, the poet recants and declares he is the lady's prisoner:

> Volo virum vivere viriliter:
> diligam, si diligar equaliter;
> sic amandum censeo, non aliter.
> hac in parte fortior quam Jupiter
> nescio procari
> commercio vulgari:
> amaturus forsitan volo prius amari . . .
>
> . . . Ecce mihi displicet, quod cecini,
> et meo contrarius sum carmini,
> tue reus, domina, dulcedini,
> cuius elegantie non memini.
> quia sic erravi,
> sum dignus pena gravi;
> penitentem corripe, si placet, in conclavi.

(I would like a man to live in a manly way; I would love, if I were loved equally. It is thus I believe one should love, not otherwise. Stronger than Jupiter in this respect, I do not know how to entreat in a common commercial way. In order to love, perhaps, I would like to be loved first . . .

. . . Alas, I am displeased with what I have sung, and I am at odds with my song, a debtor, lady, to your sweetness whose grace I have not mentioned. Because I have strayed thus, I deserve heavy punishment; bring the penitent to trial, if it pleases you, in your chamber.)

The poem suggests humour rather than the torment of the unrequited lover, with the last stanza being a comic reversal of the poet's previous complacency. References in the poem to Jupiter and Hippolytus, to commercial bargaining and to playing dice create an Ovidian and non-courtly context for love's pursuit, but the last line alludes to physical consummation in a manner reminiscent of troubadour verse.

Goliardic poems on the joys and despair of love inevitably share motifs with those of the court-poets, while being more overtly learned in style and diction in order to enhance emotion. The poem 'Dira vi

amoris teror' (Hilka and Schumann, no.107), describing the poet's
sufferings from love, echoes the sentiments of many vernacular court-
poems, but the poetic impulse behind the secular theme is distinctively learned rather than courtly:

> Dira vi amoris teror
> et Venereo axe feror,
> igni ferventi suffocatus;
> deme pia cruciatus . . .
>
> . . . Meret cor, quod gaudebat
> die, quo te cognoscebat
> singularem et pudicam,
> te adoptabat in amicam.
>
> Profero pectoris singultus
> et mestitie tumultus,
> nam amoris tui vigor
> urget me, et illi ligor.
>
> Virginale lilium,
> tuum presta subsidium.
> missus in exilium
> querit a te consilium.

(I am worn out by the terrible force of love, and I am driven on the
wheel of love, suffocated by the raging fire. Merciful one, take away
this torment . . .

. . . My heart grieves for that which made it glad; on the day when it first
knew you, it chose you, unsullied and unparalleled, to be its love.

I bring forth from my breast a sobbing and a tumult of sorrow, for a
strong love of you urges me on, and I am bound to it.

Virgin lily, show your support. He who has been sent into exile seeks
comfort from you.)

The use of metaphor, such as the fire of love, of ornate diction, and of
long syntactical phrases all contribute to a learned and sophisticated
poetic technique. In addition, the appeal to the Virgin, 'Virginale
lilium', reminiscent of hymns, and the reference to Venus to represent
love, in contrast to the courtly *amors*, identify the poem as clerical
rather than courtly.

Another poem on a similar theme, 'O comes amoris, dolor' (Hilka
and Schumann, no.111) also uses the motif of exile, inherited from
earlier Latin poems. Originally a form of voluntary withdrawal from
society for religious reasons, a self-imposed penance, the theme of
exile became associated with secular pursuits, notably love. The
troubadours developed the notion of distance and separation from

the beloved into *amors de lonh*, an important aspect of courtly love. In this Latin poem, the poet's exile expresses the same torment of separation. The poet has also made use of a number of rhetorical devices, such as *exclamatio* in the opening line, *traductio* in 'Gaude vallis insignita, vallis rosis redimita, vallis flos convallium, inter valles vallis una' (11.10.–13) (rejoice, distinguished valley, valley wreathed in roses, a valley the flower of surrounding ones, the one valley among valleys); and *interjectio* in 'dolor urget me, nec mirum' (1.4) (pain oppresses me, and no wonder). The traditional devices of rhetoric, taught as a means of constructing a rational argument or sermon, have thus been applied by the poet to a secular topic, in combination with lyrical description, in order to heighten the impact of his sorrow.

The poem 'Anni novi rediit novitas' (Hilka and Schumann, no.78) is also significant for its use of classical techniques to heighten the expression of emotion. The lyric is a celebration of love, and the thread of flower imagery running through the poem—'lovelier than lily or rose', 'thorn blossom', 'flower of flowers'—is reminiscent of earlier Latin lyrics and hymns in which the Virgin Mary is compared to flowers.[12] The references to Venus and Cupid, the rhetorical *exclamatio* of 'Vale, flos florum', and the skilful repetition (*adnominatio*) in phrases such as 'cuius flos adhuc est in flore' (whose flower is still in flower), 'dulcis fit labor in hoc labore' (it were sweet to be weary in such a labour), and 'dolor dolori' (grievous pain) contribute to the learned style of the goliardic poem. At the same time the nature opening and the courtly concepts of love, as a spear and a captor, remind us that the poem is also borrowing from popular and vernacular poetry.

The use of nature openings to enhance the poet's mood in love also occurs in troubadour poetry, and is probably popular in origin.[13] The poem 'Terra iam pandit' (Hilka and Schumann, no.140) makes a connection between the spring season, singing, and love. Nature description pervades the whole piece and has a specific function, to describe the advantages of summer as a time for pursuing love, and to emphasize by contrast the unhappiness of the poet who suffers unrequited love in a wintery atmosphere. This contrast is also made by Dafydd ap Gwilym in his seasonal poems, particularly 'Mis Mai a Mis Ionawr' (GDG 69).

In their use of nature imagery to enhance or undermine the lover's mood, the goliards are in fact much closer to the vernacular court-poetry of the Minnesingers, which makes extensive use of folk-song elements. The goliardic poem 'Omnia sol temperat' (Hilka and Schumann, no.136) consists of three stanzas, the first extolling the joys of spring, the second combining season and mood, and the last affirming the loyalty of the poet and his beloved; thus the poet's mood is here in complete harmony with the season. The format of this poem can be compared with that of 'In dem aberellen, sô die bluomen springen'[14] by the Minnesinger Heinrich von Veldeke. The first stanza contains a description of April and the joy inspired by the season; the second relates the feeling of renewal to the poet's participation in the seasonal activity. In the third stanza, however, the poet's mood changes abruptly: because of his lack of success in love, he cannot give himself up completely to the joys of spring around him. The function of the seasonal description is the same in each poem, to relate nature and love as part of an inevitable cycle and to add definition to the poet's mood.

Many of the goliardic love-poems are therefore related to vernacular court-poetry in terms of their choice of love and nature as principal themes. Some of the key images of courtly love—love as a spear or a prison, the notion of suffering and dying for love—appear in both the Latin and the vernacular poems, but the classical orientation of the former is as unique to them as is the rich texture of courtly love terminology to the latter. For the troubadours, sleep is denied to the lover who must struggle to win the regard of his *domna*; but for the author of 'Dum Diane vitrea' (Hilka and Schumann, no.62) sleep and love are both seen as ways of achieving peace of mind. The poetic significance of sleep and night have been shaped by classical and learned, rather than courtly, conventions.

The use of nature openings, on the other hand, seems to owe little to the classical tradition. Though nature imagery was employed by the earliest predecessors of the goliards such as Alcuin, Strabo, and Venantius Fortunatus, the function of nature description to define and intensify the expression of love seems to be a vernacular tradition.[15] The classical Latin mode of nature description was used to present a specific aspect of the natural world, such as Alcuin's poems on the cuckoo and the nightingale, or as a symbolic means of supporting a generalized statement about the world, as in the lament by Fredugis on the death of Alcuin, where the poet describes Alcuin's cell in the woods and reflects on the transience of earthly beauty.[16] The goliardic use of nature openings and seasonal description corresponds to its function in the court-poetry of the Minnesingers

and, to a lesser extent, of the troubadours, all of these genres
ultimately drawing on and refining the kind of nature imagery found
in popular vernacular poetry.

The love-poems from the *Carmina Burana* which I have discussed
so far display many affinities with classical and courtly traditions and
obviously belong to the type of learned Latin lyric which is widely
exemplified beyond the confines of the Benediktbeuern collection.
The theme of unrequited love, and the motifs of the spear of love and
the beloved whose beauty is unequalled, which are all associated with
vernacular court-poetry, are also found together in 'Ecce letantur
omnia', a twelfth-century poem from a Saint-Martial manuscript.[17]
Nature introductions to poems about love are also common
throughout medieval Latin poetry: consider, for example, this
opening stanza from a thirteenth-century manuscript:

> Ver prope florigerum, flava Licori,
> iam rosam aspicis, egressam tunicis,
> credere celo tepidiori
> tenera germina floris odori.[18]

(Spring nearly in bloom, golden Lycoris, already you behold the rose
emerging from its covering to entrust the tender buds of a sweet-
smelling flower to a warmer sky.)

Nevertheless, despite the similarities of theme and motif between
the love-lyrics of the *Carmina Burana* and those of other medieval
collections, it seems to me that the learned and classical traditions of
the former are regularly leavened by popular vernacular influences in
a way not commonly found among the latter. The diction and syntax
tend to be simpler and less ornate; the pursuit of love is undertaken
with a greater subjective intensity and fewer references to classical
ideals of beauty; and nature description is less elaborate and stylized,
making use of popular conventions of seasonal imagery rather than
the classical references to specific flowers and birds.

The love-poems of the *Carmina Burana* therefore seem to represent
a development away from the contemporary Latin lyric tradition and
towards the conventions of vernacular poetry. This movement is
expressed most explicitly in a group of love-poems modelled on
popular dance-songs, mainly of German origin, singing of love and
springtime and the joys of youth. In these poems, separated in the
manuscript from the more formal and artistic love-lyrics, learned
poetry has virtually become popular song, in all but language.

Discussing the poetry of the goliards, W.P. Jones says:

> Most of the popular elements in the goliardic poetry are of a general nature, but there are some particular things, such as folk phrases, Germanisms, and especially themes. One of the chief evidences of the popular character of goliardic poetry, particularly in the love songs, is that of the popular metres, mostly rhymed, the counterparts of which occur frequently in later German lyrics.[19]

The 'folk phrases and Germanisms' in many cases appear as a complete stanza in German added to some of the second group of love-poems (the dance-songs celebrating love and spring), and Bischoff quotes Hans Spanke as saying 'the added strophes [in German] were intended to arouse interest among or to make possible the active participation of an audience not capable of understanding the Latin.'[20] Many verbal echoes of these German stanzas have been found in the poetry of the Minnesingers and other medieval German poems by Richard M. Meyer, who has done an extensive comparative study.[21] Inevitably, these textual correspondences concern love and nature and indicate the pervasiveness of certain motifs and phrases in both popular and courtly German poetry. Allusions to the seasons, to the month of May, to flowers and birds, and to the poet's mood, provide a common factor between the German stanzas of the *Carmina Burana*, and the German folk- and court-poetry of the same period.

The same kinds of motifs also predominate in the Latin poems to which the German stanzas are appended. Most of these are in celebration of the coming of spring and its associated pleasures, and are clearly intended to be sung at spring festivals. A typical example is 'Ecce gratum et optatum' (Hilka and Schumann, no. 143):

> Ecce gratum
> et optatum
> ver reducit gaudia:
> purpuratum
> floret pratum,
> sol serenat omnia.
> iam iam cedant tristia!
> estas redit,
> nunc recedit
> hiemis sevitia.
>
> Iam liquescit
> et decrescit
> grando, nix et cetera;

> bruma fugit,
> et iam sugit
> veris tellus ubera.
> illi mens est misera,
> qui nec vivit
> nec lascivit
> sub estatis dextera!
>
> Gloriantur
> et letantur
> in melle dulcedinis,
> qui conantur,
> ut utantur
> premio Cupidinis.
> simus iussu Cypridis
> gloriantes
> et letantes
> pares esse Paridis!

(Behold the spring, welcome and wished-for, brings back joy: the meadow blooms, clad in purple, the sun makes everything bright. Now indeed let sad things go away. Summer returns, and now winter's rage retreats.

Now hail, snow and the rest melt away and diminish; the winter cold takes flight, and now the earth suckles at the breasts of spring. For that man who neither lives nor plays beneath the right hand of summer, his mind is wretched.

They exult and rejoice in the sweetness of pleasure, who strive to enjoy the gift of Cupid. Let us, by command of Venus, exult and rejoice to be the equals of Paris.)

The first two stanzas are constructed with a simple series of images which describe the coming of spring and contrast with the retreat of winter. Key words such as 'ver', 'floret pratum', 'sol serenat', epitomize the spring season, while 'hiemis saevitia', 'grando', 'nix', 'bruma' represent the contrasting rigours of winter. Similarly, the appropriate moods of joy and sadness are also set in opposition through 'gaudia', 'tristia' in the first stanza and 'misera', 'lascivit' in the second. The verbs, though simple in meaning and tense, also convey the opposite movements of approach and withdrawal: 'reducit', 'redit', 'recedit', 'fugit', with the repeated prefix *re-* suggesting the cyclical nature of the passing seasons.

The mood and content of the poem is obviously popular in inspiration to a great extent, although evidence of goliardic transmission is present in the balanced structure and syntax of the poem, as well as in the classical allusions to Cupid, Venus and Paris. In its diction, theme, and mood it can be compared to a number of other songs in the *Carmina Burana*, such as 'Cedit, hiems, tua durities', 'Ver redit optatum', and 'Iam iam virent prata' (Hilka and Schumann, nos.135,137,144), in which the principal ideas of spring, joy and love as mutually inclusive elements are set out in the same type of tightly structured schema. Those poems which have a refrain, for example 'Veris dulcis in tempore' (Hilka and Schumann, no.85), in which each stanza ends with the line 'dulcis amor', or 'Tempus est iocundum' (Hilka and Schumann, no.179), containing a refrain stanza beginning 'o! o! totus floreo', belong more obviously to the dance-song genre, and their regular rhyme scheme and alliterative diction reinforce the effects of music and singing.

P.S. Allen includes refrains among his criteria for distinguishing lyrics of popular origin from those of a more classical provenance, along with diction, popular paraphrase, impersonality, music, and terseness.[22] There is certainly a stylistic distinction to be made between poems such as 'Dum estas inchoatur' (Hilka and Schumann, no.160), a simple love-song, and 'O comes amoris, dolor' (Hilka and Schumann, no.111), for example, if we compare these stanzas:

> Dum estas inchoatur
>   ameno tempore,
> Phebusque dominatur
>   depulso frigore,
>
> Unius in amore
>   puelle vulneror,
> multimodo dolore,
>   per quem et atteror . . .

(When summer is beginning at the delightful season, and Phoebus is supreme, with the cold driven away, I am wounded with many kinds of pain from love of one girl alone, because of whom I am being wasted away.)

> O comes amoris, dolor,
> cuius mala male solor,
>   an habes remedium?
> dolor urget me, nec mirum,
> quem a predilecta dirum,
>   en, vocat exilium,
> cuius laus est singularis,
> pro qua non curasset Paris
>   Helene consortium . . .
>
> Gaude, vallis insignita,
> vallis rosis redimita,

> vallis, flos convallium,
> inter valles vallis una,
> quam collaudet sol et luna,
> dulcis cantus avium!
> te collaudat philomena,
> vallis dulcis et amena,
> mestis dans solacium!

(O grief, comrade of love, whose evils I can ill assuage, do you have a cure? Pain oppresses me, and it is no wonder, since dreadful exile summons me away, alas, from my chosen one whose glory is unique, because of whom Paris would not have cared to be Helen's consort . . .

. . . Rejoice, distinguished valley, valley wreathed in roses, a valley the flower of surrounding ones, one valley among valleys, which sun and moon extol, and the sweet song of birds. The nightingale extols you, sweet and pleasant valley, offering comfort to the gloomy.)

Both poems juxtapose nature description and the expression of love, and both contrast their grief with the pleasant environment around them. Clearly the second poem is far more sophisticated in its language and style than the first: apart from its use of rhetorical devices to heighten the mood and description, there is also a greater use of figurative language and a higher degree of complexity in its syntax. The nature imagery in the first poem is of a fleeting and conventional kind, with the more or less obligatory contrast between summer and winter, whereas the description of the valley in the second poem glorifies the place where the girl lives and so achieves a genuine fusion between the two themes of love and nature. It is therefore not unreasonable to consider the first poem as a 'popular' creation and the second as a 'learned' one.

Even in these two poems, however, there are similarities which undermine this distinction to a certain extent. Both are highly subjective, using verbs and pronouns in the first person and addressing the girl as 'she'. Both poems also employ imagery which is often associated with the tradition of courtly love, such as wounding, pain, wasting away, exile from the chosen one. Moreover, the diction of the two poems contains many similarities, including references to classical figures, Phoebus, and Paris and Helen. In some ways, then, it is misleading to separate these two poems into entirely different categories, even though they are separated in the manuscript; one is more popular and one is more learned but both are goliardic transformations of the same set of conventions found in the Latin love-lyric and shared by vernacular lyrics.

The distinction between learned and popular elements is even harder to make when we examine poems such as 'Salve, ver optatum' and 'Cedit, hiems, tua durities'.[23] Both poems are found among the 'popular' group of love-songs in the manuscript, but whereas the latter finishes with a German stanza in common with most of this group of poems, the former is a longer piece entirely in Latin. The first two stanzas describe the long-awaited arrival of spring, with its usual associations of joy and rejuvenation and a selection of images reminiscent of other poems in a popular style, referring to the flowers, birds and gentle breezes. Mingled with these are rhetorical flourishes and a type of diction connotative of a school-trained composer— 'salve ver optatum' (hail, wished-for spring), 'gaudeat iuventus' (may youth rejoice), 'umbre crescunt' (shadows grow longer), 'Venus subditos titillat' (Venus touches her subjects).

In the third and fourth stanzas, the poet describes his beloved in the best rhetorical tradition, starting from the top and working downwards, from her golden hair to her slim neck and fingers. This type of *effictio*, giving an itemized description of a girl's beauty, is characteristic of Latin love-poetry; the sequence of golden hair, rosy cheeks, red lips, white teeth, and slender throat, is mirrored almost exactly in the twelfth-century poem, 'Lydia', a formal and ornate example of scholarly lyric.[24] Though the goliardic poem uses techniques from classical learning, it inclines towards the pole of popular treatment rather than continuing in the tradition of learned lyric-poetry.

In 'Cedit hiems' we have an even simpler spring song, uniting images of spring with the reinforcement of love, where learned influences are confined to mere allusions in the diction, such as 'pallor et ira, dolor, macies' (paleness and wrath, pain and poverty), 'nocte micant Pliadum facies' (the faces of the Pleiads flicker at night). The contrast between winter and spring, the call to love, the exchange of pledges, the bird-song and enjoyment of youth, are all part of the repertoire of popular song imagery. Nevertheless, the poem is not without some sophistication in its composition: it maintains a single rhyme throughout; there is a series of balanced pairs in the first stanza to capture the bleakness of winter (stiffness and ice, wintry and wild, numbness and evil, paleness and wrath, pain and poverty); the contrasting images of day and night are emphasized by the juxtaposition of 'dies' and 'nocte'; and the opposition between the first and second person verbs, 'tendo manus; mihi quid facies?' (I stretch out my hand; what will you do to me?), establishes fleetingly the personal relationship between the poet and the girl in the middle of an otherwise unbroken series of third person verbs of description.

I have been arguing that both popular and learned elements appear in nearly all of the love-songs of the *Carmina Burana* in varying degrees. Learned elements, such as complex syntactical structures, ornate diction, figurative language, rhetorical devices, biblical and religious imagery, and classical allusions, predominate in those poems which are primarily concerned with love and its effect on the poet. Popular elements, on the other hand, such as simple diction and syntax, brief images with short qualifying epithets, repetitive rhyme scheme, paucity of figurative language, specific references to natural phenomena, and refrains or repeated phrases, are especially characteristic of those poems capturing the spirit of vernacular (particularly German) dance-song, in which the coming of spring and the joys of youth and love are pervasive themes.

So the love-poems of the *Carmina Burana* offer a range of themes and moods in both genres, the formal classical lyric and the simpler kind of spring love-song. The former presents love as a conflict between joy and despair, just as the troubadours also interpreted love in terms of conflict. But for the goliardic poets, the dualities inherent in the pursuit of love are expressed in terms of the rhetorical and philosophical structures which belong to classical scholarship and Latin learning. Since the poems do not have the same kind of social context as the troubadour lyrics, they refer to the inherited and highly specialized imagery of the classical world rather than to the chivalric demands of the courtly world, and they are located in the Elysian fields of classical literature rather than the martial and aggressive atmosphere of the Provençal castle. The women to whom the goliards addressed themselves are personified not as noble ladies but rather as classical deities who are remote and disdainful because of their Olympian status, not because of their birth. There is a sense in which the goliardic poems lack a precise social and historical context as much as the poets themselves lacked a distinctive and accepted place in medieval society; the alternating sterility and excess of their love-pursuits suggest the conflicting demands of desire and celibacy. Ultimately, the more formal love-lyrics resemble elaborate learned exercises with which the poets amused each other and sharpened their poetic and rhetorical skills: unlike the troubadours who were mouthpieces for the knights, the goliards spoke for no-one but themselves, since they had virtually no other audience.

The latter group, the spring-songs, present the theme of love in an essentially popular though idealized context, the world of seasonal celebration and folk-song. The pursuit of love is shown to be as significant and cyclic a ritual as the changing of the seasons and the welcoming of each new spring. By incorporating love into the world of nature, the poets suggest that it is ultimately a harmonious and stabilizing ritual, taking its place among other natural rhythms of the world, so that conflicts will eventually be resolved just as the harshness of winter will give way to the mildness of summer. Here again, the philosophy of the goliardic poets, the product of classical and clerical training, is very different from that of the troubadours who were supplying the needs of an upwardly mobile social group.

The main contribution of the secular Latin poets to the lyric tradition is their transformation of popular song material into a learned and sophisticated form. This transformation provided parallels and models for the court-poets of the vernacular tradition, who were also interested in drawing on a rich and versatile popular tradition. Both the Latin and vernacular poets were therefore appropriating a majority culture and interpreting it in a literary form which was palatable and appropriate to an élitist minority. Just as the Provençal nobility was defined as a class by the troubadour courtly love-lyric, so the educated clerics and churchmen had their corporate identity reinforced by their enjoyment of secular Latin lyrics composed in a learned and classical style.

CHAPTER 3

Popular Song and Courtly Transformations

THE court-poetry and Latin lyrics discussed in the previous chapters were composed by men of education and learning for the entertainment of scholars and noblemen; in other words they represent the secular lyrics of a minority group. The poetry of the majority was folk-poetry, dance-song, carols, nature poems, and love-songs, developing out of a rural way of life largely governed by seasons and festivals. I have already referred briefly to ways in which popular conventions were adapted by the troubadours and Latin poets. The purpose of this chapter is to examine folk-poetry and its assimilation into courtly lyrics, before looking at the parallel process which took place in Dafydd ap Gwilym's poetry.

I will be referring primarily to medieval French verse—lyric, romance and fabliau—since it is this literature which offers the widest range of evidence for surviving popular themes and genres. It is important to recognize a distinction between the French lyrics of the trouvères, court-poets who transmitted the Provençal ideal of *fin' amors* to an established northern French aristocracy, and those of minstrels such as Colin Muset who addressed a newly emerging nobility based on wealth rather than birth.

New audiences for courtly literature were emerging in northern France during the twelfth and thirteenth centuries as a result of social and economic changes. The growth of towns as centres of trade and commerce, and the corresponding development of a cash economy, facilitated the emergence of a powerful bourgeoisie. Its status was based on the acquisition of material wealth rather than on hereditary landownership, marking a departure from the earlier feudal structure characterized by patronage in return for service.

Also during this period, the sphere of influence of the French monarchy, once rivalled by the great provinces such as Burgundy, Normandy and Provence, became wider and stronger. A complex system of royal administration developed to deal with matters of law and justice which were no longer under the sole control of individual feudal overlords. Educated men were recruited into the royal administration as ministers and officials, and these were drawn from the new bourgeoisie as well as from the clergy and the nobility.

As a result of these developments, the feudal system of organization, based on independent manorial hierarchies, began to merge into a more centralized system of government, responsible to the monarchy. The impact of the increased availability of money in return for material goods led to a blending of social classes. The land-based aristocracy spread to the towns, which offered consumer products, while the urban bourgeoisie acquired lands as a symbol of their wealth and status.

The contemporary literary traditions of lyric, romance and fabliau clearly reflect these social changes. Courtly love was taken up by the new nobility as an indication of their status in society, to connect them with the old feudal aristocracy and the noble world of knighthood. It is in this literature that we find the fusion of popular and courtly elements which was to prove highly influential for Dafydd ap Gwilym and the *cywyddwyr*.

The antiquity of popular folk-songs, which long pre-date the medieval period, can be judged from their periodic condemnation by the Church, which saw heathen festivals and their celebratory songs as a threat to religious doctrine.[1] Early popular verse was therefore suppressed and rarely preserved, despite attempts by the clergy to give it a religious rather than pagan function. The most important evidence for popular song in Europe is provided by the German verses of the *Carmina Burana*, the English Harley Lyrics, and the popular themes and forms used by medieval court-poets and minstrels. All these sources suggested a prolific and widespread popular tradition throughout Europe, dating from pre-medieval times in association with pagan beliefs, and later reflecting the influence of the more sophisticated courtly and learned literature.

The popular lyric was only one manifestation of non-courtly entertainment for the people, and was itself capable of multiple variation depending on factors such as the function and the setting of the entertainment. The performance of the lyric, however, is commonly associated with the figure of the minstrel or *jongleur* who played a crucial part in the composition and dissemination of French popular song.[2]

Despite strenuous disapproval from the Church, the minstrels acquired considerable significance in medieval society, particularly those reputable singers and musicians who entertained the nobility and resented the rival existence of the wandering minstrels. But it was this lower grade of minstrel which had the greatest influence on popular thought, satirizing the authorities and encouraging the people to free themselves from restraints imposed by Church and State. The more established entertainers, on the other hand, embellished popular themes with courtly conventions to satisfy an emergent nobility and to confirm its place in the ruling hierarchy.

In its simplest and perhaps oldest form, the popular song of northern France functions as a celebration of the seasons, using forms and imagery which seem to be prototypes of those found in courtly song. The courtly forms of the *pastourelle* and *aube*, discussed previously, are examples of this kind of popular influence. In particular, the French May-songs contain many of the elements which, combined with courtly love-themes, produce popular love-songs. Gaston Paris maintains that these early popular forms, as well as the *chansons à personnages* and *débats*, can all be traced back to the *fêtes de mai* celebrated by the rural communities of France. He further suggests that the court-poets took over many of these popular genres which then became aristocratic modifications of 'jongleresque' songs.[3]

A more moderate view is expressed by Joseph Bédier, who disagrees that the whole body of European lyric-poetry stems from the May festivals.[4] Bédier supposes that the process of popular influence on courtly themes was less conscious than Paris' theory allows; he envisages a gradual transference and refinement by the court-poets of themes held in common by all poets, under the impetus of particular social conditions. Thus the similarities between May-songs and troubadour poetry, such as the motifs of spring, joy, and youth, need not be seen as a direct development of one out of the other, but rather the reflection of a stock of conventions common to all types of love-poetry.

In his examination of French lyric-poetry, Jeanroy defines popular forms strictly as those which precede and are entirely independent of any courtly influence from the south. Evidence for this early native poetry survives only in later compositions, largely in the form of borrowings into court-poetry and into the lyric-poetry of other languages, particularly German, Italian, and Portuguese. Thus the so-called 'popular' genres—*pastourelle, aube, débat, chanson dramatique*—are in fact courtly transformations of earlier popular themes and cannot be considered, according to Jeanroy, as genuinely popular material which is 'autochtone' and 'spontanée'.[5] This means that the kind of love-lyric composed by the *jongleurs* is not recognized by Jeanroy as truly 'popular'. Clearly, his understanding of popular forms and courtly transformations corresponds to the distinction between spontaneous oral song and any kind of literate verse. However, a less limiting and more valuable distinction can be made between popular and courtly lyrics in terms of their composition, theme and audience.

Court-poetry was composed by poets officially attached to specific courts, employed a limited number of recognized themes connected with chivalry and courtly love, and was directed at a particular audience of learned and noble listeners. Popular poetry, on the other hand, was composed by a range of entertainers, from court-poets down to wandering minstrels, used themes and genres familiar to the common people from oral literature, and was directed at a majority audience comprising all social classes.

The most significant difference was that whereas courtly literature was accessible only to the established nobility, the feudal aristocracy and knightly class, popular poetry had relevance for society as a whole. Peter Burke refers to an anthropological model of society to stress the distinction between the 'great tradition' of the educated few, and the 'little tradition' of the rest:

> Thus the crucial cultural difference in early modern Europe (I want to argue) was that between the majority, for whom popular culture was the only culture, and the minority, who had access to the great tradition but participated in the little tradition as a second culture.[6]

The definitive feature of northern French poetry is its preservation of much older poetic conventions associated with seasonal celebration, together with the assimilation of courtly material. The 'little tradition' of the majority thus contributed substantially to the 'great tradition' of the minority. The importance of non-courtly material, found throughout Europe, is demonstrated in the works of the early German court-poets composing before the influence of Provençal *fin' amors*. The poetry of Dietmar von Aist and Der von Kurenberg, for example, supports the existence of an ancient popular lyric in Germany, reflected also in the German poems of the *Carmina*

Burana. In this poetry, the themes of nature and love are closely related, as in the French lyric, and there are also examples of the *pastourelle* and *aube* modelled on the French genres, but not necessarily influenced by the courtly examples of these forms. Borrowing from French poetry both before and after Provençal influence is therefore indicated, but this does not preclude the existence of a native German poetry originally independent of external influences.[7]

Perhaps the most pervasive element common to all types of lyric-poetry is the nature description, which is undoubtedly popular in origin.[8] In the French lyric it takes the form of the *reverdie*, a term used by a number of early French poets to refer to a nature song specifically composed for the spring season. The *reverdie* survives in a small number of French songs as well as in German, Italian, and Latin poetry, usually at the head of a love-poem. This song from twelfth-century France illustrates many of the conventions of the *reverdie*:

> En mai au douz tens nouvel,
> que raverdissent prael,
> oi soz un arbroisel
> chanter le rosignolet.
>> saderala don!
>> tant fet bon
>> dormir lez le buissonet.
>
> Si com g'estoie pensis,
> lez le buissonet m'assis:
> un petit m'i endormi
> au douz chant de l'oiselet.
>
> Au resveillier que je fis
> a l'oisel criai merci
> q'il me doint joie de li:
> s'en serai plus jolivet.
>
> Et quant je fui sus levez,
> si conmenz a citoler
> et fis l'oiselet chanter
> devant moi el praelet.
>
> Li rosignolez disoit:
> par un pou qu'il n'enrajoit
> du grant duel que il avoit,
> que vilains l'avoit oi.[9]

(In the sweet new time of May, when meadows have grown green again, I heard beneath a bushy tree the nightingale singing. Tra la la!

how pleasant it is to sleep beside the grove. As I grew pensive, I sat down by the grove; for a little while I slept, to the sweet song of the little bird. When I woke up, I gave thanks to the bird, for he had given me joy on her account; I would be the merrier because of it. And when I stood up, I began to play the lute, and made the little bird sing before me in the meadow. The nightingale said: for once he had not been tormented by great sadness because a churl had heard him.)

The springtime setting is evoked throughout the poem, with references to May, meadows, tree, grove, and above all to the song of the *rosignolet*. The poet identifies himself with the bird, as a creator of song, and at the end of the poem there is a fusion of the poet's music and the beautiful song of the nightingale, which is usually wasted on mere *vilains*. The implication is that the poet's audience, too, does not comprise ignorant peasants, but sophisticated listeners able to appreciate musical talent.

This *reverdie* provides a theme from within itself, without depending on external themes such as love. Similar examples can be found in the *Carmina Burana* where the mood of traditional spring-songs is re-created by learned composers. More frequently, however, surviving examples of the *reverdie*, in both popular and courtly poetry, are found in conjunction with the theme of love. The court-poets in particular made use of nature openings to emphasize their own experience of love, as in this stanza from Guiraut de Bornelh:

> Can lo glatz e.l frechs e la neus
> S'en vai e torna la chalors
> E reverdezis lo pascors
> Et auch las voltas dels auzeus,
>   M'es aitan beus
> Lo dolz tems a l'issen de martz
> Que plus sui salhens que leupartz
> E vils non es chabrols ni cers.
> Si la bela cui sui profers
>   Me vol onrar
> D'aitan que.m denhe sofertar
> Qu'eu sia sos fis entendens,
> Sobre totz sui rics e manens.[10]

(When the ice and the cold and the snow depart, and the heat returns and the pasture grows green again, and I hear the swelling song of the birds—this sweet time at the end of March is so joyful to me that I am springier than a leopard and I am more lively than a goat or a deer. If the beautiful one to whom I have offered myself would honour me to the extent of allowing me to be her faithful suitor, I would be rich and powerful above everyone.)

The familiar motifs of bird-song and seasonal renewal provide a background for the poet's hope of winning love, and also form an introduction to the plea for love expressed during the poem. The German court-poets tended to use nature imagery throughout their poetry rather than as an introduction alone, balancing it against their declarations of love. In his poem 'Sô die bluomen ûz dem grase dringent', Walther von der Vogelweide compares his lady's beauty to that of the summer season:

> Sô die bluomen ûz dem grase dringent
> same si lachen gegen der spilnden sunnen
> in einem meien an dem morgen fruo
> und diu kleinen vogellîn wol singent
> in ir besten wîse die si kunnen,
> waz wünne mac sich dâ genôzen zuo?
> ez ist wol halt ... melrîche.
> Suln wir sprechen waz sich deme gelîche,
> sô sage ich waz mir dicke baz
> in mînen ougen hât getân, und taete ouch noch,
> gesaehe ich daz.[11]

(When the flowers push up through the grass as though they are laughing at the shining sun, early one May morning, and the little birds sing well in the best way that they know, what joy can compare with this? It is truly the kingdom of heaven. But if it comes to saying what can compare with it, thus I will say what has often given pleasure to my eyes, and would even do so still, if I could only see it.)

Thus Walther uses the motifs of the *reverdie*—flower, grass, birds—to describe the May season and to praise the beauty of his lady, which surpasses even the glories of summer. The association of the springtime with a joyful, celebratory mood was a convenient motif for the court-poets singing of love's bliss.

In France, the *reverdie* was similarly used by some of the trouvères and by *jongleurs* to create a simple love-poetry in the popular rather than courtly mood.[12] Colin Muset composed many lyrics which combine popular themes with the techniques of a court-poet, as in this example:

> Volez oïr la muse Muset?
> En mai fu fete, un matinet,
> En un vergier flori, verdet,
>   Au point du jour,
> Ou chantoient cil oiselet
>   Par grant baudor,
> Et j'alai fere un chapelet
>   En la verdor.

> Je le fis bel et cointe et net
> Et plain de flor.
> Une dancele
> Avenant et mult bele,
> Gente pucele,
> Bouchete riant,
> Qui me rapele:
> Vien ça, si viele
> ....
> Ta muse en chantant
> Tant mignotement.[13]

(Would you like to hear the Muset song? In May it was sung, one fine morning, in a flowering green orchard at the break of day, when those little birds were singing with great gaiety, and I went to make a garland in the greenery. I made it pretty and elegant and neat and full of flowers. A damsel, comely and very lovely, a noble girl with laughing little mouth, calls me back: 'Come then and play your song, singing so sweetly'.)

The nature opening is explicitly related to the May celebration but also provides an appropriate setting for the poet's courtship. In the rest of the poem, the nature imagery fades away and the poet declares his love through conventions borrowed from *amour courtois*, maintaining the relationship of humble minstrel towards his noble mistress.

Thus the form of the *reverdie*, originally a song in its own right, survives most frequently as an introduction to a love-lyric, either popular or courtly. The popular lyric developed from its early folksong tradition to include the celebration of love along with the beauties of nature. Once it became a love-lyric, it was open to receive the influence of courtly-love themes and motifs, resulting in a 'popularized' kind of courtly love, expressed in a framework of popular conventions. In addition the composers of these lyrics, which form the bulk of our evidence for popular song, were themselves court-poets or minstrels working in a consciously non-courtly tradition yet inevitably influenced by the conventions of *amour courtois*. This kind of overlap can be seen in the *Carmina Burana*, representing a range of moods from the most classical to the most vulgar; in the poetry of Walther von der Vogelweide, who celebrates 'hohui minne' (high love) as well as 'nideriu minne' (low love); [14] and in the poems of Dafydd ap Gwilym.

The assimilation of courtly motifs and popular poetry is exemplified in French poetry by Colin Muset, a professional minstrel who also entertained the nobility as a trouvère. Amid idyllic surroundings, Colin enjoys the kind of carefree love, free from restraints and as essential to life as nature itself, which is familiar from goliardic poetry. Yet he also experiences the two-sided love of the court-poets, describing both joy and pain in his pursuit of reward:

> En ceste note dirai
> D'une amorete que j'ai,
> Et pour li m'envoiserai
> Et bauz et joianz serai:
> L'en doit bien pour li chanter
> Et renvoisier et jouer
> Et son cors tenir plus gai
> Et de robes acesmer
> Et chapiau de flors porter
> Ausi comme el mois de mai.
>
> Tres l'eure que l'esgardai
> Onc puis ne l'entroubliai,
> Ainz i pens et penserai;
> Quant la vois ne puis durer,
> Ne dormir, ne reposer.
> Biau tres douz Deus, que ferai?
> La paine que pour li trai
> Ne sai conment li dirai.
> De ce sui en grant esmai
> Oncore a dire li ai.
> Quant merci n'i puis trouver
> Et je muir por bien amer,
> Amoreusement morrai.
>
> Je ne cuit pas ensi morir,
> S'ele mi voloit retenir
> En bien amer, en biau servir;
> Et du tout sui a son plesir,
> Ne je ne m'en qier departir,
> Mes toz jorz serai ses amis.
>
> Hé! bele et blonde et avenant,
> Cortoise et sage et bien parlant,
> A vous me doig, a vous me rent,
> Et tout sui vostres sanz faillir.
> He! bele, un besier vous demant,
> Et se je l'ai, je vous creant
> Nul mal ne m'en porroit venir.
>
> > Ma bele douce amie,
> > La rose est espanie:
> > Desouz l'ente florie
> > La vostre conpaignie
> > M'i fet mult grant aïe.

Vos serez bien servie
De crasse oe rostie
Et bevrons vin sus lie,
Si merrons bone vie.

Bele tres douce amie,
Colin Muset vos prie
Por Deu n'obliez mie
Solaz ne compagnie,
Amors ne druerie,
Si ferez cortoisie!
Ceste note est fenie.[15]

(In this song I will tell of my sweet young love, and because of her I shall enjoy myself and I shall be merry and joyous: one should sing well on her account, and rejoice and play and hold one's body more gaily, and dress up in robes and wear coronets of flowers, as in the month of May.

From the hour when I saw her, since then I have not forgotten her; rather do I think of her, and will think of her; when I see her, I cannot endure, cannot sleep or rest. Dear God so gentle, what shall I do? The pain which I suffer for her, I do not know how to tell her; from this I am in great trouble, yet I have to say it to her; if I cannot find mercy there and I die from loving well, I shall die as a lover.

I do not think I will die thus if she wishes to hold me back in good love, in good service; and in everything I am at her pleasure, nor do I intend to leave her, instead I will be her lover every day.

Alas, beautiful and fair and comely one, courtly and wise and eloquent, to you I give myself, to you I give myself up and I am all yours without fail. Alas, beautiful one, a kiss I ask of you, and if I get it, I promise you no harm could come to me because of it.

My beautiful sweet lover, the rose is full-blown; beneath the flowering fruit-tree your company helps me greatly. You will be well served with a roasted fat goose and we will drink clear wine: thus will we lead the good life.

Beautiful lover so sweet, Colin Muset begs you for God's sake not to forget in any way solace or company, love or affection: thus may you act courteously. This song is finished.)

The opening stanza of the poem evokes the mood of a spring-song, expressing the notion of celebrating love as one celebrates the coming of May. In the next stanza, however, the diction is reminiscent of courtly love-poetry as the poet describes his suffering and his hope of mercy. His declaration of continued loyalty, 'en biau servir', his praises of the lady, and his request for a kiss, all reflect the influence of the courtly love tradition. In the last two stanzas, marked by a change of rhythm and metre, the poet reverts to a simpler kind of courtship in which he envisages the two of them sharing a rustic meal and benefiting from each other's company. This is Colin's idea of 'cortoisie'—not the artificially imposed social virtues of the courtly love-poets, but a true sharing of love and affection.

This kind of 'popularized' minstrel love-poem has affinities with some of the poems of the goliards and of Walther von der Vogelweide. The goliards are influenced more by classical than courtly love traditions in their pursuit of love but they, like Walther and Colin Muset, find their ideal of love in a rural setting. Unlike Walther, however, the French poet is not concerned with offering a new philosophy of courtly love; Colin celebrates love just as he celebrates the changing seasons, the material comforts of life, the patronage of a generous nobleman. For him, love is one of the perquisites of the good life to which he aspires, rather than a complex relationship to be defined and analysed. Though Colin borrows motifs and vocabulary from courtly love-poetry, his songs reflect the non-courtly attitude of a minstrel or *jongleur*.

Minstrel love-songs thus express many of the courtly love motifs in a popularized form, making them accessible to non-courtly audiences. Other minstrel songs similarly evoke a courtly atmosphere but are based on popular themes and appeal to a range of social classes. The *chansons de toile*, for example, the 'weaving songs' sung by women, often suggest the presence of noblewomen sewing rich fabrics but in form and content they resemble ballads and non-courtly minstrel songs, as in this example:

> Siet soi bele Aye as piez sa male maistre,
> sor ses genouls un paile d'Engleterre;
> a un fil file, i fet coustures belles.
> > hé hé! amors d'autre pais,
> > mon cuer avez et lie et souspris.
>
> Aval la face li courent chaudes lermes,
> q'el est batue et au main et au vespre,
> por ce qu'el aime soudoier d'autre terre.
> > hé hé! amors d'autre pais,
> > mon cuer avez et lie et souspris.
> >   (Abbott, p.34)

(Beautiful Aye sits at the feet of her harsh governess, on her knees a length of English silk; with a single thread she stitches, to make a lovely garment. Alas, alas! Love in another land, my heart you have bound and overcome.)

Down her face the warm tears run, for she is beaten morning and night because she loves a mercenary from another country. Alas, alas! Love in another land, my heart you have bound and overcome.)

This simple love-song owes little to *fin' amors*, although the motif of *amors d'autre pais* resembles Jaufre Rudel's *amors de lonh*. Here, however, the motif does not function as part of a philosophy of love, but rather serves to create the mood and focus of the refrain.

More significant as a type of minstrel song are the *chansons de mal mariées*, which according to Jeanroy form the bulk of a larger group of *chansons dramatiques*, where a protagonist other than the poet himself expresses the sentiments of the poem.[16] Most frequently, the speaker is a woman who describes her unhappy marriage to a man who ill-treats her. Like the *chanson de toile*, the *chanson de mal mariée* attempts to evoke a courtly atmosphere but actually derives from the popular form of the 'woman's lament', found particularly in German poetry.

The tone of the *chansons de mal mariées* ranges from the colloquial to the pseudo-courtly, but the theme of the jealous cruel husband is consistent and pervasive. In this minstrel song, courtly diction is used to enhance the fate of the ill-treated wife:

> En un vergier lez une fontenele,
> dont clere est l'onde et blanche la gravele,
> siet fille a roi, sa main a sa maxele:
> en sospirant son douz ami rapele.
> > 'ae cuens Guis amis!
> > la vostre amors me tout solaz et ris.
>
> Cuens Guis amis, com male destinee!
> mes pere m'a a un viellart donee,
> qui en cest mes m'a mise et enserree:
> n'en puis eissir a soir n'a matinee.'
>
> Li mals mariz en oï la deplainte,
> entre el vergier, sa corroie a desceinte:
> tant la bati q'ele en fu perse et tainte.
> entre ses piez por pou ne l'a estainte.
> > (Abbott, pp.24–5)

(In an orchard by a fountain, whose stream was clear and gravel was white, sits a king's daughter, her hand to her cheek; sighing, she remembers her sweet lover. 'Ah, Count Guis my love. Your love takes from me comfort and happiness.'

'Count Guis my love, what an evil destiny. My father has given me to an old man who has put me in this estate and locked me up: I cannot leave it, night or morning.'

The wicked husband heard her complaining of it, he enters the orchard, he has undone his belt: so much does he beat her that she was black and blue from it. He has almost killed her between his feet.)

The opening description of the orchard, the refrain calling on Count Guis, and the status of the girl as a king's daughter create a courtly and aristocratic setting for the poem, while the woman's lament and the figure of the wicked husband belong to popular tradition. The jealous husband appears as a stock character in several types of popular literature, particularly humorous poems and fabliaux, and was usually an integral part of the *chansons de mal mariées*. As in other popular love-songs, these poems borrow images and motifs from courtly literature, but the kind of love described does not conform to the poetic ideal of *fin' amors*; instead it represents a specifically non-courtly view of love and marriage.

The *débat*, or dialogue poem, is another popular form which often includes the familiar topoi of nature, love, and marriage. Both Paris and Jeanroy agree that this is one of the oldest forms of popular song in northern France, having affinities with the classical *conflictus*, and it also provides the base for other genres, particularly the *pastourelle* and *aube*. Debates between personified characters such as Summer and Winter, Body and Soul, Water and Wine are familiar from medieval Latin poetry and versions are also found in the vernacular.[17] In the northern French *débat*, the subject of the argument is usually love and the interlocutors are real personae, rather than allegorical figures—such as a mother and daughter, a lover and his mistress or two friends. In this *débat*, a lady accuses her lover of treachery:

> 'Dites, seignor, que devroit on jugier
> d'un traïtour qui faisoit a entendre
> que il avoit m'amour sanz destorbier?
> Mais ce n'iert ja, Dex m'en puisse deffendre!
> Prenez le moi, sou me faites lier
> et sor l'eschiele monter sanz lui descendre,
>   que nul avoir
>   n'en porroie je prendre,
>   ainz morra voir.'

> 'Dame, merci: confession requier.
> De mes pechiez me vuil corpaubles rendre
> vers vos, dame, cui cuidoie engignier.

Li deables me le fist entreprendre.
Cuidiiez vos que deüsse endurer
les maus d'amer? Nenil, mie le mendre;
            por vos avoir
        jel vos faisoie entendre
            por decevoir.'

'Par Deu, ribautz, quant li autre savront,
li tricheour, que tex est ma justise,
que vos avroiz les ieuz sachiez dou front,
ja mès par aus n'iert tel dame requise.
De la paour li autre s'en fuiront:
lors verra l'en les lëaus sanz faintise
            apertement,
        quant la lengue iert jus mise,
            qui d'amors ment.'[18]

('Tell me, my lords, how one ought to judge a traitor who has indicated that he would have my love without any hindrance? But that shall never be, may God defend me from it. Take him for me, and bind him, and have him taken up onto the pillory, and don't bring him down again, for I'll accept no ransom for him, rather shall he die instead.'

'Lady, have mercy: I wish to make a confession. I wish to say *mea culpa* for my sins to you, lady, whom I thought to trick. The devil made me do it. Do you think that I ought to suffer the pain of love? Not in the least; to have you, I pretended to deceive you.'

'By God, libertine, when the others know, the seducers, that this is my sentence, that you will have your eyes torn out of your head, no longer shall such a lady be sought after by them. Out of fear the others will run away: then one will see the loyal ones openly and without pretence, when the tongue which tells lies about love will have been laid down.')

Again, in this poem, we find elements of courtly love superimposed upon popular forms and conventions. The lover begs his lady for mercy and claims he suffers the pain of love. The lady, however, is by no means the passive, idealized object worshipped in troubadour poetry. Here, she exercises to the full her social and conventional power as *dame*.

The poems I have been discussing represent the range of northern French lyrics which have transformed popular and courtly conventions into a different literary tradition addressed to a changing audience. The popular elements consist primarily of nature imagery and seasonal celebration, echoes of a simple rustic way of life. But for contemporary audiences of a newly emergent nobility, many of them town-based, the idyllic nature settings are not only an appeal to their aesthetic appreciation, they are a link with the landowning power of the established aristocracy with whom they desired to connect themselves.

The courtly elements in the lyrics are associated primarily with courtly love. This represents, not a direct borrowing from troubadour poetry, but a received northern French version, *amour courtois*, which developed out of romance and chivalric literature. The trouvères held a monopoly on courtly love in its narrowest sense since they addressed themselves to an aristocratic minority. It was through their poetry that the idealistic doctrine of *amour courtois* was disseminated to a knightly audience.

The minstrels and *jongleurs*, catering for a wider section of society, borrowed not only from the traditions of the trouvères but also from various kinds of majority entertainment including romance and fabliau. Their presentation of courtly love, therefore, is not identical to either *fin' amors* or *amour courtois*, since it is broader in both literary definition and social function. This type of extended courtly love retained many of its 'courtly' features—notably the lover's sufferings for an unrequited love—in order to appeal to an audience aspiring to nobility, to imply that they shared the élitism of the aristocracy. In many cases, the sought-for lady, pursued in a natural setting, clearly represents the established landowning class, while the persona of the lover invested with 'knightly' qualities such as *courtoisie*, represents the emerging bourgeoisie.

More significantly, it is in this kind of minstrel entertainment that a connection is made between courtly love and marriage. Such a connection was never part of the original *fin' amors*: in troubadour lyric, marriage was never an issue, either an impediment or an ultimate goal. The whole code of courtly love was constructed as a metaphor masking the realities of patronage and political marriage. But the songs and romances of the northern French nobility, especially the emergent wealth-based nobility, took courtly love literally as a form of aristocratic behaviour, whose practice guaranteed noble status. At the same time, expedient marriage was crucial to the successful rise of the emergent classes into the upper nobility, and the trading of new wealth in return for old aristocratic status, through the medium of marriage, was common practice. Not surprisingly then, the literature of the new nobility attempted to show that courtly love was the appropriate prelude to noble marriage, a progression which was never envisaged as part of the *fin' amors* construct.

That this progression from courtly love to marriage was successfully established as the model of noble behaviour is clear from the bulk of surviving songs and romances. H.A. Kelly has pointed out that, contrary to modern opinion, love and marriage were not always held to be mutually exclusive in medieval literature. In fact, 'marriage was considered the most desirable conclusion to serious love. There was no tradition of incompatibility between love and marriage, except in the literature of satire and complaint'.[19] Thus the stereotypes of the *mal mariée* and the jealous husband belong to a tradition of satire and complaint which highlighted the difficulties of assimilating courtly love, a literary ideal, with the practical reality of political marriage. The fact that this satirical and explicitly anti-feminist tradition was so widespread in medieval literature indicates that the progression from courtly love to noble marriage—presented in courtly verse as the defining characteristic of the noble classes, and a 'natural' part of their social practice—was simply an idealized construct designed to legitimate the bourgeois rise to power through marriage.

The significance of love and marriage in medieval society is further indicated by the types of literature based on discussion and analysis of these topics. Such types are mainly non-lyric forms, since the lyric itself was too limited in scope to allow for much in the way of argument. The *débat*, for example, was a popular vehicle for discussion, either in the form of a light-hearted dialogue, as in the previous example, 'Dites, seignor, que devroit on jugier'; or in a more courtly and learned form, particularly as part of the French and Anglo-Norman bird-debates and dream-visions.[20] The rival claims of the clerk and knight as lovers, a topic ultimately derived from Ovid's *Amores*, was a popular subject for debate within a longer poem. The clerk was thought to be familiar with all aspects of love, from his detailed study of classical masters such as Ovid, while the knight automatically doubled as the ideal courtly lover. Other questions concerning love could be discussed by birds rather than human protagonists, holding a kind of 'court of love', and conventions such as the *demande d'amour* were often incorporated into the debates and dream-visions, allowing the nobility to examine matters concerning love and marriage at a safe literary distance.

Such poems are evidently the work of clerical or courtly composers writing for the ruling classes, both emergent and established. The poems set out a complex and witty argument, involving allegory and symbolism, with the intention of stating a moral or provoking further discussion. Love becomes reified, the sum total of courtly love conventions, dissociated from the individual and subjective experiences conventionally described in the lyrics. Unlike the lyrics, the debate poems are presented by an objective narrator who is often detached from the action of the poem, and the aim is to instruct as well as to entertain. Dilemmas of love are therefore based on dilemmas of courtly behaviour—conflicts of loyalties, proving one's honour, and so on—which further confirm the noble status of the audience while suppressing the sensual aspect of courtly love so offensive to the Church. Satires on marriage, usually directed against the wife, are also powerful statements of Church ambivalence regarding sexual activity, particularly by women, even within the bonds of holy matrimony.

The ultimate example of the moralizing love-poem is of course the *Roman de la Rose*[21], a poem which incorporates many of the most significant literary conventions of its time: the dream-vision framework, an idealized natural setting, bird protagonists, love-debate, and stock characters, such as the jealous husband. The register of the poem shifts from the allegorical to the satirical, so that accepted literary conventions acquire new shades of meaning.

In the first part, love is presented as an allegorical pursuit of happiness, and the dreamer is entirely committed to love's worship as were the Provençal troubadours. His initiation into the mysteries of love as a formal art is conducted by the god of love who explains the rules, the suffering, and the rewards in terms familiar from trouvère lyric and chivalric romance:

> Grant joie en ton cuer demerras
> De la biauté que tu verras,
> E saches que dou regarder
> Feras ton cuer frire e larder,
> E tot adès en regardant
> Aviveras le feu ardent:
> Qui ce qu'il aime plus regarde,
> Plus alume son cuer e larde;
> Cil larz alume e fait flamer
> Le feu qui fait les genz amer.
> Chascuns amanz suit par costume
> Le feu qui l'art e qui l'alume;
> Quant il le feu de plus près sent,
> E il s'en vait plus apressant.
> Li feus si est ce qu'il remire
> S'amie qui le fait defrire;
> Quant il se tient de li plus près,
> E il plus est d'amer engrès.
> Ce sevent tuit sage e musart:
> Qui plus est près dou feu plus art.
> (Langlois, vol.II, 11.2339–58)

(You will have great joy in your heart from the beauty which you will see, and know that gazing upon her will make your heart blaze and burn, and gazing on her constantly will keep the ardent fire alive: the more a man looks upon the one he loves, the more his heart catches alight and burns; this taper ignites and sets ablaze the fire which makes people love. Each lover customarily follows the fire which burns and inflames him; when he feels the fire is closest, then he goes nearer to it. The fire is what he admires—his mistress—who causes him to burn up; when he keeps closest to her, then is he the more consumed with love. Every wise man and fool knows this: he who is closest to the fire burns the most.)

Because of the narrative structure of the poem, the conventions and motifs which are merely suggested or alluded to in the lyrics can here be fully expanded and illustrated, so that Guillaume is virtually offering a handbook to the practices of courtly love and thus exposing them to examination and perhaps criticism.

In his continuation of Guillaume's poem, Jean de Meun allows the dreamer to become increasingly detached from the persona of the poet. Allegorical characters express a variety of opinions about the nature of love, many of which are cynical and corrupt, in antithesis to the dreamer's idyllic vision of love earlier in the poem. The relationship between men and women as a struggle for power, hinted at in the *chansons de mal mariées*, is here fully developed, with advice to women on how to manipulate and exploit men balanced by the anti-feminist complaints of *li Jaloux*:

> Las! pour quei nous entreveïsmes!
> Las! de quel eure fui je nez,
> Quant en tel vilté me tenez
> Que cil ribaut mastin puant,
> Qui flatant vous vont e chuant,
> Sont si seigneur de vous e maistre,
> Don seus deüsse sires estre,
> Par cui vous estes soutenue,
> Vestue, chauciee e peüe,
> E vous m'en faites parçoniers
> Ces orz ribauz, ces pautoniers,
> Qui ne vous font se honte non!
> Tolu vous ont vostre renon,
> De quei garde ne vous prenez
> Quant entre voz braz les tenez;
> Par devant dient qu'il vous aiment,
> E par darriers putain vous claiment...
> (Langlois vol.III, 11.9224–40)

(Alas!, why did we come together? Alas, at what hour was I born, when you hold me in such contempt that those stinking adulterous curs, who go flattering and deceiving you, are so much lords and masters over you, over whom I alone ought to be lord, by whom you are maintained, clothed, fed and shod. And you make me an accomplice of these hateful debauchers, these whoremongers, who do nothing but disgrace you. May you have taken from you your good name, which you do not take care of when you hold them in your arms; in front of you they say that they love you, but behind your back they call you a whore.)

The jealous husband epitomizes a satirical and anti-feminist view of marriage which sees it as antithetical to courtly love. Of this character, H.A. Kelly says:

> He is usually opposed to marriage, not because it interferes with love or makes love impossible, but because love itself, in the romantic and ennobling sense, is impossible, given the fundamental and irremediable perversity of women. Women can only pretend a genuine love in order to entrap men into marriage, which from their point of view is simply a means of exploiting their husbands and indulging their vices all the more.[22]

The attitudes to love presented in the poem as a whole are thus polarized into two discrete categories: a vision of love in its most courtly and idealized form, and its debasement to an undignified battle of the sexes. Both views are narrow and extreme, in contrast to the popular lyrics and romances which admit aspects of both these opposites into their extended definition of love. Some evoke a courtly atmosphere and describe a knight's pure love for his lady, while others describe an unhappy marriage or a spirited *pastourelle* meeting, these often representing clerical attacks on sexual activity.

The satirical moralizing function of poems like the *Roman de la Rose* was highly influential in shaping the French literary interpretation of courtly love. Above all, the satirical poems popularized the 'bourgeois–realist' view of love and marriage which was the exact opposite of that spread by the court-poets. While courtly love was used to mask the economic and political motivations of noble marriage alliances, the bourgeois tradition attempted to reveal the truly venal and materialistic nature of non-courtly marriage. The result of this 'realism' was to polarize courtly love and non-courtly marriage, one being noble and altruistic, the other being mercenary and constricting. The emergent middle classes were determined to preserve the myth of courtly love as their guarantee of *courtoisie*, by denying, through satire, their participation in bourgeois marriage practices.

The genre of fabliau, as a type of satire, presents the negative extreme of love and marriage.[23] It also exemplifies the process of transforming a bourgeois tradition of comic and satiric tale into a genre addressed to a more diverse social group, including the nobility. The fabliau specializes in satirizing non-courtly marriage practices. The characters and settings of these humorous narrative poems can be either amusingly rustic-provincial, or they can be mock-courtly and sophisticated. In either case, the fabliaux display the concerns of an upwardly mobile audience, under the guise of light entertainment.

The non-courtly fabliaux, such as Chaucer's *Miller's Tale*, are exaggerations of low-class life from the safe vantage point of the wealthy middle classes. High-spirited students, dour millers, corrupt priests, and cunning farmers' wives act out gross and farcical scenes in provincial towns and peasant farmhouses, with the aid of props such as wooden beds, breeches, barrels of wine, and assorted pots and pans and domestic items. In such a context love and marriage are inevitably one-dimensional and static. Love on a spiritual, emotional plane is non-existent; there remains only lust, a physical desire which must be satisfied as quickly as possible. Within marriage, there is no respect or dignity, only a constant effort by the wife to thwart the possessiveness of the husband.

Fabliaux on this model seem to project the concerns of an emergent moneyed class eager to align itself with the nobility. By satirizing the spiritual emptiness and physical coarseness of urban and rural commoners, the new nobility is reassured about its own refinement and superior social status. The debased love of the fabliaux affirms by contrast the significance of courtly love conventions as a symbol of noble marriage.

Many of the surviving fabliaux explicitly make use of courtly conventions for the purposes of parody or contrastive humour. Nykrog maintains that these courtly references presuppose an aristocratic audience and way of life[24], but they would also have significance for the new rich seeking to establish themselves in courtly society. The intention of such fabliaux is evidently to expose the pretensions of those who adopt courtly manners without possessing the appropriate social status. Such an intention is clear in tales combining courtly characters, such as knights and lords, with bourgeois themes and settings, to enhance the grossness of the plot. In the tale of 'Berengier au Long Cul',[25] for example, the satire hinges on the unequal marriage between a peasant 'knight' and a noble lady. By making fun of such marriages, in an exaggerated form, noble audiences can defuse the threat of upward pressure from the socially mobile middle classes, and can also direct attention away from the fact that these 'unequal' marriages were often of great economic advantage to the nobility themselves.

Another example of a mock-courtly fabliau is 'Le Chevalier qui recovra l'amor de sa dame', which tells of a knight who pretends to be a ghost in order to win back the love of his lady.[26] Here again, the apparently courtly appearance and behaviour of the characters contrast with their decidedly materialistic and selfish motives. Typically, love is shown to exist only outside marriage, and even then the supposedly 'courtly' love conventions thinly disguise what is merely lust and the desire for possession. The humour of the story lies firstly in the cause of the lady's anger—the knight fell asleep at their rendezvous—and secondly in the trick played on the husband. The knight first wins the lady in a manner worthy of romance, by defeating the husband in a tournament, but the description brings out the humour and parody:

> Li dui qui pristrent lo tornoi
> En la place furent premiers
> Armé sor les coranz destriers
> Tuit prest de lances depecier.
> Lors saillent sus sanz delaier;
> Les escuz joinz, les lances baissent,
> Lachent les regnes, si s'eslaissent,
> Noblemant es estriers s'afichent;
> Les lances brisent et esclicent,
> Onques de rien ne s'espargnerent;
> Des espees lo chaple ferent,
> Chascuns au mialz que il savoit.

> Li chevaliers qui pris avoit
> Lo tornoi et juré par s'ame
> Envers lo seignor a la dame
> Que il voldra a lui joster
> Par tans, cui qu'il doie coster,
> Lores s'eslaisse cele part
> Plus tost que foille qui depart
> D'arc, qant ele est bien entesee;
> Jus l'an porte lance levee;
> Nel pot tenir poitraus ne cengle,
> Tot chaï en un mont ensanble.

> Et qant la dame a ce veü,
> Q'a son seignor est mescheü,
> D'une partie en fu dolante,
> De l'autre molt li atalante
> Que ses amis l'a si bien fait.   (11.56–83)

(The two who had undertaken the tournament were the first in their places, armed upon their swift horses, all ready to shatter lances. Then they surged forth without delay; their shields at the ready, their lances lowered, they loosened the reins, and they charged, nobly bracing themselves in the stirrups; the lances broke and slivered, but they spared themselves nothing; they carried on the battle with swords, each one as best as he could.

The knight who had undertaken the tournament and sworn on his soul that regarding the lady's lord he would joust with him immediately, whomsoever it might harm, at once he hurled himself in his direction more swiftly than an arrow leaves the bow, when it has been pulled taut; he brought the other down with raised lance; nor could breast strap or girth hold him up, he fell in one heap.

And when the lady saw this, that misfortune had come to her husband, on the one hand she was grieved by it, on the other she was greatly pleased that her lover had done so well.)

The wealth of technical and courtly diction—'escuzs joinz', 'lances baissent', 'tornoi', 'juré par s'ame', 'poitraus', 'joster'—emphasizes the essentially ridiculous nature of the tournament, while imperfectly concealing the triangle structure of husband, wife and lover which is basic to the fabliau genre. The combination of courtly diction and sexual humour (a combination found also in the burlesque poems of the troubadours) results in something approaching a comic romance. Its function is to offer an alternative entertainment to the serious dilemmas about love and marriage often posed in the romance and debate poems. At the same time, these 'courtly' fabliaux have the effect of reaffirming the class identity of their audiences. They share in the courtly traditions of the aristocracy, which means appreciating the political and social significance of marriage.

The fabliau genre is characterized by its humorous satire of non-courtly marriage, with the implicit intention of reassuring its audiences that they are entitled to participate in the truly courtly practices of the established aristocracy. The range of situations represented in the fabliaux, from the overtly sexual to the witty and satirical, suggests a basic intention to amuse and entertain, rather than to moralize. The fundamental assumptions of the fabliau—that love is nothing more than physical desire, marriage is a restriction of personal liberty, wives are devious and unfaithful, and husbands are jealous and boorish—are also common to the genre, whether a tale is uncompromisingly bourgeois in style and mood or is combined with courtly influences for the purpose of parody and social comment.

Nevertheless the aim of the fabliaux is to draw a clear line between the bourgeois marriage practices parodied within them, and the noble alliances celebrated in the romances. It is the commoners and the pretentious bourgeoisie who disguise lust as love and greed as noble courtship. The figure of 'knight' or 'courtly lover' in the fabliaux represents a caricature of the emergent bourgeois aspiring to enter, via marriage, the portals of the aristocracy.

The humour of the fabliau is not merely social. There is also a strong anti-feminist bias, ultimately of clerical provenance. Women are shown to be lustful, devious and adulterous, thereby confirming the need for male control through marriage and economic power. The struggles for *maistrie* between husband and wife, which feature prominently in many of the fabliaux (and indeed in some of the romances as well) suggest a real ambivalence towards women, who were desirable for their wealth and status, but who traditionally had limited personal freedom of action.

The popularity of the fabliau genre can therefore be explained not only by its content but also by its variety of functions. In effect it soothed the anxieties and confirmed the intentions of both the old aristocracy and the new wealth-based nobility. The former were reassured of their established position through satire of the socially ambitious, while the latter were encouraged to participate in courtly customs, including political marriage, as a means of cementing their alliance to the old aristocracy.

All the types of popular poetry which have been discussed so far with reference to French literature are also found in Middle English, testifying to the strong influence from one to the other. Chaucer's *Canterbury Tales* draw on many French conventions and genres, such as romance in the *Knight's Tale*, fabliau in the *Miller's Tale* and the *Merchant's Tale*, anti-feminist satire in the *Wife of Bath's Tale*. In most of the tales, the relationship between courtly love and marriage is a significant issue. This clearly indicates its importance for Chaucer's audience of Anglo-French nobility, whose position was based on, and maintained by, political marriage.

The lyric mood of popular French poetry is conveyed in Middle English particularly through the Harley Lyrics, a unique group of poems dating from the late thirteenth or early fourteenth century. The extent of French influence is difficult to assess, since English, French and Latin had been coexistent in England for nearly three centuries. John Speirs points to both similarities and differences between lyrics in the three languages and suggests that the 'resemblances arise from something deeper than conscious imitation; that there *was* a European community in which the diverse local communities belonged'.[27] Arthur K. Moore tends to minimize the extent of French influence on the Harley Lyrics, and makes a distinction between the English poems, which draw on existing native traditions, and French or Anglo-Norman *chansons* of the late thirteenth century.[28] As with the Latin and vernacular poetry of the Continent, overlapping influences from one language to another provide a pool of poetic conventions which are then given a variety of interpretations.

Though the Harley manuscript contains both religious and secular works in Latin, French, and English, the Middle English love-lyrics are recognizably popular rather than courtly in tone. Some critics have associated the manuscript with the *clerici vagantes*, but the classical and learned background of the Continental goliardic tradition is scarcely evident in the Middle English poems.[29] On the contrary, the apparent location of the manuscript and the alliterative metre of some of the poems suggest an amalgamation of an older native poetic tradition with borrowed conventions from Anglo-French sources.

The French theme of the *reverdie* is well represented in the Harley Lyrics, both on its own and as a prelude to a love-song. The poem 'Spring' ('Lenten ys come wiþ love to toune') contrasts a description of spring's abundance with the poet's lack of success in love. Each stanza catalogues some of the activities of the natural world, conveying a sense of vigorous movement which emphasizes the poet's passivity:

> Lenten ys come wiþ love to toune,
> wiþ blosmen ant wiþ briddes roune,
>   þat al þis blisse bryngeþ.
> Dayeseȝes in þis dales,
> notes suete of nyhtegales,
>   vch foul song singeþ.
> Þe þrestelcoc him þreteþ oo;
> away is huere wynter wo
>   when woderoue springeþ.
> Þis foules singeþ ferly fele,
> ant wlyteþ on huere wynne wele,
>   þat al þe wode ryngeþ.
>   (Brook no.11, 1–12)

Though the general suggestions of bird-song and blooms in full flower are reminiscent of French lyrics, the diction and alliterative metre are unmistakably English. *Dayeseȝes, þrestelcoc, woderoue,* and *foules* are all Old English forms which give a specifically native colouring to the woodland scene described.

A spring setting is similarly used in 'Alysoun' to preface an expression of the poet's unhappiness, and again the poet's mood is intensified by being out of harmony with nature. The description of his *love-longinge* clearly relies on French conventions but the mode of expression is recognizably native, to such an extent that the French loan-word *baundoun* strikes with particular effect. In another poem, 'Advice to Women' ('In May hit murgeþ when hit dawes') the *reverdie* opening introduces a general theme of love rather than an individual experience, and the poet exhorts women to beware of deceivers:

> ah, feyre leuedis, be on war,
> to late comeþ þe ȝeynchar
> when love ou haþ ybounde.
> (Brook no.12, 34–6)

The general attitude to love presented in the Harley Lyrics is manifestly non-courtly, compared both to the Provençal tradition and to the French *chansons de toile* and similar minstrel songs. There is no theory or analysis of love itself; the poet merely adopts a conventional stance as the devoted admirer, often without hope of love in return, and expresses his love by means of similes and formal descriptions of physical attributes.[30] The poems are not explicitly related to any particular social milieu but a rural setting is sometimes suggested which is reminiscent of French and goliardic folk-poetry. In other poems,[31] however, comments of a moral kind concerning humanity's place in the world indicate that the lyrics are not to be dismissed as simple folk-songs, an impression strengthened by the inclusion of many religious poems.

Continental influence is seen most clearly in the expression of the lover's suffering and in the conventional portraits of the girl's beauty, a technique also found in French and classical poetry. Some of the lyrics reflect specific genres borrowed from the Continent, such as the *pastourelle* 'The Meeting in the Wood' (no.8) and the dialogue between a clerk and his lover, 'De clerico et Puella' (no.24).

Nevertheless, the native poetic tradition is much in evidence throughout the lyrics, both secular and religious. The alliterative metre and the moralizing tone of some of the poems resemble those of Old English lyrics, reflecting their common debt to Latin religious poetry. Even those poems which contain a high proportion of French borrowings in theme and imagery still retain a solid basis of Anglo-Saxon diction. In the poem 'When þe Nyhtegale Singes' (no.25) the poet expresses a conventional plea to his lady to return his love, but he addresses her as *lemmon*, asks for *a suete cos* and *a love-bene*, and in the last stanza says:

> Bituene Lyncolne ant Lyndeseye, Norhamptoun ant Lounde,
> ne wot y non so fayr a may as y go fore ybounde. (11.17–18)

Thus although the sentiments of the poet may reflect a French influence, the setting and diction of the poem are fixed firmly in England.

The Harley Lyrics exemplify the fusion of Romance and Anglo-Saxon poetic techniques, showing how the themes and forms of one language could be interpreted through the medium of another. In the secular lyrics, the extended type of love has been borrowed from French song, with its emphasis on seasonal rejoicing, the pursuit of happiness, and the ideal of physical beauty. The poets do not present themselves as courtly lovers, with all that this implies of spiritual aspiration and feudal humility. Love is seen as a secular, youthful activity, an escape from the reminders of human mortality contained in the religious poems.

Lyric verse in French and Middle English exemplifies a tradition of popular song enriched and refined by borrowings from courtly literature. The theme of love in these poems represents an extension of the restricted and specific *fin' amors* of the troubadours: conventional motifs such as the joy and pain of love, the sufferings of the lover, unrequited love, were extracted from the aristocratic context of *fin' amors* and assimilated with other topics from popular poetry, particularly the *reverdie* and woman's lament.

The non-lyric tradition of dream-vision, debate, and fabliau tests the theory of courtly love against the reality of medieval French society, in which various élitist groups—the knights, the old aristocracy, the wealthy bourgeoisie, the royal administrators—were jostling for position. These groups wanted to participate in the courtly tradition of *fin' amors* which not only conferred *courtoisie* but also masked the real purpose of courtship, a politically advantageous marriage.

Courtly love in French literature, then, has lost the complex and abstract terminology of *fin' amors* but has retained those social functions which are relevant for the ruling classes, both emergent and established. The lyric makes a version of courtly love accessible to those who do not have access to the abstract and metaphysical verse of the trouvères. Romance and fabliau, while presenting love from opposite extremes, express the same concern with marriage as a crucial social and economic institution.

The literature I have been discussing was therefore addressed to a wider audience than that of the troubadours and trouvères, and drew from a broader range of themes, popular and courtly. Nevertheless, this literature, both in French and in English, arose out of particular social changes and was addressed to a variety of influential audiences. Just as Colin Muset, Walther von der Vogelweide, and Chaucer participated in this tradition of extended courtly love, covering a wide range of topics and genres, so Dafydd ap Gwilym also drew on this tradition to enlarge his native inheritance of bardic material.

CHAPTER 4

Welsh Court-poetry and Courtly Love

THE European poetry I have been discussing was clearly influential for Dafydd ap Gwilym and his contemporaries. In terms of motifs, themes and generic types, the poetry of the *cywyddwyr* is noticeably dependent on earlier European models, particularly French and, to a lesser extent, German. There is, however, another way in which Dafydd's poetry can be regarded as derivative, and that is in relation to his own native bardic tradition. The medieval court-poets of Wales, the *gogynfeirdd*, were Dafydd's immediate predecessors, and as such exerted a considerable influence on his work. A study of *gogynfeirdd* poetry, both the earlier panegyrics to independent princes, and the later pieces to audiences conditioned by Norman rule, is therefore crucial to an understanding of Dafydd's work.

The period of *gogynfeirdd* court-poetry, from the early twelfth to the early fourteenth centuries, displays a marked development in the use of love as a poetic theme. Until about the middle of the thirteenth century, poems to women, the *rhieingerddi*, were a formal and official part of the court-poet's repertoire, composed to honour the wives and daughters of patrons. The later poems, however, coinciding with the loss of Welsh political independence and its immediate after-effects, make a much more liberal use of the theme of love and draw on traditions other than that of eulogy.

The *gogynfeirdd* attitude to love, as a general manifestation, has been explained as a historical development from troubadour courtly love-poetry, a conscious absorption of foreign ideas received indirectly through a sequence of intermediate stages. J. Lloyd-Jones has referred to 'the pervasive spirit of a literary movement brought from the Continent by wandering scholars and troubadours—courtly love', suggesting that the attitude of the *gogynfeirdd* to love has been 'borrowed' from troubadour courtly love.[1]

The early *gogynfeirdd* poems are unlikely to have acquired any direct borrowings from troubadour verse since the two bodies of poetry were composed more or less contemporaneously. Anthony Conran has expressed the view that the middle of the twelfth century, when the first *gogynfeirdd* were composing, is 'fantastically early for troubadour influence to have reached Wales', a view endorsed by J.E. Caerwyn Williams.[2] However, it is worth remembering that indirect influence from troubadour verse was being felt in England from at least the middle of the twelfth century. Many of the themes and techniques of Provençal verse were carried to England after the Conquest, mainly through the medium of northern French verse. Imitations of troubadour lyric in both Northern French and Anglo-Norman were composed for the Norman rulers of England, and may also have found their way to the substantial Norman settlements in south Wales.[3]

The poems of the later *gogynfeirdd*, composing in the late thirteenth and early fourteenth centuries, definitely reveal traces of the Continental tradition of love-poetry. But their motifs in common, such as the pain of unrequited love, sleeplessness, the plea for love, the jealous husband, and the use of nature imagery, suggest that the channels of transmission were of a popular and non-literary kind. The pre-existence of a native tradition of popular love-poetry is also a likelihood, although survivals of this kind of poetry in Welsh cannot be dated accurately enough to allow them as evidence.

Similarities between troubadour and *gogynfeirdd* poetry can also be explained by their common function as the official eulogistic verse of a social élite. Both kinds of poetry were produced by court-centred societies and fulfilled a specific function, that of reaffirming the power and prestige of the ruling class. At the same time, however, there were significant differences between the two societies. Whereas troubadour verse traces the emergence of a new aristocracy of knights, *gogynfeirdd* poetry invokes the weight of centuries of bardic tradition to reinforce the ruling power of ancient Welsh monarchies challenged by Norman baronies. While troubadour verse supported a feudal hierarchy, the poetry of the *gogynfeirdd* supported the ancient power structure of tribal dynasties.

There is also an important distinction to be made between troubadour *fin' amors* poetry and the Welsh *rhieingerddi*. Although both function primarily as forms of eulogy, the women of Provence had a very real and significant power compared to their contemporaries in Wales. Praise of Provençal noblewomen was directed at the women themselves as possessors of property and wealth, and their idealization as courtly love objects masked their desirability as marriage partners.

In medieval Wales, however, women did not generally hold land or money in their own right. Praise of Welsh noblewomen was merely a displacement of the eulogies directed at the lord in whose court they lived. By honouring a patron's wife or daughter, a poet was honouring the patron himself, and therefore fulfilling part of his obligation as court-poet. Because of this difference in women's status in the two cultures, the basic premise of *fin' amors*, that the lover must prove himself worthy of his powerful mistress, is not relevant for Welsh society. The persona of Welsh court-poetry is not the lover-knight of troubadour verse, but rather a warrior-poet who worships a symbol of aristocratic power based on landownership.

Another significant difference between Provençal and Welsh court-poetry lies in the poetic traditions to which they belong. The antecedents of troubadour lyric are obscure and diverse: the poetry came into being at a particular time in response to particular social and literary impulses. *Gogynfeirdd* poetry also appears in connection with a specific social context—the courts of the independent Welsh princes—but has clearly arisen from an existing native poetic tradition. The origins of court-poetry can be traced back in an almost unbroken line to an accredited source of inspiration and technique, that is, to the *cynfeirdd* and the heroic poetry of the sixth century.

The poetry of the *gogynfeirdd* is therefore anachronistic in a way that Provençal poetry is not. It is consciously conserving an older poetic tradition and set of values, it is reinforcing the ancient right to rule of Welsh dynasties, and it enshrines the privileges, obligations, and social status of the bard, a position of considerable influence and prestige from earliest Celtic times. These considerations of bardic tradition and function inevitably influenced the *gogynfeirdd*, as much in the *rhieingerddi* as in their eulogies and religious verse.

The conservatism of Welsh court-poetry is well attested in terms of metre, poetic techniques, diction, and subject-matter. Whereas troubadour poetry survives in a number of different forms—the *tenso* and *sirventes*, for example, as well as the *canso*—the *gogynfeirdd* compositions considered worthy of preservation are limited largely to praise-poems, *marwnadau* (elegies), and religious verse. These traditional genres, reflecting the functions of the court-poet, were continued in varying degrees after the loss of Welsh independence. But it was that group of praise-poems composed specifically to women which marked the most innovative area of *gogynfeirdd* poetry, and which survived to form the basis of *cywyddwyr* love poetry in the fourteenth and fifteenth centuries.

The *rhieingerddi* have been listed and described by T. Gwynn Jones, who isolates some thirty-one *awdlau* composed by sixteen different poets.[4] In terms of style, T. Gwynn Jones finds these *awdlau* characteristic of the *bardd teulu*, whose duties specifically included the composition and performance of songs for women. These songs were generally less complex in diction and syntax than those of the *penceirddiaid*, but clearly belonged to the same bardic tradition.

T. Gwynn Jones sees the *rhieingerddi* as comprising two types of poem, the love-song, and the official praise-poem or elegy composed for a patron's wife or daughter. Stylistically, he finds little or no difference between the two types, since they are both bardic compositions subject to similar conventions of metre and content. He isolates a number of examples of *rhieingerddi* which foreshadow the attitude to love expressed by the *cywyddwyr* or which resemble the troubadour lyrics in some ways, and he also emphasizes the similarities between Welsh and Irish poetry of this type.[5]

More recently, the whole question of the *rhieingerddi* and possible Continental influence has been intensively analysed by J.E. Caerwyn Williams, who looks at the historical and social background of the *gogynfeirdd* as well as their literary inheritances.[6] Following a point made by T. Gwynn Jones, he looks at the possibility that similar historical circumstances in Wales and southern France produced a similar type of poetry, independently of each other. He concludes that Welsh society in the early Middle Ages evolved a code of courtesy and chivalry which was quite separate from the corresponding trends in France, as the evidence of the Welsh romances proves. He also suggests that love-poetry of the kind composed by the *gogynfeirdd* was a recognized bardic type, native to Wales, and that both courtly and popular love-poetry were composed throughout Welsh bardic history but seldom preserved.

It seems clear that the *rhieingerddi* fulfil a primarily bardic function of praise and elegy and that their literary roots lie with the *cynfeirdd* and the development of Welsh court-poetry during the Middle Ages. To suggest a dichotomy between 'genuine' love-poems and official panegyrics is to create an artificial distinction in a homogeneous body of poetry belonging to the same literary tradition. In the same way, the love-lyrics of the troubadours cannot be divided into two groups, the genuine and the official, but must instead be understood as individual compositions expressed through a set of poetic conventions which fulfil an aristocratic social function.

Those motifs and attitudes of the *rhieingerddi* which appear to be 'borrowed' from troubadour poetry can be explained partly as synchronic and parallel expressions arising from a similar courtly poetic function, and partly as influences from northern French *jongleur* song. T. Gwynn Jones discusses the similarities between *gogynfeirdd* and troubadour poetry on the assumption that 'the Welsh bards, even in the twelfth century, were already familiar with customs very much like those reflected in the poems of the Troubadours'.[7] He mentions in particular the highly technical style common to both groups of poets, the social position of the court-poets, the addressing of love-poems to married women, the complaints of love-suffering, and the use of nature imagery, as features which reflect some degree of troubadour influence on *gogynfeirdd* poetry.

However, all these features are products of the same poetic function—aristocratic eulogy—and need not represent direct borrowing. Moreover, Gwynn Jones's examples of such similarities are all taken from Welsh poetry composed after 1284, by which time the literary relationships between Wales and France had increased in scope. It seems to me, then, that troubadour influence, direct or indirect, is unlikely before the thirteenth century, but that Continental literary traditions, both courtly and popular, made an increasingly effective impact on Welsh poetry after 1284.

It is significant that the primary poetic stance adopted by the troubadours, that of a knight relating to his lady as a feudal servant relates to his overlord, is entirely absent from Welsh love-poetry, both before and after 1284. Though the Welsh poets often adopt an attitude of humility and supplication, it is always in their role as court bard that they urge their suit. This reinforces the synchronic nature of Welsh and Provençal poetry, since they express similar attitudes to love through entirely different social structures.

The two bodies of poetry also represent courtly literary traditions at similar stages of development. An aristocratic poetic tradition, embodying specific social values and intended for a limited and exclusive audience, is aware of its courtly function, and makes use of only a minimum of themes from the wider body of popular material, selecting and transforming these to comply with the purpose and expectations of the courtly poetry. Thus the troubadours apply their technical skills and poetic wit to the *pastorela*, the *alba*, and the *reverdie*, raising these popular forms up to the level of accomplishment of the *cansos* in order to define further their interpretations of *fin' amors*. Similarly, the *gogynfeirdd* select and transmit native popular themes through the system of bardic poetry, enriching the range of poetic conventions available to them.

The undoubted existence of this native popular strand makes the question of later French influence on the *gogynfeirdd* even more complex. Earlier scholars such as J. Lloyd-Jones and Ifor Williams proposed troubadour influence in a fairly direct line, through the intermediary of the wandering scholars,[8] but it is more likely that any such influence would have been already tempered by conventions of northern French poetry, both courtly and popular. The Welsh attitude to love is therefore unlikely to be directly analogous to the troubadour *fin' amors*.

Welsh poetry parallels the movement from the restricted *fin' amors* of the troubadours to the extended courtly love of the French *jongleurs*, in the form of *gogynfeirdd* court-poetry and the *cywydd* tradition represented by Dafydd ap Gwilym. Since this progression is marked by a greater dependence upon popular material, at a level where French conventions are most likely to have been absorbed into Welsh, the apparent borrowings even in the later *gogynfeirdd* poetry may in fact represent a distinctively native tradition, either entirely independent from the French, or influenced by it at a much earlier stage through oral transmission.

When we look at the poems composed by the *gogynfeirdd* before 1284, we find elegies and praise-poems supporting an aristocratic culture maintained by marriage and warfare, and expressed in a conservative and anachronistic bardic style. Though the poems serve a primarily social rather than political function, their diction and imagery consistently allude to the concerns of power-struggling warrior aristocracies.

Cynddelw's *rhieingerdd* to Efa, daughter of Madawg ap Maredudd, epitomizes the formal panegyric addressed to a noblewoman. The poet takes on the persona of a lover, addressing himself to his mistress without hope of reward, but the diction and imagery are redolent of the masculine world of warfare, feasting at court, and striving for honour. The real focus of the eulogy is not Efa herself, but rather Madawg's rule over Powys at a time when its independence was under pressure from Owain Gwynedd. The girl is constantly associated with references to the court, to battle and to the land over which Madawg rules:

> Gorvynawc drythyll gortyuyn dy vyned.
> gorthrych lys leissyawn y ystlyned.
> llys y daw deon yw darymred.
> llys eva y veirt y digoned.
> llysseit y hirdwf oe heur duted.
> llaes wenn gall wenngann wenngaen deced.
> llif dragon vanon valch y thyged . . .
>
> Neum rydraeth hiraeth uetuaeth uaccwy.
> Am ary garafy kenym karwy.
> neud llutedic glann rac glas vordwy.
> Neud llawen awen awel neud mwy.
> Neud llawer ym llify lliw amaerwy tonn.
> ban llewych y bronn ger y breichrwy . . .[9]

(Eager spirited steed, prepare to go—conquer a court, Lleisiawn its name—to a court which noble people come to visit, Efa's court, bards' abundance; courtly her tall figure with her golden cloak, modest and fair, wise and bright, as fair as a white layer (of foam): a maiden from hero's stock, proud is her inheritance . . .

Now longing calls to me, a mead-nourished youth, for the one I love, though she may not love me. The shore is weary from the green swell; inspiration is joyful but the breeze is more so. Greatly she grinds me, colour of a wave's edge, when her breast glows near her bracelet . . .)

Descriptions of the girl's beauty, courtly virtues, and rich apparel serve to emphasize the aristocratic nobility of Madawg's court and his family. Clear echoes of *cynfeirdd* poetry deliberately capture the heroic past, associating Madawg's rule with an earlier greatness. The poet's attitude to Efa, expressing devotion, torment, and the hope of reward, is a displacement of his position in relation to his lord and patron: his duty is to praise in return for material gifts. His apparent humility masks the reality of special privileges and status conferred on court-poets.

Cynddelw's poem is representative of a conservative native tradition of aristocratic praise-poetry: other examples include Llywarch ap Llywelyn's eulogy to Gwenlliant and Einion ap Gwalchmai's elegy to Nest.[10] These poems to women possess the same resonance and declamatory power, arising from the linguistic effects of compounds, repetition, metaphor and unusual syntax, as poems in praise of rulers and warriors, and are clearly part of the same bardic tradition.

In poems to both men and women, the primary function of the persona is that of praise-poet. His role as warrior and as lover are convenient metaphors by which he can relate to the person being praised. The *gogynfeirdd* often refer to themselves specifically as praise-poets, include themselves in the activities of the court, and allude to the material rewards they receive for their poetry. Through their diction and imagery they identify themselves with their audience, a male-dominated warrior aristocracy, in order to praise their patrons according to its values. Thus men are praised for their valour, courage, generosity and leadership, while women are desired for their physical beauty and passive accomplishments.

In songs to princes and rulers the poet exalts his patron while remaining strongly aware of his own prestige and influence as a court bard, making frequent reference to his poetic function. Cynddelw begins his *marwnad* for Madawg ap Maredudd with these lines:

> Kyuarchaf ym ri rad o obeith.
> kyuarchaf kyuercheis ganweith.
> y broui prydu om prifyeith eurgert.
> ym arglwyt gedymdeith.   (LlH, p.118)

(I ask of my Lord a blessing of hope; I ask, I have asked a hundred times, that I may try and compose from my highest language a golden song to my Lord and companion.)

Later in the poem he says:

> Oet beirtgar bartglwm diledyeith.   (LlH, p. 119)

(He was the friend of bards, of unblemished bardic language.)

The poet is affirming the importance of his function by implying its religious aspect—God shows approval by enabling the poet to compose—and its social aspect, since a generous patron will be well rewarded in perfect poetry.

In the *rhieingerddi*, the poet's attitude undergoes a superficial change. He appears to become an earnest supplicant for love, fearing rejection and suffering physical pain because of his lady's indifference. In his poem to Gwenlliant, Llywarch ap Llywelyn says:

> Klywaf uyg callonn tonn ual tande.
> yn llosgi yrdi ar detyf kynne.
> Diameth osgeth o wisc eurde.
> diamheu anuon grann wynyon gre.   (LlH, p.290)

(I feel my broken heart like a flaming fire burning for her like a bonfire. Girl of flawless appearance in a golden gown, without doubt she sends white-maned steeds.)

Praising Efa, Cynddelw says:

> Goruynawc drythyll gorwych yolwyf.
> Gordawc pall eurawc pell nas gwelwyf.
> Goruelyn called kolledic wyf.
> colleis gall attep y nep am nwyf.
> Ym pwyllad newid neud adwyf am vun.
> ym anhun anhed ked rys porthwyf.   (LlH, p.122)[11]

(Eager spirited steed, passionately do I desire the lively one in a golden mantle, so far-off that I cannot see her, the golden one so wise, I am lost. I have missed the wise answer of the one who rouses passion in me; in my changeable state of mind, because of a woman I have become restless, sleepless, even though I suffer it.)

The poetic stance adopted by Llywarch ap Llywelyn and Cynddelw, that of the earnest lover advancing his suit, is an accepted convention of the *rhieingerddi*, a way of establishing the poet's position as praise-singer to the lady by means of a contrived love-relationship. To male rulers, the poets assume the persona of fellow-warriors and companions. To noblewomen, the poets adopt the stance appropriate to the warrior aristocracy they speak for—that is, as supplicants for love, itself a metaphor for patronage.

The plural subject (or persona) of the *gogynfeirdd* poems—representing poet, warrior and lover—certainly corresponds to that of troubadour lyric. The troubadours make conscious references to their bardic function, illustrated by a common opening phrase, 'Farai un vers'. They also dedicate their poems to specific patrons, refer to the material rewards they receive and generally remind their listeners of their role as court-poets. While the *gogynfeirdd* poets evoke a warrior society and address their poems to members of a military aristocracy, the troubadours draw on the world of chivalry and feudal service to align themselves with the interests of the knights.

In their persona as lover, however, the troubadours and the *gogynfeirdd* begin to diverge. In troubadour lyric, the lover-knight is enrolled in feudal service to his mistress, symbolizing the knights' pursuit of economic power through marriage. The conflicts arising from this pursuit, the torments and sufferings caused by unrequited love, represent a real struggle for emergence and the very effective power of noblewomen in Provençal society. In the early *rhieingerddi*, however, the court-poets are not representing the claims of an emergent social class. Rather they are representing themselves as poets, a privileged élite within the aristocratic social framework. At a time when Wales was torn by internal conflicts and threatened by

Anglo-Norman expansion, the power struggles and changing allegiances of the ruling dynasties affected dependants such as the court-poets. Gwalchmai, for example, although the poet of Owain Gwynedd in the middle of the twelfth century, also composed a eulogy and an elegy to Madawg ap Maredudd, brother-in-law and political enemy of Owain.

The privileges and status of the court-poets therefore depended on the continuation of the ruling dynasties. The duties of the poets as eulogists contributed to maintaining the power and independence of these dynasties. The lover-mistress relationship of the *rhieingerddi* is a metaphorical expression of the poets' relationship to their patrons. By identifying themselves with the warrior aristocracy, to the extent of declaring their devotion to its noblewomen, the *gogynfeirdd* are reiterating their privileged position as bards, possessors of a highly exclusive and socially important craft.

What these two kinds of love—troubadour and *gogynfeirdd*—have in common is their artificial and conventional nature, and their basic assumption that love cannot be requited but will only give rise to conflicting emotions. Eulogistic love uses a metaphorical courtship as a form of praise, and can expect no outcome or resolution. The characteristic stance of the poet is that of the lover suffering the torture of unrequited love, a stance shared by both Welsh and Continental praise-poets. The poet's declarations of love are not intended to produce any response, since they are merely an elaborate form of praise, but this very lack of response can then be poetically interpreted as indifference and rejection.

It is to be expected, therefore, that images of suffering and torment will feature in both Welsh and Provençal court-poetry. However, the troubadours went beyond the metaphorical presentation of courtship to formulate a total concept of *fin' amors* in which suffering and conflict became socially acceptable, even obligatory. The *gogynfeirdd*, on the other hand, made no attempt to construct an entire framework of ideals and expectations around their poetic function but simply exploited the convention of the lover-poet as a form of praise in exchange for patronage. The images of conflict which often formed part of this convention express the insecurity of the bards' position at a time of political disruption.

The theme of love used by the earlier *gogynfeirdd* therefore does not correspond precisely to the complex *fin' amors* construct of the troubadours. Whereas the troubadours, representing the interests of the knights, had a real reason for addressing themselves to women (to acquire wealth and status through marriage), the *gogynfeirdd* praised women only as part of their bardic function, to emphasize their own importance and prestige in the context of a warrior society. Praise of noblewomen meant indirect praise of the dynasty to which they belonged, and thus an affirmation of its power, and their own.

In the poetry of the *gogynfeirdd*, the poet's stance as earnest lover overlays but does not completely obscure his prime task as praise-poet, and the images of love's devastating effect are woven into a rich patchwork of native expressions and conventions. Unlike the troubadours, the *gogynfeirdd* did not develop this poetic stance into a complete courtly love ethic based on feudal service and spiritual fulfilment, with a set of key terms corresponding to *merce, joi* and *amors* which implied certain definable expectations. The feudal system as it was known in medieval Europe had little relevance in a Wales governed by a host of local princes and intermittently torn by civil war, and where the loyalty of a nobleman to his lord was too closely and explicitly associated with the battlefield to provide a model for a lover and his mistress. At the same time, the serious and influential function of the Welsh poet as a spiritual intermediary, echoing the ancient identification of priest and poet, virtually precluded a poetic appropriation of a religion of love.

The parallels between troubadour and *gogynfeirdd* poetry so far suggested—such as their aristocratic audiences, their basically eulogistic function, their use of the lover-mistress relationship, and their exploitation of imagery concerned with conflict and personal suffering—have been considered in the context of the social and historical circumstances which produced them. Given some funda-mental differences between these, as well as the independent bardic tradition, it is not surprising that *gogynfeirdd* poetry is by no means imitative or even highly reflective of troubadour characteristics.

However, the two groups of poems clearly belong to the same generic type of aristocratic praise-poetry, and an important feature of this genre is the assimilation of non-courtly material into formal eulogy in order to enhance the poetic relationship between the poet and his object of praise. We have already seen that the troubadours and the secular Latin poets drew on popular vernacular traditions, particularly those connected with seasonal celebration, to provide sources of imagery and analysis about love. The same fusion of poetic traditions occurs in *gogynfeirdd* poetry, where influences from a concurrent body of popular verse increase the symbolic intention of the lover-mistress relationship.

The few examples which survive, in nature poetry, gnomic verse, and the bardic Grammar, suggest that a popular tradition of love and nature poetry was available to the court-bards and that they consciously selected themes from it when appropriate. This tradition was largely rejected by earlier court-poets as being unsuitable for official bardic composition, and did not begin to emerge as an acceptable bardic resource until after 1284 when bardic conventions were changing and relaxing, and the model of French poetry, with its established assimilation of courtly and popular themes, set a precedent for the later *gogynfeirdd*. Just as the rigidity of bardic conventions began to disintegrate during the thirteenth century, so the attitude to particular themes and forms of expression also broadened.

Evidence of popular influence on the early *gogynfeirdd* can be found particularly in the work of Gwalchmai, Cynddelw, and Hywel ab Owain Gwynedd, which foreshadows the greater dependence on popular traditions reflected in the work of the later *gogynfeirdd* and the *cywyddwyr*. Gwalchmai's *gorhoffedd* begins with a nature description which has affinities both with early Welsh gnomic verse and with the popular French *reverdie* tradition, and this kind of description recurs regularly throughout the poem:

> Moch dwyreawc huan haf dyfestin.
> maws llafar adar mygyr hear hin . . .

(Early rising the sun, summer's growth approaching quickly, pleasant the bird-song, bright the fine weather . . .)

> Dymhunis tonn wyrt wrth aber deu
> dychyrch glan glaswyn glwys yfrydeu
> diessic yd gan ednan eneu . . .

(The green wave awoke me by Aber Dau, it strikes the shore of the pale blue sea, lovely its spray, lively the singing from a little bird's mouth . . .)

> Aduwyn kynteuin kein hindyt.
> araf eriw haf hyfryd dedwyt.
> aduwyn dydaw dyuyr dychwart gwyrt wrth echwyt.
> oguanw a chegin a chlawedawc drydyt.   (LlH, pp.16 and 21)

(Mild spring, beautiful weather day, gentle is the force of summer, delightful and lucky. Gently flow the waters—a green [wave] laughs for flowing—of Ogwan and Cegin and Clawedog the third.)

Interspersed with the nature description are heroic references to
Gwalchmai's prowess as a warrior and allusions to the girl he loves.
The diction often reflects official bardic praise-poetry and the poem
as a whole clearly belongs in the mainstream of *gogynfeirdd* poetry.
At the same time the juxtaposition of love and nature and the
implications of the physical relationship enjoyed by Gwalchmai as
part of his warrior persona suggest a transformation of popular ideas
through a recognized bardic medium:

> Caraf y eos uei uorehun lut.
> a golygon hwyr hirwyn y grut.   (LlH, p.18)

(I love the nightingale of May that prevents morning sleep, and the
gentle looks of the tall fair-cheeked one.)

> Pellynnic vyg khof yg kynteuin.
> yn ethrip caru kaerwys vebin.
> pell o uon uein. yduyti dwythwal werin.
> essmwyth yssyt ynn asserw gyfrin.
> yt endeweis eneu yn echlyssur gwir.
> ar lleueryt gwar gwery y lein.   (LlH, p.17)

(Far away is my mind in spring, because of loving a beautiful young
girl. Far from the slender one of Môn—you are a great ruler of people –
a quiet one who is a true friend to me, I listened to her words in a
perfect retreat, refined speech, lively the fair one.)

> Hynoeth oeth dybytaf o dybwyf ryt.
> Ac os duw o nef neu ym kynnyt
> keinuod gan lywe ymy lawr ym hunyt.   (LlH, p.22)

(Tonight I will be in wonder if I may come freely; and if God in heaven
would prosper me, [there will be] bliss for me alone with a fair one in
my sleep.)

The relationship between May-time, love, and the burgeoning of
nature evoked here by Gwalchmai is by no means unique to French
popular poetry, but also belongs to the Welsh poetic tradition.
Compare this stanza to May, as part of the 'Englynion y Misoedd':

> Mis Mai, difrodus geilwad,
> klyd pob klawdd i ddigarad;
> llawen hen diarchenad;
> hyddail koed, hyfryd anllad;
> hawdd kymod lle bo kariad;
> llafar koc a bytheiad;
> nid hwyrach mynd i'r farchnad
> croen yr oen no chroen y ddavad.[12]

(May month, vehement the ploughboy, every ditch is snug for the
abandoned; old people are joyful when lightly clad, trees are thickly

leaved, the wanton person is content; easy the reconciliation where there is love; cock and hound are noisy; no less likely for the fleece of the lamb to go to market than the fleece of the sheep.)

Similar seasonal verse in early Irish, with the conventional topoi of bird-song, tree-growth, and a mood of harmony found also in the French *reverdie*, points to an earlier Celtic tradition of popular seasonal poetry:

> Cétemain, cain cucht,
>   rée rosaír rann;
> canait luin laíd láin
>   día laí grían gaí ngann.
>
> Gairid cuí chrúaid den;
>   is fo-chen sam saír:
> suidid síne serb
>   i mbi cerb caill chraíb.[13]

(May day, fair its form, so perfect a period of time; blackbirds sing a complete song when the sun casts a thin spear. The hardy vigorous cuckoo calls; welcome to noble summer. It settles the bitterness of a storm when the wood's branches are torn down.)

In the context of this pre-medieval Celtic nature poetry, Gwalchmai's incorporation of nature imagery into a bardic praise-poem can be seen as an expedient blending of familiar elements from both popular and courtly native traditions. The placing of the nature references within the framework of the warrior celebration achieves a gnomic effect which parallels the earlier poetic function of seasonal description in Celtic verse.

The first part of Hywel's *gorhoffedd* belongs to the same register as that of Gwalchmai's. Images of the landscape, the season, his life as a princely warrior, and the girl he loves are woven together as aspects of the same sense of triumph. Hywel's use of nature imagery in his *gorhoffedd* is more stylized and figurative than Gwalchmai's gnomic juxtaposition of nature description and warrior boasting. In Hywel's poem, the features of the landscape which he celebrates are symbols of the beauty hidden in strength which characterizes the warriors themselves:

> Caraf y milwyr ae meirch hywet.
> ae choed ae chedyrn ae chyuannet.
> Caraf y meyssyt ae man ueillyon arnaw.
> myn yd gauas faw fyryf oruolet.
> Caraf y brooet breint hywret.
> ae difeith mawrueith ae marannet.   (LlH, p.316)

(I love its soldiers and its trained horses, and its woods and its mighty people and its settlements. I love its fields and the tiny clover on it, where honour found powerful rejoicing. I love its valleys, privilege of bravery, and its extensive wilderness and its wealth.)

The two *gorhoffeddau* are explicit celebrations of aristocratic warrior society and its values. Both poets refer to the lands which they defend against the English, the lords whom they serve, and the material equipment of their profession—horses, armour, shields, swords, spears. In this martial context, nature imagery, with its emphasis on the sea-coast of Wales and the fertile agricultural lands, implies the strategic significance of the coast and the need to own land to support a warband. References to the seasons, to spring, summer, May, as well as to birds and animals of the forests and woodlands, allude to popular verse traditions to evoke a mood of joy and celebration.

The two poets, Gwalchmai and Hywel, also portray themselves as lovers as an integral part of their warrior personae. Gwalchmai says he fights to win the favour of his mistress, while Hywel describes himself as 'karyadawc kerted ovyt', (a lover in the manner of Ovid). Both poets imply a single-minded devotion and loyalty, as well as the experience of physical desire, but there is little suggestion of the sufferings of unrequited love. Instead, their references to the women they love are closely associated with the celebration of their native lands. The lands, like the women, are physically beautiful, fertile and productive in a way that is crucial to the continuation of the ruling dynasty, and thus inspire loyalty and protection from the warrior class. These lands are owned by the dynasty as the essence of their power, while the women are possessed by the warriors as a token of their social status.

The five *awdlau* of Hywel ap Owain Gwynedd, sometimes singled out as 'genuine' love-poems, make the same connection between warrior-society, land, and women. In these poems, the primary function is not eulogy of an individual but rather of the aristocratic way of life. Perhaps because of his princely rank, Hywel does not assume the persona of a court-poet or draw attention to his poetic status. He sings not as a bard eulogizing his patrons but as a lover of nature and women, both of which symbolize his princely power.

As a consequence of this function, he has no need to project the persona of a suffering lover in the same way as Cynddelw or Llywarch ap Llywelyn did in their eulogies. There is not the same suggestion of social distance between himself and his lady. The poet's love is placed

in the context of his social background at court and the Welsh
landscape around him, both integral parts of his life which restore his
happiness and self-confidence. He is primarily a prince and a warrior
rather than a poet, and battle imagery is also used in his love-poetry to
contrast his two roles, as lover and fighter.

Only one of Hywel's *awdlau* expresses the suffering caused by love.
It is presented through images of Hywel's major concerns—love,
nature, and his aristocratic background—and is essentially native in
spirit as well as content:

> Karafy gaer wennglaer o du gwennylan
> mynyd gar gwyldec gweled gwylan.
> ydgarwny uyned kenym cared yn rwy
> ry eitun ouwy y ar veingann.
> y edrych uy chwaer chwerthin egwan.
> y adrawt caru can doeth ym rann.
> y edryt uy lledurydy ae llet ourwy.
> y edryt llywy lliw tonn dylann.
> llifyant oe chyuoeth a doeth atann.
> lliw eyry llathyr oeruel ar uchel uann.
> Rac ual ym cotidy yn llys ogyruann.
> chweris oe hadaw hi adoed kynrann.
> ethiw am eneidy. athwyf yn wann.
> Neud athwyf o nwyf yn eil garwy hir.
> y wenn am llutir yn llys ogyruann.   (LlH, p.319)

(I love a fair bright fortress beside a pale sea, where a modest fair girl
loves to watch a seagull. I would love to go, though I am not greatly
loved, on a wished-for visit upon a slim white steed to see my darling
with the quiet laughter, to speak of love—since it has come to my share
to declare my sadness and the extent of her beauty—to the home of the
fair one, colour of the ocean wave. From her realm a current has come
to us, colour of cold bright snow on a high peak. Because of the way I
was offended in the court of Ogrfan, there happened from her dwelling
a prince's sorrow. She has taken my life away and I have grown pale.
Now I have become from passion a second Garwy Hir, for the fair one
who has been refused to me in Ogrfan's court.)

The images of 'lliw tonn dylann' (colour of an ocean wave), 'lliw eyry'
(colour of snow), 'gaer wennglaer' (fair bright fortress), all belong to
the native tradition, just as the proper names Ogrfan and Garwy Hir
place the poem firmly in a Welsh context. However, Hywel's use of
'karafy' (I love), in this and other of his *awdlau*, creates a mood of
subjectivity and an illusion of the poet's individual involvement
which is not matched by other *gogynfeirdd*. The use of the first person
to draw attention to the presence of the poet is an accepted technique

of Welsh court-poetry, as in 'gweleis' (I saw), 'molaf' (I praise), and 'kyvarchaf' (I greet), but such verbs tend to express aspects of the poet's function as court-bard. Hywel's 'karafy' exposes a more sensitive, non-official persona which has something in common with the poetic identity of the European court-poets.

Though Hywel shares this conventional subjectivity with other composers of love-lyrics, as well as a similar awareness of love as a purifying and essential life-force, there is very little in his work to suggest direct influence from troubadour poetry. The love he seeks is courtly in the sense that the protagonists and their social setting belong to an aristocratic élite, but it is untrammelled by any of the considerations of *fin' amors* which preoccupied the troubadours. Instead it is interpreted as one of many sources of emotional response, available to the ruling élite, including the beauty of nature, the call to battle, or the loyalties of court life. In this respect his poetry is more akin to the other *rhieingerddi* than to either courtly or popular lyrics of Europe, which are concerned primarily with the theme of love.

It is interesting to compare Hywel's *gorhoffedd* with one of Bertran de Born's *sirventes* to see how differently the two poets interpret and define their mood. The verbs 'caraf' and 'e platz mi' are used to introduce images of the environment to which the poets respond with joy and a sense of belonging. This technique gives the two poems a superficial similarity which in fact emphasizes their cultural differences. The *gorhoffedd* opens with images of the Welsh landscape:

> Caraf trachas lloegyr lleudir goglet hediw.
> ac yn amgant y lliw lliaws callet.
> Caraf am rotes rybuched met.
> myn y dyhaet myr meith gywrysset.
> Caraf y theilu ae thew anhet yndi.
> ac wrth uot y ri rwyfaw dyhet.
> Caraf y morua ae mynytet.
> ae chaer ger y choed ae chein diret.
> a dolyt y dwfyr ae dyfrynnet.
> ae gwylein gwynnyon ae gwymp wraget.   (LlH, p.315)

(I love—England's hatred—the open land of the north today, and in the region of the Lliw a multitude of trees. I love what has given me my desire of mead, where the seas approach in ceaseless turmoil. I love its retinue and its crowded settlement, and at the will of the king, to go to war. I love the sea-strand and its mountains, and its fortress near the woods and its fine lands, and its meadows with water and its plains, and its white seagulls and its fine women.)

Bertran de Born's *sirventes* begins in the same spirit of enthusiasm and delight in the familiar scene around him:

> Be.m platz lo gais temps de pascor,
> Que fai fuolhas e flors venir,
> E platz mi, quan auch la baudor
> De.ls auzels, que fan retentir
>   Lor chan per lo boschatge,
> E platz mi, quan vei sobre.ls pratz
> Tendas e pavilhos fermatz,
>   Et ai gran alegratge,
> Quan vei per champanha rengatz
> Chavaliers e chavals armatz.
>   (Hill and Bergin, vol.I, no.80)

(I love the gay season of spring which makes leaves and flowers appear, and it pleases me when I hear the rejoicing of the birds, who make their song echo through the woods; and it pleases me when the meadows are covered with tents and pavilions, and I feel great delight when throughout the countryside there are ranks of knights and horses in armour.)

Both poets are using conventional imagery, but the conventions belong to separate and independent poetic traditions. In his nature description, Hywel is specific in naming key features of the Gwynedd landscape which immediately evoke its grandeur—sea-marsh, mountains, fortress by the woods. Bertran, on the other hand, uses a more generalized spring opening, with the key terms 'temps de pascor', 'fuolhas', 'flors', and 'auzels' to suggest the revival of nature after winter and the corresponding lifting of his own spirits, an association of ideas which richly pervades courtly and popular poetry of Europe.

Martial activity as a continuing and integral facet of the poet's life is suggested by the juxtaposition of images in Hywel's poem. The *gorhoffedd* begins: 'tonn wenn orewyn a orwlych bet' (a foaming white wave washes a grave), and the line is repeated at different points of the poem. There is a parallel between the endlessly flowing sea and the inevitability of death, and also an implied reference to the sea-battles which were often strategically decisive. The images which evoke the warrior aristocracy belong specifically to Welsh society and suggest strong echoes of the heroic age of Taliesin and Aneirin: 'teulu' (retinue), 'tew anhet' (strong settlement), 'ri' (king), 'caer' (fortress), 'met' (mead).

In Bertran's poem, martial imagery is also appropriate to the knightly aristocracy for whom he is composing, but it already prefigures the great chivalric ethos of medieval European literature. References to tents and pavilions, knights and horses, for example, anticipate the world of Chrétien's romances. The spring opening prefaces the whole theme of the poem, which is a call to arms after a long stretch of idle peace, a return to vigour and productive activity after inertia, just as the spring heralds a new wave of life after the barrenness of winter. The two poems are therefore celebrations of a similar way of life, that of a warrior nobility, but each evokes a different social context.

The use of nature imagery by the earlier *gogynfeirdd* is not the only evidence of influence from a native popular tradition. Some informal love-poems suggest that there was a concurrent tradition of court-poetry meant for entertainment rather than eulogy. The second half of Hywel's *gorhoffedd*, for example, is sometimes treated separately from the first half, since there is a marked difference in tone and subject matter.

In this second part, Hywel deliberately lowers the register of his poetry and uses bardic techniques and an elevated style to describe the girls he has wooed with his praise-poems. Most of the women seem to be married, and Hywel's courtship is presumably no more than a eulogistic convention, but the informal, almost humorous tone implies a more personal relationship. This informal tone, the emphasis on physical love, and the simple narrative structure of the verse, all characteristic of popular poetry, have been taken up by Hywel to amuse and implicitly flatter the group of women named in the poem. Thematically, the two halves of the *gorhoffedd* fit neatly together, the first part celebrating land and the second part celebrating women, both important symbols of possession for the warrior aristocracy.

The same kind of lowered register occurs in the *awdl* attributed to Cynddelw, distinguished principally by its use of the epithet *eiddig* for the jealous husband. The very concept of the 'jealous husband' suggests contact with French popular poetry, but may also refer to a native tradition. Since women were regarded as, and equated with, material property in both French and Welsh society and literature, the related idea of the 'owner' jealous of his 'property' may easily have arisen independently in both cultures.

Like Hywel's poem, Cynddelw's *awdl* combines a technically polished bardic style with a non-courtly attitude to love. The achievement of the *awdl* lies in its humorous punch-line which contrasts in tone and style with the rest of the poem:

> Mynych ym anfon dygn gofion dig—erof,
> Arien gannwyll rhyfyg,
> Mal ydd wyf yn celu calon ysig,
> Ni mad gyrchawdd gwen gwely Eiddig.[14]

(Often she sends me painful enraging memories, [she is like] a hoar-frost candle of presumption to me; because I am concealing a bruised heart, it's unfortunate that the fair one made for Eiddig's bed.)

Through his use of bardic diction and rhetorical ornaments, Cynddelw builds up the expectation of a conventional praise-poem, only to replace this expectation with the realization of a humorous purpose, which makes a joke at the expense of the poet himself.

These two poems by Hywel and Cynddelw differ in tone and function from the more formal love-songs. The element of conflict and suffering for love is replaced by a humorous acceptance of love's unpredictability. This is a tone typically used in medieval satire to describe women who are sexually active, as in these two poems. It has the effect of diminishing the possible threat of their sexual power by not taking it seriously.

In addition, the possession of women is explicitly regarded as the poet's reward for his praise-songs. Hywel says at the end of his *gorhoffedd*: 'kyveis y wyth yn hal pwyth peth or wawd yr geint' (I had eight [women] as a reward, payment for the praise I sang). This clearly implies the social and economic value placed on women in a male-dominated society, and equates women with the material possessions of the warrior élite.

The use of nature and love imagery by the earlier *gogynfeirdd* presages a shift in poetic function and attitude which developed gradually during the period of the later *gogynfeirdd* and achieved its fullest expression in the poetry of Dafydd ap Gwilym. The conservative bardic tradition, bereft of its social relevance, began to lose contemporary significance after 1284. Although praise-poetry continued to be a dominant poetic genre throughout the medieval period, the court-poets could no longer depend on a stable audience of independent native rulers. The changing style of their poems, drawing increasingly on popular forms and French models, is directly related to the changing social conditions of composition and performance.

In the wake of the English conquest of Wales, which authorized the already considerable Norman settlements in Wales, marriage became an increasingly significant means of assimilating the new rulers. Women from noble Welsh families were highly prized by Norman lords who wished to secure their power bases in Wales. At the same time, the old ruling hierarchy of the native dynasties had been seriously weakened, and poets were seeking patronage from new lords, both Welsh and Norman. These changes meant that the primarily eulogistic function of the *gogynfeirdd* was gradually given a new focus. Poems to women no longer emphasize their symbolic value as the possessions of an entrenched and ancient warrior aristocracy, but rather their new value as symbols of assimilation between Norman overlords and the traditional culture of the Welsh nobility.

This shift in focus is strongly apparent in the poems of the later *gogynfeirdd*. These are more overtly love-poems: the women are described in terms of their physical beauty, instead of being associated with the world of warrior activity. The persona of the poet approaches nearer to that of lover than warrior, though his primary function as court-poet, and therefore eulogist, is still made explicit. In terms of style, much of the court-centred imagery, archaic expressions, and references to the heroic past, are stripped away from the love-poems, in order to concentrate on the figure of the girl.

There is more emphasis, too, on the sufferings caused by love, in the manner of European court-poetry. Earlier *gogynfeirdd* poems merely alluded to the pain of unrequited love in order to reinforce the eulogistic function of their verse. As praise-poets, they described a love-worship which was a metaphor of eulogy in return for patronage. It was a 'rhetorical love' which, like a rhetorical question, required no response. In the work of the later *gogynfeirdd*, which displays increasing influences from Continental poetry, both popular and courtly, the emphasis changes from eulogy to the love-worship itself. This results in a greater emphasis being placed on the idea of physical reward, as in Continental court-poetry, so that bardic love is not merely rhetorical but is now pressing for a resolution.

The changing emphasis of *gogynfeirdd* poetry is exemplified by a poem composed by Iorwerth Fychan towards the end of the thirteenth century. Here the relationship between poet and mistress is the central focus of interest, unencumbered by references to martial vigour or landscape glories. Now it is the woman and the desires she

arouses which are the main themes, lovingly evoked through a series
of crystallized images:

> Medwl a dodeis medwid vy kofein
> am twf mirein mein kein kyfyrdelid.
> medyant pop nwyfyant naw gofid am treul
> nym llut lliw gwenheul gwan edewid.
>
> medweis prydereis pryd tonn eruid.
> madeu dyn goreu nym goruygid.
> medylyaw yd wyf am dilid lliw gwawr
> lle red olwynawr o elenid.
>
> mi awyf yrdi ardelw ermid.
> mwyuwy ym tramwy tramawr edlid.
> a meinoeth ym doeth o detholid nep
> lliw ar vy wynep ny llwyr edid.
>
> Mynawc dawedawc dec kyfnewid.
> meingan wedeidwan h[u]an ho[y]wnid.
> mynygylwen yn llenn yn lle rennid gwyrd
> mynychsathyr miluyrd milueird ganlid.
>
> Morwyn a weleis mor drybelid.
> mireingall o ball a bell glywid.
> mawredus ueinus ven yd vernid kreir
> mor wen y hesgeir wch y hesgid.   (LlH, p.324)

(I set my thoughts, my senses intoxicated, on a fair slim flower,
beautiful and dignified. The power of all energy, nine sorrows consume
me, [she with] the colour of the fair sun does not hinder me with a weak
promise.

I was drunk, I was anxious [for her with] the form of the breaking
wave. The best girl does not cause me to depart. I am considering
pursuing [the one with] dawn's colour where wheels run from Elenid.

For her sake I am like a hermit. More and more, very great longing
passes through me. And at midnight, if there was anyone chosen, there
came to me colour to my face that was not allowed to stay at all.

Noble silent girl, of fair conversation, slender and white, graceful and
frail, bright sun, fair neck in a veil where green was shared out,
frequent footsteps at a thousand tables where a thousand bards keep
company.

I saw a maiden who is far-famed, so brilliant, beautiful and prudent,
wearing a mantle. Noble and graceful girl wherever treasure was
assessed, so white her leg above her shoe.

The metrical choice of *gwawdodyn* quatrains rather than the
cumbersome sequences of *awdlau* favoured by earlier praise-poets

immediately liberates the poem from the more elaborate technical devices and also implies an intention which goes beyond that of praise. References to the poet's bardic function and the court setting are kept to a minimum; instead the focus is directed to a detailed description of the girl herself and the emotions she arouses in the poet.

In contrast, Cynddelw's poem to Efa praises her in terms of her noble position—'llys eua' (Eva's court), 'llysseit y hirdwf oe heur duted' (courtly her stature in her golden cloak), 'om rieu om rwyf ry gystlynir' (for my lord and my ruler there is an allegiance)—and his description of Efa is confined to lists of virtues interspersed with references to the misery she causes him—'llaes wenn gall wenngann wenngaen deced' (gentle-voiced, prudent, fair white skin, so beautiful), 'a dywed yno eniwed o hanaf' (and tell there of the harm which I have). The poet's consciousness of his bardic office and the weight of his accumulated images result in a stylized, one-dimensional portrait of his object, and a contrived, conventional statement of his own emotions.

In Iorwerth Fychan's song, however, Gweirful is represented as an object of love rather than praise. His descriptions of her include individualized details as well as general references to her noble birth, for example 'meingan wedeidwan huan hownid' (slender and white, graceful, frail, bright sun), 'mireingall o ball a bell glywid' (beautiful and prudent, wearing a mantle, far-famed) 'mor wen y hesgeir wch y hesgid' (so white her leg above her shoe). Similarly, the poet's position as the rejected suitor is described more specifically than in Cynddelw's praise-poem, the economy of the imagery enhancing the intensity of emotion—'mi awyf yrdi ardelw ermid' (because of her I am like a hermit), 'mwyuwy ym tramwy tramawr edlid' (more and more an excessive sorrow passes through me). The poet does not dwell on his sorrow but explicitly relates his bardic role to his personal feelings: in the last stanza the poet draws a comparison between great Welsh praise-poetry, born out of political misfortunes, and the glory it brought for its composers, and his own creation, arising out of personal anguish, which he hopes will bring him Gweirful's individual approval and reward.

Stylistically, the poem unquestionably belongs to the *gogynfeirdd* tradition, though the bardic techniques have been scaled down to lose some of their power as well as their obstructive complexity. Thus Iorwerth uses the device of *torymadrodd*, a break in the sense unit, with his parenthetical *sangiadau*, and also an accumulation of predicated phrases depending on a single main clause: 'morwyn a weleis' (I saw a maiden), is followed by fifteeen lines of descriptive imagery defining the maiden and the predicative construction with *yn* also provides a unifying repetition. This can be compared with Cynddelw's expansion of 'gorthrych lys' (she conquers a court) (LlH, p.122, 11.20–8), where the images are linked by alliteration. Alliteration and word-play are also an important element in Iorwerth's poem, and these combined with internal rhyme create sound-patterns which approach those of strict *cynghanedd*.

In this poem, the idealized bardic love of the earlier *gogynfeirdd* is less a vehicle for praise and more a set of conventional ideas through which to present an individual experience. Compared to troubadour poetry, however, this poetic realization of love is static and dependent on the interrelationship between the poet's suffering and the girl's perfection. Arising from this are the tensions and conflicting emotions associated with courtly love, but the poet's pursuit of love is presented as a personal quest rather than a function of his poetic role.

This kind of bardic relationship, in which the poet's grief is set in opposition to his beloved's virtues, is given an individual inter-pretation combined with traditional skills in the poems of Gruffudd ap Dafydd ap Tudur, composing about 1300. This poet was mentioned particularly by T. Gwynn Jones as being possibly influenced by troubadour poetry, since his poetic attitude and imagery are very similar.[15]

In one of Gruffudd's three *awdlau*, he begs for a favourable answer from his beloved, which will release him from torment:

> Gwyl vun adry hun drwy hut kur ortho
> car wrthyf dywedut.
> nyt diboen nam attebut
> nyt hawd ymadrawd a mut.
>
> Mut a balch hil gwalch gweilch nwyf yth welaf
> oth uarnaf ieith vawrnwyf.
> mon oed henw menydhenwyf.
> minneu llaes gofeu llesc wyf.
>
> Gwanllesc wyf hut rwyf hoet drwc am vn geir
> o du maengaer amlwc.
> gwannach adicyach ymdwc
> gwennllys hil gwanllaes olwc.
>
> Dy olwc treiswc trossof wyf alltut
> aa villtir hebof.
> dyn aryd geuyn argof.
> dywet eir diwyt yrof.

Dywet eir kyweir yn ol kawat nwyf.
can gorwyf cwyngirat.
ae yr gwerth cannerth kennyat.
ae oth uod enw rod yn rat.

Ym ny chat yn rat reit atteb eilwyd
eilyw gwendon moreb.
nac yr gwerth nac yr nerth neb.
y gan honn etton atteb.

(*Red Book of Hergest*, p.82)

(Modest maiden who disturbs sleep with a spell, mantle of pain, love to speak to me! It is not painless that you do not answer me, it is not easy to converse with a mute.

Mute and proud, of a hero's lineage, of the spirit of heroes, I see you, if I should assess you in my language of great passion. Môn was the name of the place I come from: as for me I am feeble with sad memories.

I am pale and weak from the madness of magic and evil longing, for a single word from the direction of a conspicuous stone fortress. Weaker and more angry [still] does she make me, [she of the] pale lingering glance, [of the] lineage of a fair court.

You cast a contemptuous frown over me—I am an exile—which will go a mile beyond me. Girl who puts a fetter on memory, speak a true word for my sake.

Speak a proper word, after a rainstorm of passion—since I have wrought a complaint of sorrow—either for payment—message of comfort—or willingly—pattern of generosity—for free.

For me there has not been got freely—necessary response for an assignation—she of the hue of the white wave of the harbour—neither for payment nor because of the strength of anyone, an answer from her yet.)

The englyn metre, the references to Môn and later to Eitun and Caer Rhun, and the use of traditional diction such as 'hil gwalch' (offspring of a hawk), '(m)awrnwyf' (great yearning), 'gwanllesc' (weak and frail), 'gwanllaes' (a soft voice), all indicate the poet's conscious adherence to a native poetic tradition. Moreover, he is aware of it as a courtly tradition as we see from his reference to 'maengaer' (stone fortress), 'gwennllys hil' (offspring of a fair court), and his portrait of his beloved as a refined, learned, and noble girl. The poet is addressing the girl primarily as a suitor, but the references to his bardic skills remind us of his function as a praise-poet:

Amyl drwy hiraeth yd aethan.
amot rwyd awyd awen.

> om geneu eryeu eiryan.
> eurdylat attat eittun.
> (*Red Book of Hergest*, p.82)

(Often through longing they went—generous terms for the muse's ardour—brilliant words from my lips, a golden flood towards you in Eitun.)

This bardic role becomes secondary to the poet's courtship of the girl, and the fluency of his poetry is used as a motif to contrast with the silence of his beloved.

So the poem moves beyond the confines of eulogy and sets up a bardic relationship based on the poet's expression of suffering and the girl's silence of indifference. The poet's grief manifests itself as sleeplessness, weakness, pain, and longing, symptoms which also afflict Hywel ab Owain Gwynedd and Cynddelw and which therefore have a precedent in the native poetic tradition. Gruffudd's use of this convention as a motif counterbalancing the girl's silence has the effect of establishing the love relationship as something real and tangible, an accepted fact beyond the limitations of bardic expedience.

The motifs of silence and speech run right through the poem, linking the loosely-structured stanzas of praise and complaint. These motifs also symbolize the dual nature of his beloved, who is both perfect and cruel. The poet associates deceit—'brat' (treachery), 'godwyll' (deceit), 'twyll' (fraud)—with silence, which can be more powerful and effective than speech:

> Trwy hut bwyll astut a bell ystyr gwenn
> tu ae gwann ae hepkyr
> tro mwy vwy traha myvyr
> trech odwyll nogwirbwyll gwyr.
> (*Red Book of Hergest*, p.83)

(Because of enchantment—assiduous study—which the fair one long contemplates towards her weakling who has to do without her (cumulative effect of the violence of contemplation), stronger is deception than the true wisdom of men.)

The two-sided nature of the beloved, who causes both joy and pain, is a commonplace of Provençal and French love-song and one of the primary sources of grief and conflict. Its appearance as a convention of the later *gogynfeirdd* love-poems marks the change of stance from all-admiring praise-poet to manipulative love-poet. The convention is not developed in the earlier *rhieingerddi* since the object of praise could not be accused of any faults such as cruelty or deceit. But as the poet's attitude changes from that of praise-poet to love-poet, he becomes more critical of his beloved and uses this criticism to press his claim.

Gruffudd's poem ends on a *carpe diem* note reminiscent of Latin poetry. Having shown by a carefully plotted argument that physical love is not sinful, the poet urges his beloved to reward his suit as soon as possible:

> Ynol adaf naf nwyfrad
> kynn kyfreith pab nae drablud
> y goruc pawb y gared
> ae gares yndigeryd.
>
> Digeryd uyd ryd rwydgael
> da y gwnaeth mei dei ordeil
> deuoet dan goet y dan gel
> y minneu ui am annwyl.
>
> Gwylya bwyll hirdwyll hwyrdwf
> golwc kynn mod diodef
> ac ennill dysc ac ynnif
> ac antur byd yn gyntaf.
> (*Red Book of Hergest*, p.83)

(After Adam, lord of high passion, before the law of the Pope and his trouble, each man fulfilled his lust with his lover without punishment.

It will be without punishment, the free and easy enjoyment (well has May made houses from leaves) of two meetings, beneath trees in hiding, for myself and my beloved.

Take note of the operation of long deceit of late growth, look before [starting on] a course of suffering, and gain learning and vigour, and venture into the world first.)

This syllogistic argument—by re-creating the Garden of Eden, the poet and his lover can also return to a state of pre-lapsarian grace—is a more explicit and literal association of physical and spiritual ideas than the type of reconciliation attempted by the troubadours. The reference to 'kyfreith pab' (Pope's law), suggests an anti-clerical viewpoint, but the poet makes use of scholastic learning to construct his argument, and the reference to his learning in the last stanza emphasizes his range of bardic and religious knowledge.

The conflict between spiritual ennoblement and physical consummation which was the perennial dilemma of the troubadours is not explored to the same extent by the Welsh bards, since they do not explicitly seek spiritual ennoblement through love. Love is an extension of praise and is therefore openly material and physical, a love of external beauty rather than inner virtue. The conflict of *gogynfeirdd* poetry lies in the attempt of the praise-poet to justify his pursuit of physical love.

Gruffudd's reference to May and the sinless enjoyment of love in the woodland represents a further stage in the process of assimilating popular and bardic native traditions, which has already been observed in the earlier *gogynfeirdd*. Seasonal imagery is a particularly strong poetic tradition in Welsh verse, and is used in heroic and gnomic poetry to comment on the human earthly condition. An association between love and nature is also made occasionally as part of human life on earth, as in the poem 'Cân Yr Henwr' from the Llywarch Hen cycle. In this poem, the speaker mourns the loss of his youth and virility, using images of the passing seasons to emphasize his senility:

> Baglan brenn, neut gwa[ea]nnwyn.
> Rud cogeu; goleu e gwyn.
> Wyf digarat gan uorwyn. (CLlH,
> p.9)

(Wooden crutch, it is spring. Red the cuckoos, bright and fair. I am unloved by a maiden.)

In the work of the early *gogynfeirdd*, nature imagery fulfils its traditional function of enhancing heroic and martial themes, and by extension comes to be associated also with the expressions of love in the *rhieingerddi*. The connection between love and nature is therefore already established in Welsh court-poetry as part of the bardic tradition.

This fusion of popular traditions—seasonal description and the joys of physical love—with formal bardic skills results in a poetic purpose and register which is very similar to the extended courtly love-poems in French, introduced by a *reverdie* opening. In both cases, popular forms have given a new direction and impulse to an outdated and cumbersome use of themes and stylistic devices. Gruffudd has taken a motif from praise-poetry, reflected in a line from Llywarch ap Llywelyn's *rhieingerdd* to Gwenlliant, 'neud adneu cogeu coed neud atre' (cuckoos deposit [eggs], woods rise up), and associated it, not with eulogistic bardic love, but with the kind of physical love belonging to non-courtly poetry, in which the relationship between poet and beloved can be extended beyond the restrictions of eulogy. Gruffudd's poem therefore prefigures the transference of the popular view of love as ultimately capable of resolution to the genre of bardic poetry, a process completed by Dafydd ap Gwilym.

Another poem by Gruffudd ap Dafydd ap Tudur has been used by T. Gwynn Jones as evidence for a Welsh version of the theme of the 'court of love' based on French models.[16] In this poem, Gruffudd brings a complaint against his beloved:

> llyma vy mawrgwyn, –
> nyd am eurgeis, –
> rac lliw tonn ertrei, –
> mae vy llw arnei,
> rei ae ryfedei
> nas rwy vedeis, –
> llifaw vyng grudyeu,
> am llad heb arveu,
> minneu, y madeu
> nys medylyeis.

(Here is my main complaint, not in order to seek gold, against one the colour of a breaking wave, this is my oath on it—some have wondered that I have not possesed her completely—that my cheeks were flooded and I was killed without weapons, but as for me, I have not thought of renouncing her.)

The central section of the poem sets out the accusation in mock-legal jargon, naming the exact place and date of the offence, calling on witnesses, and nominating an appropriate compensation. The rest of the poem, however, is a conventional plea by the poet, interspersed with a disclaimer by the lady herself, who absolves herself of all guilt since the poet exaggerated the charge and is not actually dead:

> 'Dy gwyn vu gynneu
> dy lad heb arveu
> â llafneu geireu
> gwyron, lledneis;
> am llw, bei'th ledid,
> â geir,—llesmeir llid, –
> yn vyw na'th welid,
> edlid adleis;
> a byw y'th welaf,
> y bawb y tystaf,
> a brawd a archaf,
> ac a ercheis.'

('Your complaint just now was that you were killed without weapons by blades of deceptive gentle words; on my oath, if you had been killed with a word—swoon of passion—you would not be seen alive to voice your longing. But I see you alive, I testify to everyone, and I will claim the judgment just as I have claimed.')

While this poem clearly foreshadows the kind of extended metaphor and elaborate wit often employed by Dafydd ap Gwilym, it bears little relationship to medieval 'court of love' poems. In these, a topic connected with love is debated by a number of speakers, often represented by birds, and a final verdict is delivered by a prominent figure presiding over the debate. Gruffudd's poem is not consciously following this genre but merely utilizing legal jargon as a source of metaphor.

However, the humour and wit of the poem again illustrate the assimilation of a popular mood into bardic poetry and the consequent extension of the bardic representation of love. Though the poet fails in his quest for love, his failure is presented as a humorous set-back, almost a parody of the love-longings of court-poets. The diction and imagery, redolent of *gogynfeirdd* praise-poetry, form a humorous contrast to the consciously hyperbolic metaphor of the accusation, and combine with the localized references and place-names to give an indisputably native flavour to the whole poem.

Far from being suggestive of foreign influence, therefore, this poem testifies to a rich native tradition of popular love-song which was increasingly accessible to the court-poets. Elements from this tradition which were analogous to contemporary French conventions were elevated into the bardic repertoire, resulting in court-poetry which moved beyond the fundamental stasis of the eulogistic bardic love relationship and suggested a kind of love which was as dynamic, productive and attainable as that celebrated in French popular poetry.

The poems of the later *gogynfeirdd*, typified by Gruffudd ap Dafydd ap Tudur, illustrate a movement in Welsh court-poetry away from archaic eulogy and towards a native genre of love-poetry. This genre developed from a synthesis of native popular forms and Continental courtly love-poetry. The influence of the latter was facilitated partly by Norman contact, and partly by the analogous social functions of the two bodies of poetry. Just as the emergent nobilies of France required a form of courtly love-poetry to identify themselves as a social élite, so the changing nobility of Wales after 1284 required a new type of élitist verse to replace the old native eulogistic tradition.

The development of a native love-poetry relies on conventions similar to those of Continental love-poetry. In both types, the excessive worship of the beloved mistress symbolizes the social and political importance of noblewomen as marriage partners. This love-worship is expressed through images of suffering and conflict symbolic of a struggle for acceptance, experienced in Wales by the court-poets as well as by their audiences of emerging Welsh and Norman overlords. In contrast to the poems of suffering and worship are those of humour and parody, which satirize the pretensions of the lover and undermine the potential power of the beloved.

This developing genre of Welsh love-poetry shares significant social and literary characteristics with the corresponding Continental genre, either through borrowing or as a result of analogous native forms. Clearly the two bodies of love-poetry are addressed to comparable types of audience –noble, élitist, emerging from an older hierarchy—and are composed by court-poets dependent on patrons.

However, even in the work of the later *gogynfeirdd*, the native bardic inheritance strongly outweighs any foreign influence. The concepts of knighthood and feudalism so crucial to Continental love-poetry are not part of the ideological basis of Welsh love-poetry. Instead, the developing themes of love pursuit are placed in the context of native power structures, the warrior aristocracy, and the new nobility arising to replace the old independent princes.

The court-poetry of the *gogynfeirdd* therefore displays consider-able evolution during the course of two centuries. Starting as a rigidly defined set of poetic conventions, and fulfilling a specific functional expectation, it gradually develops into a native love-poetry based on more flexible forms and techniques. Entirely native traditions of language and imagery and a strictly defined standard of bardic verse are undermined by influences from popular verse, both Welsh and French, creating a lighter and more evocative type of bardic love-poetry. This gradual development from bardic eulogy to love-lyric provided the formative context for the emergence of Dafydd ap Gwilym's verse.

CHAPTER 5

The Court-poetry of Dafydd ap Gwilym

I N the previous chapter I argued for the development of a native Welsh love-poetry addressed to the ruling élite and arising out of the eulogistic tradition of the earlier *gogynfeirdd*. It is possible to view Dafydd ap Gwilym's poetry as a further extension of this native poetic development, making accessible the bardic skills and themes of the *gogynfeirdd* to a society which was more flexible and heterogeneous than the limited aristocratic world of the earlier court-poets.

The eulogistic purpose of Dafydd's court-poems suggests they were addressed to the contemporary ruling class, like their troubadour and *gogynfeirdd* predecessors. The troubadours composed to and for an emergent class of neo-aristocrats, the knights, and the code of courtly love evolved as an analogy of the code of chivalry or knightly behaviour. The *gogynfeirdd*, on the other hand, were supporting an ancient and entrenched nobility increasingly under threat from internal and external forces.

The power structure of Dafydd's audience was different yet again. Descendants of the old Welsh nobility and the newly elevated Welsh administrators had merged into the *uchelwyr* class. This class itself was in the process of assimilating with the old Anglo-Norman baronial order by means of marriage and economic ties. The *uchelwyr* therefore wanted to preserve the traditions, culture and status of their Welsh predecessors, while also needing to unite their interests with those of the Anglo-Norman rulers against the emergent bourgeoisie of the borough towns.

These are precisely the concerns we see expressed in Dafydd's poetry. His eulogistic poems, continuing the traditions of the *gogynfeirdd*, remind the *uchelwyr* of their native cultural inheritance while also reassuring them of their own status as a nobility. The majority of Dafydd's love-poems move beyond eulogy to celebrate love as the pursuit of sensual and spiritual comfort, a fusion often symbolized by a woodland location. Themes and motifs from European love-poetry attest to the shared literary traditions of Welsh and Anglo-Normans and thus to their social and political integration as a ruling nobility. Finally, a group of humorous and satirical poems express an élitist contempt for the bourgeoisie, largely comprising English settlers in the borough towns of Wales.

In this chapter I will be concentrating on the first of these groups, the eulogistic poems and formal love-lyrics. The issue of Continental influence is particularly relevant for these poems which often seem to be imitating the 'courtly love' attitudes of the troubadours. Certainly Dafydd draws on external literary traditions, particularly imagery concerned with the suffering of love, and we need to balance the extent of this influence against the weight of the native bardic tradition.

Because of the undeniable evidence of European influences in Dafydd's work as a whole, it has become customary to define his poetry as a synthesis of native conventions inherited ultimately from Taliesin and Aneirin, and literary influences from the Continent which had permeated Welsh culture at least since the Norman Conquest. Dafydd's debt to the *gogynfeirdd*, and indirectly to the *cynfeirdd*, is not in doubt, but the extent of Continental influence on his work has long been a matter for critical consideration. The poet's social position as a member of the *uchelwyr* justifies the assumption that he understood French and therefore had access to foreign material, either written or oral, in the original. The appearance of certain classical themes suggests a more indirect knowledge of Latin poets, particularly Ovid, either in translation or through the medium of French adaptations.

Traditionally, Dafydd's debt to the Continent is seen to exist primarily in his use of courtly love conventions, apparently derived in a direct line from the twelfth-century troubadours. One of the first scholars to draw attention to this link was E. Cowell, who believed that 'Dafydd borrowed the first idea of his new form of poetry from the troubadours of Provence'.[1] The features in common which bring him to this conclusion include poetic references to Ovid, debates between poets, dialogues between lovers, and the Provençal practice of addressing love-poems to the sister or wife of a patron, mirrored in Dafydd's poems to noblewomen.

Cowell therefore finds that 'Provençal influence must bear the blame of the somewhat immoral shadow which hangs over parts of Dafydd's poetry'.[2] However, it seems certain that Cowell was not familiar with *gogynfeirdd* poetry, especially of the later period, since most of the Provençal features he mentions are also found in the native Welsh tradition of praise-poetry. References to Ovid and dialogues between lovers occur in later *gogynfeirdd* poetry and cannot be attributed to Provençal influence since neither is characteristic of *fin' amors* poetry. They are more likely to have reached Dafydd not only from his predecessors, but also through the medium of popular poetry, both Latin and vernacular, which was accessible to him through French and Anglo-Norman.

Another early scholar, W. Lewis Jones, supports Cowell's suggestion of Provençal influence but defines the nature of this influence in a different way.[3] He concentrates on the Provençal verse-types which seem to have been models for many of Dafydd's poems, in particular the *canso, sirventes, tenso,* and *alba.* He also draws a parallel, rather than assuming actual influence, between the poems to Morfudd and the Provençal concept of courtly love:

> The entire series of odes addressed to Morfudd are based upon a relationship which finds its nearest analogue in the *amour courtois* which evoked from the Troubadours their service of song. But Dafydd's passion for Morfudd . . . had little of the chivalric courtliness, or of the idealism, which usually characterized the homage [of the troubadours.][4]

Lewis Jones is recognizing here that Dafydd's poetry, like that of the *gogynfeirdd* before him, received no direct influence from troubadour courtly love-poetry, but was caught up in the main current of popular literature which carried many of the extended courtly love conventions along with it. *Fin' amors* in its original form is even further removed from Dafydd's work than from the *gogynfeirdd* and cannot be considered as a significant influence on his poetry.

In fact, more recent scholars are now recognizing that direct troubadour influence on Dafydd's poetry is not a justifiable assumption. Gwyn Thomas says of the troubadours:

> Ond ar y cyfan y mae agwedd Dafydd at serch yn gwbwl wahanol i'w hagwedd nhw. Y peth pwysicaf a dreiddiodd i Gymru o'r cyfandir i waith beirdd Cymraeg, a Dafydd yn eu plith (h.y. os mai o'r cyfandir y daeth) ydyw diddordeb cyffredinol mewn serch.[5]
>
> (But on the whole Dafydd's attitude to love is completely different to their attitude. The most important thing which penetrated to Wales

from the Continent in the work of Welsh poets, Dafydd among them (that is, if it came from the Continent), is a general interest in love.)

He goes on to say that Dafydd's attitude to love is closer to that of the wandering scholars, but points out that the secular poems of the goliards had ceased to be part of contemporary Continental literature even before Dafydd's time.

In an article on the *cywyddwyr*, Gareth Davies emphasizes the variety of Dafydd's poetry and of the *cywydd* style in general, saying 'the outstanding feature is that the treatment of love is varied, and not subject to the strict limits of the courtly love convention'.[6] He argues that Continental influences are less important than other aspects of *cywydd* poetry, and that Dafydd's poetry in particular uses the theme of love as 'an expression of a personal attitude towards life, and of the poet's belief in love as a manifestation of what God has created in nature'.[7]

Clearly then, Continental influences on Dafydd's work cannot be regarded simply as attitudes derived directly from *fin' amors*. Dafydd is drawing on a more generalized tradition of courtly love which has expanded from its original social context—the emergence of the knights—and become associated with other influential classes, both in France and in Wales. This non-specific courtly love, constructed from conventional imagery shared by a number of literatures, courtly and popular, can be interpreted by different poets depending on the audiences to whom it is addressed. As we shall see, Dafydd takes full advantage of the potential of courtly love conventions to be used in a variety of ways.

It is important that a consideration of Continental influences on Dafydd's poetry does not obscure the native tradition in which he is working, or his individual contribution to what was a highly socialized, and therefore unavoidably conventional, literary form. The *gogynfeirdd* inheritance is particularly strong in the religious poems and those dedicated to Ifor Hael and other members of the *uchelwyr*.[8] These poems are deliberately reminiscent of the bard's duty to praise God and his patron. Dafydd is consciously re-creating the old order of court-poetry, when bards were attached to particular dynastic courts under an ancient and codified system of duties and privileges. By composing such poems for members of the *uchelwyr*, Dafydd is implying their connection with the old independent rulers of Wales.

This association between the *uchelwyr* and the old native aristo-cracy is made clear in Dafydd's elegy to Angharad (GDG 16), which is very much in the style of the later *rhieingerddi*. The purpose of the poem, to mourn the death of a patron's wife, refers back to the *gogynfeirdd* and their duties as court-poets. Angharad is specifically praised for her noble virtues and generosity to poets:

> Didyr deigr difyr adafael—o'm drem
> Am drymed ym gof gael
> Dodiad hoyw Angharad hael
> Dan ddaear, duon ddwyael.
>
> Aele yw nad byw buail—win aeddfed;
> Awenyddfeirdd adfail;
> Alaf glod waesaf wiwsail,
> Aelaw fu o'i hoywlaw hail.
>
> Heilwin fu, medd llu, lleuer,—cain Indeg
> Cyn undydd breuolder;
> Hoedl dangnef dref, ond nef nêr,
> Hudol yw hoedl i lawer.
>
> Llawer bron am hon ym Mhennardd—a hyllt,
> Ail Esyllt wiw lwysardd;
> Llawer cyfarf galarfardd,
> Llwyr wae, ni chwarae, ni chwardd.   (GDG 16, 1–16)

(Tears break out—unrelentingly wrested—from my eyes because it is so sad for me to remember that Angharad, lively and generous, has been laid beneath the earth, she of the two black brows.

It is sad that the lady of ripe wine is not alive, the ruin of inspired poets; famed for wealth and the pledge of fitting gifts, liberal was the feast from her lively hand.

She was a generous wine-giver, said a host—source of light, beautiful Indeg – before the day of [her] mortality; an illusion is every life except in God's heaven, the home of peaceful life.

Many a heart breaks for her in Pennardd, a second Esyllt, fitting, fair and beautiful; many a comrade of the grieving poet (a thorough grief) does not play, does not laugh.)

The *englyn* metre used in the first nine stanzas and lack of strict cynghanedd recall the *rhieingerddi* of the later *gogynfeirdd*, as well as the formalized structure of the poem, with stanza-linking (*cyrch-gymeriad*) between the first ten verses and line-linking (*cymeriad*) in the last ten. Courtly and heroic references, such as 'buail' (lady), 'awenyddfeirdd' (inspired poets), 'heilwin' (wine-serving), 'medd llu' (host's mead), evoke a Welsh society existing before 1284, and serve to enhance the status of Angharad and the impact of her death. The poet's sadness is repeatedly emphasized as his personal sense of loss, creating a relationship between himself and Angharad. The device of accumulated imagery is also used, as in the second stanza, and the whole poem is bound together by an elaborate network of allitera- tion, rhyme, and word-play.

Despite these indications of conservatism, there are other char- acteristics of the poem which may be associated particularly with Dafydd's work. Some of the expressions and imagery used here are applied by him throughout his poems as familiar tokens of praise and approval—for example, 'hoyw' (lively), 'ail Esyllt' (second Esyllt), 'duon ddwyael' (two black brows). Because of their contextual associations in other love-poems, they automatically indicate a set of connotations about the subject: that she is beautiful, noble, worthy of being loved. Key terms such as these are not merely conventional line- fillers but form an important and transferable substructure in Dafydd's love-poems.

Syntactically, Dafydd's poetry tends to use more finite verbs than that of the *gogynfeirdd*, as a means of linking a series of images or stressing a mood, such as 'ni chwarae, ni chwardd' (does not play, does not laugh), 'didyr deigr difyr adafael' (tears break out unrelentingly wrested). Though Dafydd's imagery is often intricate and lengthy, he uses syntactic markers to divide up strings of juxtaposed phrases and compounds, thereby avoiding the obscurities of much of the earlier *gogynfeirdd* poetry.

This group of bardic poems (GDG 1–21) composed, for the most part, in the traditional metres of the *awdl* and *englyn*, reflects Dafydd's awareness of contributing to an established and well- defined native tradition. His direct inheritance from the earlier Welsh court-poets reveals itself to varying degrees throughout the whole corpus of the poetry. Though Dafydd's use of the *cywydd* metre is innovative, *gogynfeirdd* techniques of diction and ornamentation are used by him with a consciousness of their archaic value. Lexical and syntactic structures associated with court-poetry are also taken over by Dafydd to give weight and connotation to new subject-matter.

The comparative conservatism of these eulogistic court-poems addressed to patrons and influential members of the Welsh nobility clearly connects them with *gogynfeirdd* poetry in terms of function as well as form. The poems are a reminder of the long and noble tradition of Welsh culture under the independent princes, and an assurance that the *uchelwyr* are worthy successors to the noble obligation to maintain that tradition. In form as well as function, then, they are much closer to their native predecessors than to the Continental tradition of courtly lyric.

In his formal love-poems, Dafydd is again drawing on *gogynfeirdd* tradition, that of the later *rhieingerddi*, together with the more obvious Continental borrowings. Like the *rhieingerddi*, Dafydd's poems use the persona of the court-poet or praise-poet who composes eulogy in the form of love-pursuit. They also develop the theme of unrequited love as the principal dynamic of each poem, with its accompanying imagery of suffering and pain. This love is part of the metaphor of the poet–patron relationship, in which praise of the patron in return for material reward is one of the underlying functions of the poetry.

This metaphorical structure follows on from *gogynfeirdd* praise-poems to patrons, but can also be compared to the troubadour use of metaphor in their love-poems. Rachel Bromwich has already commented on this similarity:

> Just as the Troubadours had envisaged an implicit parallel between love's service and the feudal relation which bound a man to his lord, so Dafydd conceived of his relation to the girl he was praising in his poetry in terms of a bard's relation to his patron, from whom he would inevitably expect and demand a fitting reward.[10]

The feudal relationship between lord and vassal was a fundamental social structure from which poets could draw their analogy to love-service. Similarly, the relationship between praise-poet and patron in early Welsh society was one of great social significance, related as it was to the power and supremacy of the ruling families.

It is not surprising, then, that Dafydd, developing a tendency first manifested by the *gogynfeirdd*, should use the poet–patron relationship as a metaphor for love pursuit. His presentation of himself as a court-poet in his eulogies corresponds to the *gogynfeirdd* role as praise-poets, explicitly referred to in their poems. But whereas the *gogynfeirdd* had a definable and culturally significant position as court-poets, Dafydd represented a new era of court-poetry in Wales. In his time, poets were not associated with specific courts of the established aristocracy, but were more mobile and dependent on a wider circle of patrons. Though their audiences were still élitist, they now included wealthy members of the administrative class or of the Church, who may not have possessed their own 'courts' in the traditional sense of the word.

Dafydd's role as court-poet, to which he frequently refers, is more in the manner of an assumed persona than it was for the *gogynfeirdd*. While the latter identified themselves literally as court-poets and metaphorically as warriors and lovers, Dafydd identifies himself through a whole range of personae, including court-poet, *clerwr*, courtly lover, rustic suitor, adulterer, young squire, old man, and so on. This shifting authorial perspective is one of the main reasons why Dafydd's poetry appears to be so dynamic and varied. It also suggests the lack of a unified and static social position for poets in Dafydd's time. The old identity of court-poet, whether *prydydd* or *bardd teulu*, had become fragmented into a variety of composers and entertainers with a number of functions, whose duties and privileges were interpreted differently by different patrons. It should also be noted that, significantly, Dafydd never refers to himself as a warrior, in the way the *gogynfeirdd* did. The old social structure of the warrior aristocracy had disappeared as a reality by Dafydd's time, and such a persona would have had little relevance for audiences of noblemen and royal officials.

Dafydd's assumption of the role of court-poet as a consciously stylized and conventional device allows him to develop the metaphor of the poet–patron relationship in more imaginative ways than the *gogynfeirdd* attempted. In particular, the physical desire expressed by the lover becomes increasingly relevant as a metaphor of the poet's desire for material rewards. Whereas once these rewards were an accepted part of the court-poets' privileges, understood by patrons and poets alike, by Dafydd's time there was little security of this kind, even for trained bards. Though Dafydd came from a wealthy and noble family, his need for financial support from patrons may have been very real, and had to be articulated through his poems. His desire for love's rewards is therefore associated quite often with compensation of a more material kind, and the anguish of the unrequited lover mirrors the despair, and even outrage, of the unpaid poet. The women of the poems are constantly appealed to as the dispensers of both love and money, the two-sided poetic reward, an apparently flattering appeal which actually serves to conceal their purely functional and economic role among the new nobility.

The social function of Dafydd's court-poems, the use of a metaphorical structure, and the imagery of unrequited love, relate the poems generically to those of the troubadours and also of the *gogynfeirdd*. All of them represent a type of eulogy to a particular ruling class, and an affirmation of a particular way of life, in return for financial support. This similarity of purpose, despite differences in the way it is realized in the different poems, allowed French influences to penetrate easily into Dafydd's verse, given the proximity of the two cultures at that time.

It is here that Dafydd's poems show most clearly their growth away from the preceding *gogynfeirdd* tradition—in their assimilation of Continental courtly love material, particularly the imagery associated with love's suffering. This imagery seems to have had a fairly potent effect on noble Welsh audiences, both in the later *rhieingerddi* and even more strikingly in Dafydd's verse. Perhaps the appeal lies mainly in the courtly context of such imagery, which is associated so strongly with Provençal *fin' amors*. But it also expresses a relationship based on conflict which had wider implications for both the troubadours and the Welsh poets. The knightly class, represented by the troubadours, and the *uchelwyr* class, represented by Dafydd and his contemporaries, needed to assert themselves to emerge from an older aristocracy. Women as marriage partners were a crucial factor in assisting this emergence, and the poetic sufferings of unrequited love, which endowed women with an illusory power of choice, actually functioned to disguise women's economic value and their lack of choice. In addition, the imagery of grief and desire for reward has a particular relevance for the poets of Dafydd's time who were seeking patrons to support them in the absence of an established system of poetic privileges.

What we find, then, are strong echoes of *gogynfeirdd* tradition in Dafydd's eulogistic court-poems, as well as conscious references to the courtly tradition of unrequited love in his formal love-lyrics. These two sets of literary traditions must have had a particular appeal for Dafydd's audiences. The first reminded them of their native cultural inheritance as successors to the old Welsh nobility, while the second reinforced their identification with the Anglo-Norman aristocracy.

Dafydd's court-poems to women have a specific function as a reinforcement of *uchelwyr* status. Courtly love-poems were addressed to the noblewomen of Provence, France, and Germany, and it was therefore fitting that Welsh noblewomen should be honoured in the same way, using the same kind of imagery and metaphorical structures. In this manner, they and their families, indeed their whole way of life, were brought into the courtly aristocracy of Europe, and included in the ruling Anglo-Norman culture, through their participation in the courtly love tradition.

The way of life of the *uchelwyr* is the real object of Dafydd's praise, just as the *gogynfeirdd* were eulogizing an earlier warrior aristocracy, and the troubadours a feudal knighthood. Dafydd's poems to individual women, couched in the form of exquisite love-poetry, are open to a more general interpretation as celebrations of the sophisticated and courtly culture achieved by the native nobility. His combination of native poetic traditions and Continental literary influences perfectly reflects noble Welsh culture as a synthesis of the native aristocracy with the ruling Anglo-Norman power-lords.

Dafydd's formal bardic love-poems are best exemplified by the poem 'Dyddgu' (GDG 45), addressed to the daughter of Ieuan ap Gruffudd ap Llywelyn. The figure of Dyddgu, with her aristocratic background and noble virtues, provides an obvious focus for the pursuit of an idealized bardic love. The primarily eulogistic function of the poem is reinforced by the probability that Dyddgu was a real person, the daughter of a patron whom Dafydd wished to honour.

The structure of the poem follows a tripartite scheme which is found in many of Dafydd's love-poems. This scheme begins with a statement of poetic intent, the circumstances out of which the poem arises, in this case the desire to honour the daughter of a noble lord in return for gifts and hospitality. The central section conveys the argument or purpose of the poem, here a description of Dyddgu herself and the effect she has on the poet, culminating in the extended comparison between her features and the colours of the snow, the bird, and the blood, which is taken from the Welsh romance of *Peredur*. The conclusion of the poem, in this case contained briefly in six lines, reinforces the central argument, often by making an emotional demand or offering some new and conclusive reason why the poet's suit should be rewarded.

The formal tone of the poem is achieved partly by the device of referring to Dyddgu only in the third person, and addressing Ieuan, her father, directly. This tone is then sustained by the imagery of the noble lord in his hall—'iôr gwaywdan gwiwdad' (spear-fire lord, fitting father), '(g)wyn wingaer' (fair wine-fortress), 'radlawn rydd dy loyw win' (liberal and gracious your bright wine)—which consciously evokes a tradition reaching back to the *cynfeirdd*. Similarly, the descriptions of Dyddgu follow three conventional lines of praise-poetry, but they are deliberately arranged in a pattern of contrasting images of black and white, leading up to the extended comparison— 'gwynnach nog eiry y gwanwyn' (whiter than the spring snow), 'du yw'r gwallt' (black is her hair), 'duach yw'r gwallt' (blacker is her hair).

Dafydd's persona as a court-poet is explicitly mentioned several times: Dyddgu's father is his patron who rewards him with gold and wine; one of the effects of his love is that he cannot compose any poetry—'ni weais wawd' (I have not woven poetry)[11]—and he also refers to himself as 'ei phrydydd' (her poet). At the end of the poem he implies that he expects a reward for his devotion:

> Barned rhawt o'r beirniaid draw
> Ai hywaith, fy nihewyd,
> Ymy fy myw am fy myd.   (GDG 45, 56–8)

(Let the troop of judges yonder judge whether my life is profitable because of my darling, my desired one.)

By the terms of his conventional role as court-poet, Dafydd is also able to express his love through references to his suffering. His sleeplessness—'hun na'i dryll' (not a fragment of sleep), 'ni'm gad hun' (she allows me no sleep)—and his sickness—'heiniau drallawd' (fevers of tribulation), 'neu'm curia haint' (fever makes me pine)—are already associated with bardic love in the native tradition so that they merely reinforce his bardic role rather than explore a particular state of mind.

Dafydd's assumption of this bardic role is evidently conscious and expedient, since he also suggests other personae for himself. In the extended comparison, Dyddgu is compared to the girl whom Peredur loved, and therefore Dafydd himself, by analogy, is Peredur. As a result, he acquires by implication all the virtues of a chivalric knight and fleetingly moves his love out of the context of praise-poetry and into the world of courtly romance with its associations of spiritual questing. By this shift of literary connotation, we can see that Dafydd's persona as court-poet is just as much a stylized convention as is his identification with Peredur. By sustaining this role as court-bard, Dafydd provides a framework and a rationale for his formal love-poetry, just as the troubadours assumed the role of knight to provide their poetic framework.

Dafydd's deliberate assumption of the role of court-poet is seen clearly in another poem to Dyddgu, 'Dagrau Serch' (GDG 95). Though the metaphorical level of the poem deals with the sorrow of the unrequited lover, the message of the poem is the court-poet's appeal for payment in return for his praise-songs. In his persona of unrequited lover, Dafydd describes his suffering through the central hyperbolic image of tears falling: 'digroenes deigr ei wyneb' (tears excoriate his cheeks), 'dau lygad swrth yn gwrthgrif' (two sullen protesting eyes), 'diystyr wallawyr llif' (heedless outpourers of the deluge). These images are supported by others indicative of love's torments, such as 'dyn fal corfedw yn edwi' (a man decaying like a dwarf birch), and 'dodaist wayw llon dan fron friw' (you placed a spear of distress beneath a broken heart).

But parallel to these emotional reproaches are reminders of a more material kind. In his *alter ego* of court-poet, Dafydd is asking to be paid. References to his bardic function are recurrent and explicit: 'dy gerddawr' (your minstrel),[12] 'dy fardd mad' (your fortunate poet), 'dêl i'th fryd dalu i'th frawd, dyfu yt wawd â'i dafawd' (may it come into your mind to pay your brother for growing poetry for you with his tongue), 'dylyaf ffawd am wawdair' (I am owed good fortune for a word of praise), 'dylyy fawl' (you are owed praise). The mutual obligations of praise-poet and patron are clearly being invoked here, reinforced by references to Dyddgu's material wealth and hence her ability to pay what she owes: 'didawl main ar dy dâl mawr' (unstinting the gems on your wide forehead).

So the poet speaks here, as in many of the poems, with two voices, that of courtly lover and that of court-poet, both of which must be regarded as to some extent conventional and non-literal. Nor is it easy to decide which voice is the 'real' one and which is the figurative inversion of it, especially as Dafydd himself links them inextricably and makes one depend on the other. He describes Dyddgu as wearing 'didawl main' (unstinting gems), symbolic of her rank and right to be praised, but he also describes himself as 'didawl o'th gariad ydwyf' (I am without a share of your love), playing on the two meanings of *didawl*. He also makes an implicit contrast between his own tear-filled eyes and Dyddgu's beautiful and praiseworthy eyes, again linking his two functions of lover and praise-poet.

A more explicit link between the two personae is found in the poet's direct reference to himself as Dafydd—'Dyfed a ŵyr mai difyw . . . a Dafydd yw' (Dyfed knows that Dafydd is lifeless).[13] The implication of this, and the later 'dwfn fynegais' (deeply have I expressed), is that the poet has spread the news of his suffering, and therefore also of Dyddgu's virtues, throughout the land in fulfilment of his bardic function. But there is also an identity suggested between Dafydd the lover and his persona as a court-poet, so that the bardic love which the latter has publicized can also be interpreted as the private and individual emotion of the former.

The poem therefore has elements of praise-poem and love-poem skilfully mingled and expressed through metaphor and traditional bardic devices. It has clear affinities with the native courtly tradition, in which the poet and his subject belong to an aristocratic society and understand the mutual obligations of eulogy. But it also works on the level of a courtly love-poem, in which the lover seeks emotional stability and release from torment in exchange for his declarations of love, a release also sought by the troubadours. As an object of praise, Dyddgu owes the poet some form of reward or payment, but as the object of love she has no clearly defined obligations and her presence in the poem is as a passive and negative recipient.

The importance of metaphor in conveying Dafydd's praise of Dyddgu is seen again in 'Caru Merch Fonheddig' (GDG 37), in which the bardic relationship is given less prominence and Dafydd's presence as a noble lover is more strongly felt. There is one reference to the craft of the praise-poet, 'oni'th gaf er cerdd erddrym ddidranc' (if I do not get you for a fine endless song), which implies that Dyddgu's love is his ideal reward for immortalizing her in song.

The argument of the poem expresses Dafydd's dilemma in pursuing a girl of an aristocratic family, and he uses a series of three metaphors to describe his position. In the first, he is like a climbing animal which gradually reaches the top of the tree; in the second, he is like a sailor who navigates the stormy sea to reach the shore at last;[14] and in the third he is like an archer who makes a hundred attempts before his arrow finally hits the bull's eye. Each of these images makes a comment about his courtship—that he is seeking a girl too far above him, that his life has been a purposeless wandering until he found Dyddgu, and that he will keep trying until he wins her. The fact that each of the metaphorical attempts ends in success only reinforces the poet's hope of eventual joy. The ideal love he seeks is only enhanced if he must go to some trouble to obtain it.

Dyddgu's courtly background is suggested by a minimum of references, such as the bardic 'naf gwaywsyth' (spear-straight lord), and her noble virtues are described in the opening lines, beginning with the striking compound, 'Dyddgu ddiwaradwyddgamp' (Dyddgu of faultless excellence), to justify Dafydd's determined pursuit of her. The argument develops through the successive stanzas, with the extended metaphors following the poet's statement of his dilemma:

> Od wyf fi ŵr, nid af fyth
> I geisio merch naf gwaywsyth,
> Rhag fy ngalw, gŵr salw ei swydd,
> Coffa lwybr, y cyfflybrwydd.   (GDG 37, 7–10)

(If I am a man, I will never go to seek the daughter of a spear-straight lord, lest I be called, a man whose office is base, (memorable course of action) some such thing as that.)

Through the metaphors, he implies his confidence of success and his justification for pursuing Dyddgu, expressing this openly in the last part of the poem—'nid drwg fy ngobaith', (my hope is not harmful). The poet's persistence is emphasized at the end of the poem when he says he will simply wait until all the other suitors have given up and he is the only one left. He then refers briefly to his role as a bard praising a noble subject, reminiscent of the *rhieingerddi*, but the mocking tone of familiarity shows that the poem is not merely an official praise-poem. The final lines also indicate that Dafydd's attitude as a court-poet does not correspond to the subservient and pleading tone of the troubadours. Unconstrained by the code of chivalry and *courtoisie*, Dafydd displays the confidence of the poet whose place in society is traditionally an honoured one.

The courtly tone of the poem is partly a product of the language and style, but is also related to the figure of Dyddgu, who represents the poet's ideal of aristocratic womanhood. As in the other poems, her role is passive, she is merely the symbol of beauty and nobility who functions to inspire the intense emotions expressed by the poet. Dafydd's aspirations to achieve Dyddgu's love clearly represent a celebration of the native Welsh nobility, in which his audience can also participate.

The same role of noble feminine ideal can also be taken by Morfudd. Traditionally, Morfudd is seen as fickle and unreliable, and her association with Bwa Bach is the subject of a number of Dafydd's humorous and non-courtly poems. However, *cywyddau* such as 'Talu Dyled' (GDG 34), 'Cystudd y Bardd' (GDG 102), 'Morfudd fel yr Haul' (GDG 42), and 'Edifeirwch' (GDG 106) are composed in the same courtly style as those to Dyddgu, and Morfudd herself is presented as noble and refined.

In 'Talu Dyled', Dafydd describes himself specifically as Morfudd's praise-poet, and laments the fact that she has not paid the debt she owes Dafydd for spreading her fame. The recurrent emphasis on Morfudd's widespread fame as a result of Dafydd's songs recalls the importance of *gogynfeirdd* eulogy as a means of preserving the memory of heroes and rulers. In addition, the equation between secular praises and religious worship—'pater noster annistaw' (a noisy Pater noster), 'Amên mawl', (an Amen of praise)—suggests the duty of the bards to praise God as well as their patrons. It is also comparable to the troubadour convention of worshipping the beloved as a sacred object, although Dafydd's allusions to religious worship are in terms of a metaphorical rather than metaphysical expression.

In this poem, Dafydd's persona as praise-poet and his grievance that his love is unrequited are part of the conventional structure of bardic love-poetry. It is inevitable that Dafydd will not receive the reward he seeks, and his realization of this reward in a material sense, as a financial debt, reinforces the literal interpretation of the poem as a bardic euology. Like the *gogynfeirdd*, Dafydd introduces nature imagery to provide a subjective contrast to the stylized diction of praise, but he exploits it as a source of metaphor to enliven the eulogistic conventions. Thus he compares his far-flung praises to the scattering of seed, with the implication that, like the seed bearing fruit in fertile soil, his praises will only yield results if Morfudd is receptive to them:

> Heais mal orohïan
> Ei chlod yng Ngwynedd achlân.
> Hydwf y mae'n ehedeg,
> Had tew, llyna head teg.   (GDG 34, 13–16)

(Like a frenzied lover I have sown her praise throughout Gwynedd's extent. It sprang up into a strong growth, the plump seed, that was a fair sowing.)

The metaphor and its referent are closely bound together, so that their roles are almost interchangeable: 'ei chlod' (her fame), is the object of 'heais' (I sowed), the literal meaning intruding into the figurative image. In addition, Dafydd's reference to himself as 'orohïan' (frenzied lover), introduces another kind of figurative device, a simile which has the effect of further reinforcing his persona: he is a praise-poet who behaves like a lover.

The description of the cuckoo is a more extended image which has associations with popular poetry,[15] but the juxtaposition of metaphors implies a link between the cuckoo's song and doctrinal prayers such as the *paternoster*.[16] Both are recited ritualistically, repetitively, and at length, and therefore are comparable to Dafydd's own single-minded praise of Morfudd:

> Unllais wyf, yn lle y safai,
> Â'r gog, morwyn gyflog Mai.
> Honno ni feidr o'i hannwyd
> Eithr un llais â'i thoryn llwyd.
> Ni thau y gog â'i chogor,
> Crygu mae rhwng craig a môr;

> Ni chân gywydd, lonydd lw,
> Nag acen onid 'Gwcw'.   (GDG 34, 31–8)

(Where she might stand, I have the same voice as the cuckoo, serving maid of May. By her nature she cannot know, in her grey cloak, any speech but one. Nor is the cuckoo silent with her chattering, she grows hoarse between rock and sea; she sings no song—a quiet oath—or note except 'Cuckoo'.)

The single sound of the cuckoo and the distances over which her song travels are compared to Dafydd's songs to Morfudd. The association of the cuckoo with May, evoking all the connotations of springtime and joyful love celebrated in popular poetry, is used here to contrast with Dafydd's unrequited love, a use exactly paralleled in Continental courtly and learned poetry.[17]

In 'Cystudd y Bardd' (GDG 102), Dafydd is again composing as Morfudd's love-poet, voicing a conventional complaint about her indifference. He describes his suffering in terms of physical pain—'heinus wyf heno o'i serch' (I am afflicted tonight because of her love), 'garwloes gŵr' (a man's grievous pain)—and he ends by asserting 'hebddi ni byddaf fi byw' (without her I cannot live). This stance of the suffering lover is closely related to that of the later *gogynfeirdd* in their praise-poems to women, and is clearly analogous to the Continental movement of courtly love. Moreover, the technical demands of this poem, in which every line begins with the same letter, are a reminder of its function as an example of bardic expertise.

However, Dafydd's expression of his mood through a series of fast-changing metaphors is a mark of his own original contribution to the ideal of bardic love. The image of sowing a seed, which Dafydd uses in a number of poems, occurs here again, this time to describe his own condition of love-longing:

> Heodd i'm bron, hon a hyllt,
> Had o gariad, hud gorwyllt. (GDG 102, 5–6)

(She sowed in my breast—this will break—a seed of love, cruel magic.)

The idea of magic and enchantment is sustained throughout the first part of the poem, with 'hud' (magic) occurring in other forms such as 'hudai' (enchanted), and 'hudoles' (enchantress). This image is replaced in the second half with that of 'herwr' (outlaw), a metaphor both for Dafydd's exile from Morfudd's company, and Morfudd's theft of his heart, leading to his death. The terms 'cyhudded' (accusation), and 'galanas' (compensation), impart a semi-legal tone to Dafydd's complaint which is reminiscent of Gruffudd ap Dafydd ap Tudur's accusation against his beloved because of her cruelty to him. The whole poem is bound together not only by the *cymeriad* but also by the repetition of words involved in the *cymeriad* such as *hudoles, hud;*[18] *heddwch* (peace); *hwyr, hwyrach* (late, later); *hualwyd, hual* (fettered, fetter); *hawdd* (easily); *herwr* (outlaw).

Dafydd's finest courtly poem to Morfudd, and one of the most successful pieces in the whole canon, is 'Morfudd fel yr Haul' (GDG 42), in which the comparison between Morfudd and the sun is extended throughout the length of the poem. John Rowlands has pointed out that the comparison itself is not new since the *gogynfeirdd* often used the sun as a source of imagery in the *rhieingerddi*,[19] but Dafydd's treatment of it surpasses anything that went before. This use of extended metaphors is particularly characteristic of Dafydd's poetry as a means of exploring his attitude to love, and is a technique apparently unparalleled in earlier Welsh poetry.[20]

In this poem, Morfudd is praised for her beauty and brilliance, assuming the role of a eulogized love object. Dafydd describes himself as 'oferfardd' (foolish poet), a rhetorical undervaluing of his bardic skills, and says of Morfudd, 'Gŵyr obryn serchgerdd o'm pen' (she is able to buy a love-song from my head). His persona is clearly that of the praise-poet who is eulogizing his subject rather than declaring his love, and Morfudd's association with a courtly setting—'fy nyn gan mewn llan a llys' (my fair girl in parish and court), 'ddyn galch falch fylchgaer' (girl of a proud lime notched fortress), 'ar lawr neuadd' (on the floor of the hall)—implies that she is a worthy recipient of praise from a court-poet. The images of brightness used to reinforce the equation of Morfudd and the sun are reminiscent of *gogynfeirdd* poetry, as well as courtly diction such as 'hil naf' (offspring of a lord).[21]

The underlying assumption of the poem, that Morfudd herself as well as the poet's pursuit of an idealized bardic love are subject to irreconcilable conflicts, is also characteristic of the *rhieingerddi* and the court-poetry of Europe. The notion of the two-sided beloved who can be cruel or kind, causing pain but also joy, is a central theme of *fin' amors*, and many of the troubadours explicitly complain of this duality, as in the *canso* 'Can lo boschatges' by Bernard de Ventadorn:

> Ai! can brus sui, mal escharnitz!
> qu'eu no posc la pena durar,
> de tal dolor me fai pasmar,
> car tan s'amistat m'esconditz!
> ab bel semblan sui eu träitz.[22]

(Alas, how dark I am, and so badly scorned. I cannot bear the pain which makes me swoon from such grief, since she refuses me her love so much. I am betrayed by her fair appearance.)

The paradox implicit in 'bel semblan' corresponds exactly to that which Dafydd perceives in Morfudd: she appears and then vanishes, offers herself and then withdraws, behaviour which he describes with pejoratives such as 'ei thwyll a'i hystryw' (her deceit and her cunning), 'eiddungam ddangos' (deceitful appearance). The later *gogynfeirdd* also recognized this fundamental duality in the nature of their beloved, particularly Gruffudd ap Dafydd ap Tudur who emphasized the beguiling, deceptive qualities of the girl from Eitun.[23]

The difference in Dafydd's treatment of this conflict is that Morfudd herself is presented as actively establishing her dual nature rather than passively receiving complaints about it. She appears in court, she walks on the battlements, she is like a merchant or a shepherdess, she disappears with 'y dyn oerddrwg' (the cold evil man), she comes to the clearing at Penrhyn. The extended metaphor of the sun allows Dafydd to incorporate other inherent paradoxes: he desires to touch the sun but to succeed means certain death, to look on the sun is to be blinded. Morfudd therefore has the same powers and limitations as the sun, and the comparison helps to establish her identity as more than just a reified love object. Dafydd is also acknowledging in the poem that the pursuit of love itself is fraught with difficulties and insoluble dilemmas, an acknowledgement frequently made by other court-poets, both Welsh and European. This arises partly from the eulogistic function of court-poetry which automatically implies that eulogistic love can never be requited, but again Dafydd adds a new dimension to this common dilemma by associating it specifically with the girl herself. His love cannot succeed, not only because he is Morfudd's praise-poet and she, by virtue of her birth and marriage is inaccessible to him,[24] but also because Morfudd chooses to be elusive and provocative. His complaints of suffering and unrequited love are therefore given a more personal and individual significance, despite their conventional expression and context.

Dafydd's poem of repentance, 'Edifeirwch' (GDG 106), explicitly confirms his role as Morfudd's praise-poet, and his simultaneous fulfilment of this role as well as that of lover. Morfudd's rejection of him causes him pain and ultimately death, which means the end of his career as a poet. Dafydd is making a formal declaration of his occupation as a *prydydd*, a chief poet whose function is to praise

Morfudd. It is in terms of this eulogistic relationship that Dafydd formally declares his love and his consequent suffering. As the object of this bardic love, Morfudd is typically passive and non-responsive; the declaration is a rhetorical device with no opportunity for reply.

The poem is in the style of a prayer, that of a man about to meet his Maker, when honesty is the only policy, and Dafydd confesses his sin of pursuing an earthly love before seeking forgiveness. In keeping with the native bardic tradition, Dafydd shows an awareness of the ultimate authority of God over human affairs. Though his pursuit of Morfudd has caused his death, he must make his peace with God before dying. The literary device of the 'retraction' and the prayer-like appeal to the Trinity and the Virgin Mary are in imitation of the *marwysgafn* of the earlier *gogynfeirdd* and provide an ironical, almost humorous, hyperbole of Dafydd's unsuccessful suit.

These formal love-poems to Dyddgu and Morfudd are significant illustrations of Dafydd's poetic purpose and the social function of his court-poetry. Dyddgu in particular, is an embodiment of the native aristocracy, and is consciously associated with images of the Welsh heroic past. By addressing love-poems to such a symbol of an old independent Wales, Dafydd is deliberately fostering and preserving the native poetic tradition and culture, reminding the nobility of their inheritance. In all the poems to Dyddgu, she remains unattainable, far above the poet's reach, talisman of a vanished and irrecoverable Wales.

The poems to Morfudd, on the other hand, suggest a slightly different purpose. She represents, not the old aristocracy, but the new class of *uchelwyr* who have to be courted by the poets in return for their patronage. While Dyddgu comes of ancient noble stock, daughter of Ieuan ap Gruffudd ap Llywelyn, Morfudd is married to Y Bwa Bach, 'y dyn oerddrwg' (the cold bad man), just as many noblewomen were placed in expedient marriages either to Welshmen or to Anglo-Normans. Unlike Dyddgu, the static and remote emblem of a distant past, Morfudd is fluctuating, undefinable, unpredictable, and therefore characteristic of contemporary Welsh society in general, and of the relationship between poets and the nobility in particular. Morfudd has to be wooed, with flattery or with censure, just as the *uchelwyr* have to be persuaded to take over the aristocratic patronage of poets.

The question of whether or not Dyddgu and Morfudd were 'real' people does not change their role in the poems as powerful emblems of contemporary social relationships. Modern scholarship tends to the view that Dyddgu and Morfudd actually existed, a view based partly on the occurrence of their names in fourteenth-century manuscripts.[25] Certainly the earlier opinion held tenaciously by Ifor Williams [26] that the names were mere pseudonyms applying to any dark-haired or fair-haired girl respectively, in the manner of troubadour and goliardic pseudonyms, seems too simplistic an explanation for Dafydd's repeated references to them.

There is no doubt that Dafydd refers to 'real' people in his poems, such as Angharad, Ifor Hael, and Madog Benfras, who belonged to his own circle of patrons and acquaintances. He also uses names such as Tegau and Esyllt as conventional labels which automatically convey to his audience impressions of beauty, nobility, and other courtly virtues. Such names clearly belong to the kind of common literary tradition suggested by Ifor Williams, corresponding to the Lydia and Phyllis of Latin verse, or the Belle Aelis of popular French verse. They are not necessarily pseudonyms, specifically used to conceal a true identity, but rather conventional titles which describe female virtues in a summarized and recognizable way.

Though the names Dyddgu and Morfudd are not uncommon in Welsh, they do not carry the same set of implications as Tegau or Esyllt, since neither of them belong to known literary traditions beyond the poems themselves. There is no reason why we should not place them in the same category as Angharad then, as people who actually existed in Dafydd's circle and were known personally to him. However, accepting the existence of a 'real' Dyddgu and Morfudd does not enable us to draw conclusions about the 'real' nature of their relationships with a person called Dafydd ap Gwilym. Attempts to deduce biographical material from the surviving poems, or indeed from any literary text, are doomed to frustration.

It is more important to decide what significance the figures of Dyddgu and Morfudd possessed for the poet and his audience, what was their symbolic value. They must have come to acquire such a value since they are both mentioned so frequently, particularly Morfudd. Any attempt to reconstruct 'real' people from the poetic figures of Dyddgu and Morfudd must fail at the outset because neither of them are presented in the poems as a consistent and identifiable individual. Dyddgu is the least complex, since she is invariably used to convey traditional courtly values and virtues, whether she is in her father's hall or out in the woodland. But her passivity, her lack of voice or emotion, the absence of any personal or individualizing information about her, apart from her name and conventional beauty, make her as 'unreal' as the idealized *domna* of Provençal verse.

Morfudd is even harder to identify as a single individual person because she is presented in so many different roles. She can represent the cruel courtly love mistress, as in 'Morfudd fel yr Haul', the carefree woodland lover, as in 'Yr Het Fedw', or a participant in an adulterous triangle, as in 'Amau ar Gam'. Whoever the 'real' Morfudd was, the poetic figure of Morfudd is perceived by the poet in a number of different forms, performing a number of different functions. It is not that there is one person called Morfudd who is presented 'inconsistently' by the poet; it is simply that the figure of Morfudd is used by the poet to illustrate various kinds of relationships and situations which had relevance and significance for his audience.

I have already tried to indicate Morfudd's function in the court-poems. While Dyddgu suggests enduring and traditional values of Welsh aristocratic society, Morfudd suggests the kinds of conflicts, compromises and fluctuations which were inevitably characteristic of *uchelwyr* society in its upward movement towards noble status. Dafydd himself is as much a figure or persona as the two women, and in the court-poems he represents the ancient order of court-bards attempting to find new patrons while preserving some of their traditional skills and functions, such as eulogy.

The conventional and stylized nature of Morfudd and Dyddgu as poetic figures is more apparent when we look at poems to unnamed women who perform similar roles and functions. It is not only Dyddgu who represents traditional noble values, nor is it only Morfudd who represents the aspirations of the *uchelwyr*. The same concerns are also evident in a small number of Dafydd's poems addressed to unnamed, but manifestly noble, women. 'Campau Bun' (GDG 56), for example, is virtually a textbook example of a formal praise-poem to a noblewoman, as defined by the bardic Grammar. Its language and style are deliberate echoes of an older poetic tradition commemorating Wales' past.

Dafydd, in his persona as praise-poet, begins with a description of his sleeplessness caused by love-longing, a motif associated with Continental courtly love-poetry but which was also used by the *gogynfeirdd*, as early as Hywel ab Owain Gwynedd. This aspect of love-suffering establishes the formal and conventional nature of the poem as an expression of praise in the form of a *rhieingerdd*. Dafydd refers explicitly to his bardic role—'fardd hardd heirddryw' (hand-some poet of fair descent), 'digollwawd bardd' (poet of perfect praise)—to reinforce the essentially eulogistic function of the poem.

The object of the eulogy, the maiden, is placed in a courtly context to suggest her inherent nobility of behaviour and lineage, unmixed with any non-native blood. He then constructs a series of negative and positive statements which follow the prescriptions laid down in the bardic Grammar:[27]

> Nid un ddihaereb nebun
> I'n gwlad ni â hi ei hun.
> Ni bu,nid oes i'n oes ni,
> Ni bydd tebyg neb iddi:
> Yn hael iawn, yn hil ynad,
> Yn heilio gwledd, yn haul gwlad,
> Yn fonheddig, yn ddigardd,
> Yn fain ei hael, yn fun hardd,
> Yn rhy ddiwair ei heirioes,
> Yn ddyn mwyn dda iawn ei moes,
> Yn ennill clod, yn annwyl,
> Yn dda ei thwf, yn ddoeth, ŵyl.   (GDG 56, 37–48)

(No-one in our country is proverbial as she is herself. There was not, there is not in our time, there will not be anyone like her: very generous, offspring of a magistrate, serving a feast, country's sun, noble, excellent, slim her brow, a beautiful maiden, too chaste her disposition, a gentle person of such good manner, winning praise, beloved, good her stature, wise, modest.)

The use of the possessive pronoun, 'in our country', supports Dafydd's function as the praise-poet of a Welsh patron's daughter, while the imagery, redolent of *gogynfeirdd* eulogy, further establishes his role. The wit of the poem depends on the list of virtues which work against Dafydd as a lover: because the maiden is virtuous, she will not agree to a tryst with him. The dual nature of the maiden, perfect and yet cruel, ensures that Dafydd's love will remain unrequited—the inevitable outcome of eulogistic 'love'.

Eulogy of an unattainable object is the theme of another of Dafydd's praise-poems to an unnamed girl, 'Rhagoriaeth ei Gariad' (GDG 51). Here, the focus is not on the poet's suffering but on the beauty of the girl herself who outshines not only the moon and sun but also the three legendary beauties, Polixena, Deidameia, and Helen of Troy. These references to classical heroines show that Dafydd is deliberately reaching beyond the limits of *gogynfeirdd* material to make use of foreign traditions, although the legends of early Greece and Rome were as popular in Wales as in France and England. Moreover, Dafydd is evidently drawing on one of the native triads for his opening description of the women.[28]

The imagery also draws strongly on the native tradition, with a series of images describing the girl's beauty compared to the sun or a lime-washed chamber. The diction implies a noble background, even a hint of French refinement in the borrowed word *siambr*. Elsewhere in the poem, religious diction is used to reinforce a sense of formality and distance between the poet and his beloved—for example, 'i'r deml' (to the temple), 'Cristion credadun' (believing Christian), 'Duw'n fach' (God as surety)—and to suggest the spiritual, rather than physical, nature of the love. The poet's rejection of worldly riches in favour of love adds to this motif, while his direct address to his audience indicates the official rather than personal nature of the eulogy:

> Pa les i minnau, wyrda,
> A maddau'r dyn, meddu'r da?   (GDG 51, 51–2)

(What advantage is it to me, lords, to renounce the girl and possess wealth?)

Implicit in this question is the assumption that true nobility of nature is not necessarily a product of wealth, that one is possible without the other, an idea that probably had some appeal for poets like Dafydd as well as for his *uchelwyr* listeners.

This assumption is reinforced to some extent by the poem 'Penwisg Merch' (GDG 44) which describes the opulent gold head-dress worn by a young noblewoman. In expressing his unrequited love, Dafydd implies that the inner qualities of the girl do not match the external display of wealth on her head. However, the real focus of the poem is undoubtedly the head-dress itself as a magnificent symbol of the wealth and prestige of the *uchelwyr*. It is described as an adornment appropriate to the girl's status:

> Fflwring aur, ffloyw reng oroen.
> Da lun ar ddail fflŵr-dy-lis,
> Ac aur bwrw o gaer Baris.
> Gem yw ar y ddau gymwd,
> Ac aur Ffrainc, unne geirw ffrwd.   (GDG 44, 22–6)

(Gold florin, bright rank of beauty, a good design on leaves of fleur-de-lis, and cast gold from the city of Paris. She is a gem of the two commotes, and gold from France, of the same colour as the foam of a stream.)

The references to florin and fleur-de-lis occur again in the nature poems as images of trees and leaves, but here they have a literal application to the appearance of the head-dress. The repeated references to gold and to French craftsmanship testify to the sophisticated material culture available to the *uchelwyr* as a hallmark of their wealth and status.

A similar kind of appeal is made by 'Hudoliaeth Merch' (GDG 84) which evokes the setting of a contemporary noble feast. The motif of magic and enchantment which Dafydd uses in many of his love-poems, such as 'Cystudd y Bardd' (GDG 102), is its central theme. Here the enchantment emanates not so much from the girl herself but from her playing of the harp during a function at which Dafydd is evidently present in his official bardic capacity. His eulogy of the fair harp-player, however, transcends the merely conventional to capture the whisper of a personal grievance like a snatched conversation behind the formal grandeur and protocol of the occasion. The poem is a rich celebration of noble status and of the tradition of bardic eulogy which reinforces and sustains it.

All the elements of the bardic relationship, familiar from *gogyn-feirdd* poetry and further embellished in Dafydd's own court-poetry, are presented with an almost dramatic flourish and sense of occasion. The poet's bardic love is expressed purely in terms of mutual obligation and his meagre payment in exchange for his praises. His suffering is exemplified by physical anguish—'gwewyr serch gwaeth no gwŷr saint a gefais drwy ddigofaint' (anguish of love worse than that of holy men have I received because of anger)—and by references to Welsh historical and legendary characters, Gwaeddan, Menw, Eiddilig, Math, Llwyd fab Cel Coed. The girl's beauty is conveyed by a liberal sprinkling of conventional imagery, such as 'gwedd memrwn gwiw' ([she whose] face is like fair parchment), 'gwenddyn gwyn-ddaint' (fair girl with white teeth), 'bryd nyf' ([you of] the beauty of snow), and also through a fragmented description of the harp itself.

The poem is not merely a courtly eulogy, however. Its central theme is the illusory and deceptive nature of bardic love, an illusion which is here created and reinforced by the playing of the harp. As an extension of this, the girl herself is seen to be cruel and tormenting, an allusion to the common dilemma of courtly love that the unavailable beloved is at once perfect and yet cruel. Just as the craftsmanship of the harp enhances the beauty of the girl, so it also represents the spell she casts over the poet.

The whole poem is a brilliant synthesis of the conventions and assumptions of native bardic love-poetry, together with some individual contributions which lift the poem out of its genre. This comment on name-calling, for example, suddenly reveals a moment of innocent, almost childish, emotion, which contrasts with the gilded and stylized imagery around it:

> Yn iarlles eiry un orlliw
> Y'th alwn, gwedd memrwn gwiw;
> Yn herlod salw y'm galwud
> I'm gŵydd drwy waradwydd drud.   (GDG 84, 9–12)

(I used to call you a countess of snow's brilliant hue, face like fair parchment; you called me a vile wretch, to my face, with dire opprobrium.)

The contrast between 'yn iarlles' (a countess), and 'yn herlod salw' (a vile wretch), balanced by the repetition of 'y'th alwn' (I called you), and 'y'm galwud' (you called me), and the similar syntactical patterns, suggest a note of pathos, even of bitterness, the same touch of irony which Dafydd injects into many of his serious love-poems. In the conclusion, however, the poetic voice is once again assured and in command, making reference to a proverb which carries with it an almost moralistic imperative:

> Gwell yw crefft, meddir, hir hud,
> Ne gwylan befr, no golud.
> Cymer, brad nifer, bryd nyf,
> Gannwyll Gwlad Gamber, gennyf,
> Lawrodd ffawd, lariaidd ei pharch,
> Le yr ŵyl, liw yr alarch.   (GDG 84, 67–72)

(It is said that artistry—[girl of] long enchantment, hue of bright seagull—is better than wealth. Receive from me—traitor to a host, beauty of snow, candle of Cambria, fortune's gift—a place at the feast, gently is she respected, swan-coloured girl.)

The central syntactic structure asserts the superiority of artistry over wealth: in other words, the poet has capitulated and ceased his reproaches and is returning to a fundamental belief in the value of artistic skill as a gift worth more than any material reward which the girl could offer him. Because of this new understanding, he then offers his praises freely, with no more desire for payment in exchange; the music of the harp is his reward. At the same time, the poet accepts that his love must necessarily remain unrequited. Like the workmanship of the harp, it transcends material compensation.

Around his central structure Dafydd distributes, deliberately disguising but also subtly reinforcing the impact of his statement, a series of *geiriau llanw* which allude to the inner and outer virtues of his beloved.[29] 'Brad nifer' (traitor to a host) and 'lariaidd ei pharch' (gentle her respect) suggest the duality of her nature and also of the harp's, an apparent mildness which nevertheless casts a treacherous spell. The reference to the seagull, with its implications of the colours of black and white, juxtaposed to 'hir hud' (long-lasting magic), reiterates this duality, the dark enchantment hidden beneath the bright exterior. The final series of images, however, 'bryd nyf' (beauty of snow), 'gannwyll Gwlad Gamber' (candle of Cambria), 'liw yr alarch' (colour of the swan), all emphasize the girl's pure and immutable beauty and spotlessness, complementing the explicit sense of capitulation to her spell and a renewed awareness of her perfection despite the impossibility of receiving her love.

The kinds of ambiguities and tensions expressed in the poem, followed by a clear statement of resolution and acceptance, suggest an underlying endorsement of *uchelwyr* claims to nobility, on the understanding that they support *crefft*, the skills and virtues of their native heritage, rather than merely pursuing *golud*, the money they earn from services to the Crown. They may take their place at the feast, provided they remember to reward the bards who support their claim.

All these poems of Dafydd's can be considered 'courtly' in the sense that they are continuing technical and thematic conventions used by the earlier court-poets, the *gogynfeirdd*. The tradition of eulogy expressed in the form of love-poetry, with in-built conflicts and paradoxes, is characteristic of court-centred medieval aristocracies, and there is thus a clear analogy between Welsh court-poetry and earlier European material, though limited evidence for direct borrowing. Just as the *gogynfeirdd* are conscious of acceptable archaism in using the heroic diction and contexts of *cynfeirdd* poetry, so Dafydd is conscious of archaism, even anachronism, in his courtly poems.

Despite this archaic basis of the courtly poems, which have developed largely within the native tradition, Dafydd has skilfully introduced innovations and original interpretations to prevent his poems becoming as unwieldy as the work of the *gogynfeirdd*. His most obvious innovation is of course the use of the *cywydd deuair hirion* metre accompanied by strict cynghanedd, in contrast to the *awdlau* and *englynion* with which he composes bardic poems to Christ and to Ifor Hael. The stylistic techniques of *dyfalu* and extended metaphor are also characteristic of Dafydd's attempt to move beyond the confines of *gogynfeirdd* poetry, while his greater emphasis on love's sufferings and ways in which he deals with unrequited love reflect his wider interest in love-poetry apart from the purely eulogistic mode.

This movement beyond the conventions of praise-poetry leads to a group of love-lyrics which, while formal in their tone and technique, are far from being comparable to courtly love-poems of the troubadour type.[30] Unadulterated by extensive nature imagery or eulogistic description, these lyrics analyse the effects of a love between two equals which is capable of resolution and yet seldom achieves it. The poet laments for what might have been as well as for his present condition of suffering. However, the persona of the distant praise-poet has not been replaced by the courtly lover of European tradition, submissive to his beloved, finding pleasure in pain, and willing to be ennobled through the ordeal of love. Instead we find a narrator who explicitly retains his poetic function along with a strong sense of his own worth and of the appropriate way in which to conduct a love-affair.

In these poems, the confidence of the lover allows him to rise above failure and disappointment and to demand the reward which is rightfully his. The metaphor of bardic patronage is thus strongly implied. Like the lover, the poet has confidence that his own skills and abilities deserve an appropriate reward. Significantly, these more assertive poems lack the same demonstrably courtly background of the eulogistic poems and simply express the poet's response to a particular event in his love relationship. There is a parallel here with the fluctuating relationship between poet and patron in contemporary Wales and the need for poets such as Dafydd to make a strong claim for support.

It is not entirely coincidental, then, that one of Dafydd's favourite themes is that of fickleness. This characteristic is associated particularly with Morfudd, as in the praise-poem 'Morfudd fel yr Haul' (GDG 42). 'Gofyn Cymod' (GDG 52) is another formal love-lyric in which the results of Morfudd's fickleness are displayed. The poet has accused Morfudd of this weakness, she has responded with anger and coldness, and the poet is now trying to effect a reconciliation. As in many of Dafydd's poems, a complex set of ideas and circumstances is laid out amongst a network of *geiriau llanw* and *sangiadau*, creating a rich texture in which the implications are as important as what is actually stated.

Dafydd's reference to himself as 'dy brydydd . . . diledach' (your noble poet) reminds us that he sees his role as that of love-poet rather than the lover-knight of European poetry. His attitude to Morfudd is not that of *fin' amors* or *amour courtois*: rather than presenting himself as submissive or supplicating, he is almost moralistic, reminding Morfudd of her Christian duty to forgive him. The *exemplum* of Jesus and Mary showing mercy to those who injured them, the reference to anger as 'pechawd' (a sin), and the use of imperatives—'dilidia' (cease from anger), 'cymod' (be reconciled)—all suggest a sermon-like delivery with an ironically irreligious text: 'cynnal faswedd i'th weddi' (support wantonness in your prayer).

The context of the poem, evoked through phrases such as 'gwynddyn gwiw' (fitting fair girl), 'hoen Dyfr o sud' (vigour of Dyfr in form), 'ddeuliw ton' ([you of] the two colours of a wave), is unmistakably Welsh rather than European. Not only the stance of the courtly lover, but also the imagery associated with love's sickness, are noticeably absent, and the poem depends instead on the resolution of a dynamic, on-going situation. The poet, though requesting a reconciliation, has not yielded all control over the relationship and in fact emerges at the end as a persuasive and dominant figure. His description of himself as 'croesan' (buffoon), implies that his criticism of Morfudd was only a joke in the first place, and also emphasizes, by contrast, his worth as a poet and as a lover.

As a variation on this theme, Dafydd presents himself as an angry, rejected lover in another poem to Morfudd which attacks her fickleness, 'Y Cariad a Wrthodwyd' (GDG 93). He begins with a formal address which establishes Morfudd's crime and his own bitter, yet resigned, response:

> Drud yr adwaenwn dy dro,
> Gwen gynhinen, gyn heno.
> Mae i'm bryd, ennyd ynni,
> Aml ei thwyll, ymliw â thi.
> Morfudd ferch Fadawg Lawgam,
> Myn y Pab, mi a wn pam
> Y'm gadewaist ar feiston
> Yn weddw hyll yn y wedd hon. (GDG 93, 1–8)

(I recognized your daring trickery before tonight, fair little piece. It is in my mind, moment of energy, frequent her deceit, to reproach you. Morfudd daughter of Madog Bent-Hand, by the Pope, I know why you have left me stranded, bereft and ugly in this way.)

Rather than attempting to woo Morfudd back by flattery, Dafydd adopts a scathing poetic tone and uses some rather gross analogies to describe Morfudd's adultery: she keeps two oxen under the yoke, and is a ball passed from hand to hand. However, this harshness is alleviated by many references to Morfudd's beauty and the poet's love for her—'seren oleuwen o liw' (you of the colour of a bright fair star), 'fy chwaer ffydd' (my faithful girl), 'bryd hardd annwyl' (dear lovely beauty). Though he rebukes Morfudd for rejecting him, her spell is still unbroken, and the closing simile indicates the poet's bitter sadness and sense of injustice:

> Bid edifar dy garu,
> Bwriaist fi, byr o wst fu.
> Ys gwir y bwrir baril
> Ysgwd, pan fo gwag, is gil.   (GDG 93, 41–4)

(May he repent, whoever loves you, you cast me off, the trouble was brief. It is true that a barrel is thrown aside with a shove when it is empty.)

Indifference and rejection are the subjects of two other poems voiced by a similar poetic persona, 'Merch O Is Aeron' (GDG 88) and 'Angof' (GDG 97). Here the dual function of poet and lover is indicated more clearly, and the tone is one of mournful devotion rather than bitter hostility. Nevertheless, the poet remains conscious of his own status and deliberately points out the lesson that is to be learnt from his experiences.

In 'Merch O Is Aeron', Dafydd describes himself as 'gwan y bardd sythardd seithug' (pale the poet, stiff and tall, futile), and describes the tears and the spear which represents his suffering in a series of sections beginning 'Gwae' (woe). He also uses the parable of the man who builds his house on sand as an analogy for the insecurity of his love:

> Gwae a wnêl rhag rhyfel rhew
> Dŷ ar draeth, daear drathew.
> Bydd anniogel wely,
> Byr y trig, a'r berw a'i try.   (GDG 88, 17–20)

(Woe on him who builds a house on sand, fine thick earth, for fear of the onslaught of frost. It will be an insecure bed, it will stay only a short time, and the foaming tide will shift it.)

Clearly Dafydd is drawing on a number of familiar literary themes, setting these firmly in an environment of native images such as 'gweunllethr gwawn' (meadow slope of gossamer), 'gwenlloer Garawn' (white moon of Carawn), but his stance is still that of the rejected poet rather than courtly lover. The use of the parable implies an analogy between wordly and spiritual affairs but also draws attention to a general moral exemplified by the poet's individual experience.

The function of the poet to instruct, as well as to praise and satirize, is again made clear in 'Angof'. Just as Dafydd preached against fickleness in 'Gofyn Cymod', so he points out the moral fault of forgetting a person to whom an obligation is due:

> O bu, ymannerch serchbryd,
> Un gair rhôm, unne geirw rhyd,
> Ac o bu gynt, tremynt tro,
> Bai ditiwr, mawl, bid eto.
> Na haedd ogan fal anhael,
> Ac na fydd adwerydd wael.
> Angof ni wna dda i ddyn,
> Anghlod mewn awdl neu englyn.   (GDG 97, 13–20)

(If there was a single word between us, mutual greeting of love's beauty, same colour as ford's foam, and if there used to be praise, extreme change, accuser's fault, let it be so again. Do not deserve satire like a miser, do not be a poor old maid. Forgetfulness does no good to anyone, dishonour in *awdl* or *englyn*.)

Dafydd thus discusses forgetfulness from the point of view of a poet who depends on continued patronage, but his persona as a lover seeking the renewal of an affair is clear from his references to the girl's beauty and his final plea:

> Nid taeredd a wnaut erof,
> Nid da, deg Efa, dy gof.
> Na fydd anghywir hirynt,
> N'ad tros gof ein wtres gynt.   (GDG 97, 25–8)

(It was not steadfastness, what you did for me, your memory is not good, fair Eve. Do not be false for a long time, do not forget our former passion.)

'Anwadalrwydd' (GDG 60) illustrates ingratitude and fickleness by examples from the natural world. Extended descriptions of animals deserting those who have fostered them when young become analogies for the poet's girl. Despite his attempts to keep her with him, she has betrayed him and left him. The same theme of fosterage and nurturing is developed at greater length in 'Y Mab Maeth' (GDG 104), a brilliantly sustained metaphor of the poet's love lodging in his breast like a wayward, uncontrollable foster-son. The poet even envisages this *mab maeth* as being the unwanted son of his mistress who has put him out for adoption, to be taken in by the unwilling poet. The whole poem conveys most vividly the poet's ambivalent feelings, his frustration and hope, his love and despair, his desperate attempts to control an uncontrollable emotion.

The pain of rejection or of indifference, despite the lavishing of love and praise upon the beloved, is the subject of 'Gwadu' (GDG 107) and 'Difrawder' (GDG 110). The first begins with a courtly image suggesting the poet's status as praise-singer to a noblegirl:

> Traserch ar wenferch winfaeth
> A rois i, fal yr âi saeth.   (GDG 107, 1–2)

> (I gave great love to a fair wine-nourished girl, like an arrow might go.)

Yet the poet receives no reward, either material or physical, for his love, and the final image, of rustic fertility symbols, forms a striking contrast to the opening image in order to reinforce the poet's sense of worthlessness and humiliation.

'Difrawder' begins with another vivid image—of the fool chasing his own shadow—to describe the futility of the poet's love pursuit. Through references to her nobility and beauty, the poet manages to praise his mistress as well as mourn her indifference to his pursuit of her. He takes comfort from the fact that her impassiveness is due to her chasteness, and that if she actually noticed his extremes of suffering, she would take pity and smile upon him. But even then, he torments himself by wondering if it would be a smile of love or of mockery.

The social relevance of these poems as the work of a court-poet seeking patronage is clear. The new nobility are being firmly reminded of their duty to support the native culture, and specifically the displaced court-poets, rather than being seduced by imported literary traditions and social structures. The poet is confident and assertive, an attitude which reflects the ancient status given to court-poets, but he is also affirming the need for loyalty in the process of cultural assimilation.

The impact of the imported tradition of love-poetry is seen particularly in a small number of Dafydd's poems based on the hyperbolic conventions of courtly love. The tone of these poems is created by the use of a different persona, a younger and less worldly character than the court-poet, one who is full of the enthusiasm and illusions of youth. In these poems, the persona is simply an eager lover, and does not have the eulogistic role of the previous group. Consequently there is no restraining framework of poetic duty to prevent a full description of love's devastating effects. These poems also seem to have an overtly ironical intention: Dafydd manipulates his youthful persona to achieve a level of hyperbole which verges on parody of all that courtly love takes most seriously. In this way, he undermines the influence of the foreign tradition and asserts the superiority of the native bardic profession.

One of his poems to Morfudd, 'Blinder' (GDG 96), exemplifies the use of this persona, and also the range of ways in which Dafydd views Morfudd. The poetic narrator is far less formidable and self-confident than the lover-poet, and in fact is deliberately described as 'gwas o nwyf a gwedd' (a lad in vigour and appearance), to emphasize his youthful looks and devotion, and also to indicate the absence of the bardic role. The reference to his reward, 'a gaf o dâl, gofud yw' (what I received of payment is sorrow), now becomes a complete metaphor, with all trace of its original referent lost.

The setting of the poem is the church where the poet gazes helplessly upon his beloved, a non-courtly setting which comple-ments the naive and non-bardic persona of the poem. The wit of the lyric depends on an extended description of the poet's tear-filled eyes, which are pricked by needles and flooded with rain 'hyd y farf' (as far as his beard). It is again noticeable in this poem that although Dafydd is illustrating a kind of unrequited love similar to *amour courtois*, he does not adopt the character of a courtly lover nor utilize con-ventional courtly love imagery. The tone of the poem, with its heartfelt cry at the end

> Cyfraith serch y sy'n erchi,
> Cymer dy hun yt, fun, fi.   (GDG 96, 39–40)

(The law of love commands it, take me to yourself, maiden.)

is clearly that of a formal love-lyric, but one which belongs neither to the eulogistic tradition of the *gogynfeirdd* nor to the European courtly love tradition.[31]

The idea of love as a betrayal and a source of affliction is pursued in 'Cystudd Cariad' (GDG 90), where the poet affects to be completely disillusioned by love, and to have grown out of his youthful enthusiasm for it, but cannot help retaining some hope that love may yet reward him. The contrast between former vigour and present sorrow is hyperbolic enough to suggest Dafydd's irony when talking of love's excesses, and also the extremes of emotion felt by the youthful persona:

> Darfu'r rhyfyg a'm digiawdd,
> Darfu'r corff, mau darfer cawdd.
> Darfu'n llwyr derfyn y llais,
> A'r campau, dygn y cwympais.

> Darfu'r awen am wenferch,
> Darfu'r sôn am darfwr serch.
>
> Ni chyfyd ynof, cof cerdd,
> Gyngyd llawen nac angerdd,
> Na sôn diddan amdanun',
> Na serch byth, onis eirch bun.   (GDG 90,15–24)

(Finished is the arrogance which afflicted me, finished is my body, a turmoil of sadness is mine. Finished to the utter limit is my voice and its accomplishments, hard have I fallen. Finished is my poetry for a fair girl, finished the talk of him who scatters love. No joyful purpose or passion arises in me—memory of song—nor is there amusing talk about them, nor any more of love ever—unless a girl should ask.)

The description of suffering contains the same references to physical debility—'gwn ganclwyf' (I know a hundred wounds)—familiar from European courtly love-poetry, yet the poet's attitude to love is not the conventional courtly stance of humility and supplication. His assertion 'darfu'r sôn am darfwr serch' (finished the rumours about love's scatterer), implies that he has, or had, a reputation of being as victorious in love as a warrior in battle, and the final line of the poem indicates his willingness to maintain this reputation if given the opportunity.

Another method used by Dafydd to examine the effects of love, apart from presenting the experiences of an individualized persona, is the isolation of certain motifs associated with the courtly love tradition. Five poems in particular exemplify this method: 'Saethu'r Ferch' (GDG 100), 'Cusan' (GDG 133), 'Y Galon' (GDG 108), 'Y Gwayw' (GDG 111), and 'Yr Uchenaid' (GDG 109). All these subjects—the arrow of love, the kiss as a reward, the lover's heart, the spear of love which causes pain, and the sigh of anguish—are familiar from both the Latin and French traditions of formal love-poetry.[32]

The symbol of the arrow is used most commonly in European poetry to signify the process by which the poet becomes enamoured of his beloved. The arrow of love pierces his eye when he looks at the lady and he then becomes her slave. In 'Saethu'r Ferch', Dafydd takes the same motif and changes its significance so that he becomes the sender of the arrow which is then repelled by his lady, as a metaphor for her rejection of his praise, a term which itself, in the context of Dafydd's poetry, represents love. The poem thus works at a level deeper than the superficial structure, and the detailed description of the arrow, alternating between literal and figurative imagery, acknowledges the conscious symbolism of the poem.

In 'Cusan', the poet celebrates the gift of a kiss which he has received from his lady. For many of the courtly love-poets, and often for Dafydd himself, this was the reward most highly prized, an indication that love was returned without the moral complexities of complete physical surrender.[33] Since courtly love is inevitably unrequited, Dafydd is moving beyond the usual conventions by describing how a poet might feel if such a reward were actually granted. The tone of the poem is triumphant and celebratory, praise is given unstintingly to the beloved, and the technique of the poem itself, with its long *cymeriad* repeating the initial letter of *cusan*, reinforces the poet's joy.[34]

In European love-poetry, the heart is often mentioned as the seat of the passions, the organ which experiences the joy and pain of love.[35] Dafydd's poem 'Y Galon', however, takes a very literal, almost anatomical, view of the heart and dissociates it from the finer feelings of love. Instead, he sees it as the seat of lust and the instigator of all the tribulations connected with love.

The poem falls into three clearly defined parts, the first describing the heart itself as an organ using a series of figurative images such as 'gwehydd-dy gwawd' (weaving-house of song), 'palmeres' (pilgrim), 'cron forwyn' (round maiden), 'cadair ceudawd' (cradle of the breast). In the second section, the poet describes three things which are 'gwraidd yr heiniau' (the roots of pestilence), drink, a woman's curse, and adultery, all of which are controlled or processed by the internal organs. The third section translates the images of lust, excess, and disease, into a more familiar language of love, linked to the earlier sections by an equation between the physical diseases of the body and the emotional difficulties of loving Morfudd:

> Hynny yw gwraidd yr heiniau,
> Henw swydd falch honno sydd fau.
> Nid mwy rhyfel dan Geli
> Dyn na mil, myn Duw, no mi,
> Yn caru, nesäu serch,
> Er anfodd pawb, yr unferch –
> Pobl wrthrych, llewych llywy,
> Pefr feinwyr, pawb a ŵyr pwy. (GDG 108, 31–8)

(Those are the roots of pestilence, the name of that proud office which is mine. There is no greater warfare under Heaven, for man or animal, by God, than my loving the one girl, approaching love, despite the disapproval of everyone—people's aspiration, fair brightness, radiant maiden, everyone knows who.)

The symbol of the heart is therefore used in a very different way from the European love-poems, providing a contrast between the grossness of physical excess and the tenuous delicacy of the poet's love for Morfudd.

Again in 'Y Gwayw', the emotional perception of love is transferred to a physical object, here a spear whose carefully observed concreteness is nevertheless merely a figure for the poet's torment. The motif of a spear or dagger representing love's suffering is known in both French and Latin love-poetry, but Dafydd goes further than the European poets in his description of the spear and its physical effects:

> Gwydn ynof gwayw deunawnych,
> Gwas prudd a wnâi'r grudd yn grych.
> Gwynia'n dost, gwenwyn a dâl,
> Gwayw llifaid, gwäell ofal.
> Esyllt bryd a'i dyd er dig,
> Aseth cledr dwyfron ysig.
> Trwm yw ynof ei hirgadw,
> Trwyddew fy mron friwdon fradw.
> Trefnloes fynawyd cariad,
> Triawch saeth fydd brawdfaeth brad.   (GDG 111,
> 25–34)

(Grievous in me is an eighteen-barbed spear, a dire agent which would make the cheek wrinkled. It hurts sorely, it is as good as poison, whetted spear, skewer of anxiety. [She of] Esyllt's form places it from anger, a stake in my bruised breastbone. Its long staying in me is wretched, piercer of my bruised, broken, worn-out breast. The awl of love is an instrument of pain, the three-edged arrow is treason's foster-brother.)

The concept of love's suffering, with its emphasis on physical pain and debility, is an integral part of the European courtly love movement, and although Dafydd is clearly aware of the foreign tradition he often diverges from it, as here, by objectifying his suffering, externalizing it and attributing it to a genuine physical cause, rather than to the more abstract power of love by itself.

The same tendency is illustrated in 'Yr Uchenaid' where the sigh of pain, caused by Morfudd's rejection of him, becomes the symbol and focus of the poet's despair. The physical act of sighing, with sufficient violence to break the poet's heart into four pieces, is described in terms of external imagery: the poet has more breath than a blacksmith's bellows, he makes a noise like a tool chipping stone from a wall, his breath is like a wind, 'awel glaw i grinaw gran' (a rainy breeze to wither a cheek), 'gwynt hydref hoedran' (autumn wind of longing). There is emphasis too, on the expulsion of air from a narrow channel, represented by the poet's reference to himself as a piper.

Throughout the poem, the figurative descriptions of the sigh lead to sadness and pain. The references to autumn, to wheat being winnowed by the force of the poet's sigh, and to his cheek withering under the force of the blast, suggest the disintegration and decay of life as time passes, so that the poet's hopes of love are blighted by his own breath. As in other love-poems, Morfudd's name is introduced only at the very end of the *cywydd*, as if she is carrying, in a structural as well as metaphorical way, the weight of responsibility for the poet's grief. The narrow limits of the poem, which isolates a single sigh from the infinity of the poet's breathing, and the mood of suffering and reproach, make this poem another example of a piece to Morfudd as a disdainful noblewoman rather than as a fickle creature of the woodland.

In this group of poems, then, the focus is on a particular object or event which forms the subject of most of the imagery and characterizes a static, unchanging situation. The poetic voice is not that of an obtrusive persona, whose point of view is integral to the events and feelings being described. Instead, the narrator's presence is discernible only through conventional expressions of joy or longing, his real energy being directed towards a central minutely examined subject.

These poems also display a tendency towards hyperbole which verges on irony and parody. This tendency emerges clearly in those poems voiced by the youthful ardent persona, such as 'Blinder', which have a kind of humorous undertone directed at the speaker's passionate outpourings. But in some of the other poems, particularly 'Saethu'r Ferch' and 'Y Gwayw', the exaggerated descriptions of love's torment suggest a parody of the more hyperbolic developments of the courtly love tradition itself.

It is well known from the 'Ymryson' between Dafydd and Gruffudd Gryg that the latter criticized Dafydd's use of exaggerated imagery in his love-poetry, and that Dafydd defended his preoccupation with love and its effects. There is nothing in the 'Ymryson', however, to suggest that Dafydd was a serious convert to the principles of *amour courtois*, and in fact most of his love-poems, which are intended to explore the very real emotions associated with love, betray a certain scepticism regarding the more excessive

European conventions, such as the spears and arrows of love, the ambivalence about physical desire, the life or death extremes of love, and the single-minded commitment to one idealized object. Dafydd's elaborate and highly magnified scrutinies of these conventions are often powerfully effective in conveying a range and depth of emotion, but they also suggest the artificial distance which such motifs place between poet and beloved, and point out the impossibility of ever satisfying a love which is based on such exaggerated and over-sensitized perceptions. Thus Dafydd clearly implies his qualified acceptance of the literary traditions introduced as a result of Norman power, and invites his audience to laugh at such poetic affectations.

The poems discussed in this chapter are all examples of Dafydd's work as a court-poet, including his official eulogies and his extensions from these to explore the bardic love relationship.[36] Dafydd is consciously working in the wider tradition of courtly love, while also maintaining many of the traditional skills of the native court-bard.

Like the troubadours in Provence, Dafydd is composing for a particular social élite, the Welsh ruling class of *uchelwyr*. His praise poetry is complimentary to them in two major ways: by using techniques and echoes of *gogynfeirdd* praise-poetry, Dafydd is implicitly identifying the *uchelwyr* as rightful successors to the old Welsh aristocracy; and by drawing on Continental themes associated with *courtoisie*—unrequited love, worship of a courtly mistress—Dafydd is clearly aligning his audience with their powerful Anglo-Norman overlords.

Again like troubadour song, Dafydd's court-poetry focuses on conflict and tension. In the social context of twelfth-century Provence, this conflict was symptomatic of the knights' struggle for autonomy. The voice of troubadour song was the voice of the lover-knight seeking social recognition and status through marriage. But the conflict behind Dafydd's court-poetry arises from different social preoccupations. The voice of his courtly *cywyddau* is the voice of the lover-poet seeking material support and patronage in exchange for eulogy and courtly entertainment. Using the role of court-poet, Dafydd's eulogies tell us something about the relationship between bards and their patrons. The theme of fickleness, which is developed much further in Dafydd's poetry than in any preceding tradition, is surely indicative of the insecurity of the poet's position in fourteenth-century Wales.

Using the persona of lover, Dafydd's court-poems suggest some of the concerns of the *uchelwyr*, of whom Dafydd himself was one. Dafydd represents himself as a noble lover in order to make observations regarding the identity of the *uchelwyr* as a social class, their aspirations towards nobility, and their loyalties to the old independent Wales. As a poet, Dafydd's goals are material reward, recognition, and some degree of security. As a lover, Dafydd seeks the same things but in the social context of wealth, status, and advantageous marriage.

Finally, I would like to isolate two of the court-poems which convey most resonantly the kind of messages that Dafydd's verse sent to his noble audiences—these are 'Caer Rhag Cenfigen' (GDG 140) and 'Yr Adfail' (GDG 144). The first represents a powerful example of Dafydd's work as an official court-poet, with its elevated register, dependence on metaphor, and projection of the poet into the poem specifically as a court-bard. The poem is constructed from an elaborate extended metaphor in which the poet's heart is a fortress being stormed by enemy hosts representing jealousy. The language of warfare and siege fighting predominates, implying that the pursuit of love is a battle to be waged, but there is also a strong contemporary relevance with references to the siege of Calais and to King Edward.

God is called the creator and owner of the metaphorical fortress, so that the poet is personified as a crusader fighting with God on his side against an enemy of God:

> Ef a roes Duw, nawddfoes nawd,
> Gaer i'm cadw, gwiwrym ceudawd,
> Cystal, rhag ofn dial dyn,
> Â'r Galais, rhag ei elyn.   (GDG 140, 19–22)

(God gave—customary protection—a fortress to protect me, fair strength of the heart, which is as effective against fear of man's vengeance as Calais is against his enemy.)

This implies that God will help the poet overcome his tribulations and win the love of his lady Angharad,[37] an assumption which is made in many of Dafydd's love-poems. The poet therefore has the spiritual legitimation of God's support for his love, and can avoid the spiritual conflict which obsessed many of the troubadours. The poem is more than just a record of love's tribulations. Its language of warfare and contemporary references have a specific appeal to the *uchelwyr*, whose power is partly dependent on the continued military strength of the English crown.

In 'Yr Adfail' (GDG 144), Dafydd describes, in the form of a dialogue, the ruin of an old house. The poet contrasts the present appearance of the building, with its gaping roof and broken walls, to its former glory as the place where he courted his beloved. The point of the poem is to evoke the transience of earthly life, including physical love, a theme which is expressed in the line 'hudol enbyd yw'r byd byth' (the world is ever a dangerous magician). The illusory nature of worldly goods and desires, their deceptive attractions, indicates the impermanent and unsatisfying quality of a love based on physical desire alone, devoid of any spiritual basis. The *contemptus mundi* theme, familiar from the clerical tradition, occurs repeatedly in Dafydd's poems as a warning to the *uchelwyr* not to place too much reliance on worldly status and materialistic values. The ruined house is symbolic of the old order of independent Wales, swept aside by the winds of change.

Dafydd's court-poetry therefore functions as an important part of his interpretation of love, but has a wider social relevance as well. His use of the persona of praise-poet indicates his understanding of the significance of this role in continuing and maintaining the native bardic tradition. There are close analogies between his work and that of the troubadours in terms of their function as representatives of a new type of nobility. Dafydd, however, is not concerned with the theme of courtly love merely as a set of stylized conventions, as is shown by his use of ironic hyperbole, nor does he adopt the suppliant role of the courtly lover. Instead, he uses his status as a court-poet to impose demands on the new nobility, while at the same time reassuring them of their élitism. Images of conflict are not as threatening and overwhelming in his poetry as they often are in troubadour lyrics, but are used as a motivation for positive action towards consensus and assimilation with the Norman ruling class.

CHAPTER 6

Popular Traditions in Dafydd's Love-poetry

THE love-poems discussed so far are those in which Dafydd's skills as a Welsh court-bard, and his debt to the native bardic tradition, are most in evidence. Composing as a praise-poet, Dafydd is following a native tradition of eulogy which is analogous to that of other aristocratic societies in Europe, but which has its own individual characteristics of style and attitude. The differences between Dafydd's formal love-lyrics and those belonging to the traditions of *fin' amors* and *amour courtois* are marked. Most obviously, Dafydd avoids the tendency to discuss a philosophy or abstraction of love and instead deals with specific events or situations. In addition, his stance is that of the lover-poet rather than lover-knight, and the paradoxical joys and sufferings of love are not deliberately juxtaposed to create a sense of virtue or of the ennobling power of love.

Thus the bardic poems are characterized by their comparative conservatism in adhering to *gogynfeirdd* techniques, and their specifically native frame of reference which is distinct, at a social and literary level, from the aristocratic and courtly environment of the troubadours. However, in many of his poems Dafydd moves away from the bardic function of the court-poems in order to incorporate foreign literary influences which reached him through popular rather than courtly channels.

Dafydd's poetry diverges most radically from the *gogynfeirdd* tradition in his extensive use of motifs and references associated with popular literature, both native and foreign. The antecedent native popular tradition is hard to reconstruct, since it was transmitted orally, but the evidence of the dialogue poems in the Black Book of Carmarthen and the Llywarch Hen cycle suggests the existence of an

145

early native poetic tradition untouched by European influence. There are in addition a number of secondary sources which indicate the existence of a widespread popular tradition which was used by professional bards. One such source is the Grammar of Einion Offeiriad, in which excerpts of poetry exemplifying particular metres provide evidence of a lost body of verse. The sixteenth-century *canu rhydd*, though considerably later than Dafydd's time, draws on a range of popular verse traditions which may pre-date Dafydd's poetry and on which Dafydd himself may also have drawn.

The prose romances and tales of early and medieval Wales are also a valuable source of evidence for a popular tradition shared by both poets and story-tellers.[1] Dafydd's allusions to native story material and characters from popular tales show that he was familiar with this tradition. In addition to the significance of his reference to the *Doethion Rhufain* (GDG 45.23) and his obvious familiarity with those tales, D.J. Bowen mentions 'Chwedl yr Anifeiliaid Hynaf' (The Tale of the Oldest Animals) in *Culhwch ac Olwen*, and the 'Chwedlau Odo', fourteenth-century tales about birds and animals, as likely sources of borrowing by Dafydd.[2]

A third source of popular tradition which is relevant to Dafydd's poetry are the non-linguistic manifestations of popular culture and folk-custom. The influence of the urban life of the borough towns of south Wales is clearly present in Dafydd's poems, though less pervasive than the rural environment with its seasonal celebrations and rituals. D. J. Bowen has remarked on the prevalence of birds, animals, and leaves in the visual arts of the medieval period, in tapestries, carvings, stone-work, and illustrated manuscripts, as an indication of the way in which the world of the forest overlapped with the world of humanity.[3] Finally, folk-customs and rituals, particularly those associated with the seasons, are often alluded to in Dafydd's poems as part of rural society, not merely as literary conventions.

The popular stratum of Dafydd's poetry comprises not only these kinds of native influences and reflections of a contemporary culture, but also non-native borrowings which suggest an indirect knowledge of the popular literary tradition of Europe. The precise sources of this tradition, and the form in which Dafydd received it, are less easy to isolate. The historical and social context in which Dafydd was composing suggests that he was familiar with French or Anglo-Norman, but may have been influenced by French poetry transmitted in an oral rather than written form.[4]

The extent of his knowledge of Latin is more difficult to assess, since important Latin works, including Ovid's *Ars Amatoria*, had been translated into French. Certain references in Dafydd's poems suggest his familiarity with monastic and clerical life which may include a knowledge of Latin, but there is no incontrovertible evidence for this. Clearly, though, Dafydd has been influenced by Ovidian material, either directly or indirectly.[5]

Dafydd's use of popular traditions and motifs can be examined in three major groups: firstly, his references to native story material such as the romances; secondly, his extensive and wide-ranging use of nature imagery; and lastly, his expedient drawing on the folk-customs and rituals of a non-courtly rustic society.

The convention of referring to characters from romance and folk-tale is widespread in Dafydd's poetry. In his bardic love-poem 'Dyddgu' (GDG 45), he refers to the tales of the *Doethion Rhufain* to emphasize the marvellous, almost fairy-tale, quality of Dyddgu's beauty. Translated from a Middle English romance which was based on a Latin original, the Welsh version of *The Seven Sages of Rome* achieved great popularity, and Dafydd is clearly including it as part of a native popular literature. Rachel Bromwich suggests a long oral history of the stories in Wales, and says 'they are presented entirely in the style and language of the *cyfarwyddiaid* or native story-tellers.'[6]

Further on in the poem, Dafydd borrows an incident from the Welsh romance of *Peredur*, a tale which is found, in a different form, as part of the Arthurian cycle in French and German. Again, however, Dafydd uses it as a familiar native source, and his allusive description of the incident is evidently meant to evoke the full detail of the prose version. Thus Dafydd mentions the bird, the snow, and the blood but leaves them as symbols for the three colours which are explicitly repeated in the story of Peredur:

> Sef a oruc Peredur, sefyll a chyffelybu duhet y vran a gwynder yr eira a chochter y gwaet, y wallt y wreic uwyhaf a garei, a oed kyn duhet a'r muchyd, a'e chnawt y wynder yr eira, a chochter y gwaet yn yr eira gwyn y'r deu van gochyon yg grudyeu y wreic uwyhaf a garei.[7]

> (This is what Peredur did, he stood and compared the blackness of the crow and the whiteness of the snow and the redness of the blood, to the hair of the woman he loved the most, which was as black as jet, and her skin to the whiteness of the snow, and the redness of the blood in the white snow to the two red spots in the cheeks of the woman he loved the most.)

The equation between the natural colours and the girl's beauty is described in detail in the prose but is merely suggested in Dafydd's poem, with *sangiadau* such as 'iôn eryrawl' (lord like an eagle), 'wych wawl' (splendid light), and 'morwyn falch' (proud maiden), interrupting the syntax of the main clause and delaying recognition of the purpose of the description. The detail of the prose description is thus translated into the elevated imagery of the poem, and the impact of this serves to emphasize the beauty and nobility of Dyddgu.

The widespread Celtic nature of this equation between natural colours and desirable beauty is suggested by a strikingly similar description in the early Irish saga, *Longes mac n-Uislenn*. In this tale, the description is applied to a man, Noisiu, who is coveted by Derdriu, and, as in the Welsh tale, the observer falls in love before knowing the identity of the desired person:

> Fecht n-and didiu baí a haite na ingine oc fennad loíg
> fothlai for snechtu i-mmaig issin gaimriuth dia funi
> di-ssi. Co.n-acca-si ní, in fiach oc ól inna fola
> forsin t-snechtu. Is and as.bert-si fri Lebarchaim:
> 'Ro-pad inmain óen-fer forsa.mbetis na tri dath
> ucut .i. in folt amal in fiach ocus in grúad amal in
> fuil ocus in corp amal in snechta.'
> 'Orddan ocus tocad duit!' ar in Lebarcham. 'Ni
> cían úait. Atá is'taig it arrad .i. Noísi mac Usnig.'[8]

(On one occasion the girl's foster-father was skinning a weaned calf on the snow outside in winter, to cook it for her. And she saw something, a raven drinking the blood on the snow. It was then she said to Lebarcham:
'He would be my beloved, the one man on whom there may be the three colours yonder, namely hair like the raven and cheek like the blood and body like the snow.'
'Dignity and prosperity to you', said Lebarcham. 'He is not far from you. He is in the house near you, namely Noisiu son of Usnech.')

The use of colours as story motifs, particularly black, white, and red, is certainly not confined to Celtic tales, but is found in the folk-tales of many countries, and is also associated with religious symbolism. However, these two examples have many features in common which are not found elsewhere, indicating a specifically Celtic version of the colour motifs.[9]

In the same poem, as well as in his elegy to Angharad (GDG 16), Dafydd compares his subject to Esyllt, the lover of Tristan. The story of this couple became one of the most widespread courtly love romances of medieval Europe, but is generally acknowledged to be of

Celtic (specifically Pictish) origin and to have derived from a number of popular Celtic elements.[10] The French versions of the tale date from the late twelfth century so that they, like Chrétien's romances cognate with the Welsh legends of *Owein* and *Gereint*, may have been accessible to Dafydd in some form, possibly oral rather than written. However, the Welsh form of the name, Esyllt, suggests a recognition of the original Celtic character of the story, and it is likely that Dafydd is consciously evoking a Celtic rather than French heroine.[11]

What we have in these and similar references to native story-telling is the implication of a substratum of themes, characters, and tales familiar to Dafydd's audience. A single reference to Peredur or Esyllt is enough to convey a whole range of impressions and understandings about these characters and why Dafydd is bringing them into his poems. Just as the conventional references to May-time and bird-song evoke a mood and setting appropriate to love, so the references to courtly romances reinforce the refinement of Dafydd's bardic love and the nobility of his beloved.

However, the tales behind the references are not inherently courtly; having started life as popular traditions they became absorbed into the movement of French romance with its emphasis on courtly love. What Dafydd is borrowing is not the tales themselves, which are originally Celtic, but their association with a courtly context. This upgrading of popular themes was accomplished by French story-tellers seeking new material with which to entertain courtly audiences, so that the connotations of Peredur and Esyllt are based on an understanding of the characters as fundamentally Welsh with the addition of external ideas of courtliness and chivalry.

Another character from popular tale used by Dafydd to suggest the beauty and nobility of his beloved is Tegau, referred to in 'Campau Bun' (GDG 56) as 'Tegau iesin ddoethineb' (Tegau of beautiful wisdom). Though there are no extant Welsh tales preserving the stories of Tegau, she has been associated, through Old French sources, with Caradawc Vreichvras, and her name also appears in several of the early Welsh triads exemplifying faithfulness and virtue.[12]

All Dafydd's references to Tegau are simply metaphors for his beloved, and the absence of any identifying detail suggests that Tegau was a well-known heroine of folk-tale, later absorbed into the Arthurian group of romances. The contexts in which the name is used vary in tone: thus in 'Gofyn Cymod' (GDG 52) and 'Breichiau Morfudd' (GDG 53), Dafydd is addressing Morfudd as Tegau, but in the first he is humbly trying to appease Morfudd's anger and effect a reconciliation, whereas in the second he is envisaging a rustic idyll where he and Morfudd will enjoy their love surrounded by natural harmony. In another poem, 'Y Fiaren' (GDG 65), Dafydd takes a humorous approach to love, and the reference to Tegau underlines the gap between the hoped-for love encounter and the reality of the poet's undignified entanglement with the briars. These differing contexts indicate that the name Tegau carried with it a set of recognized characteristics, particularly noble beauty and virtue, making the name appropriate in a courtly context and effectively contrastive when associated with natural imagery and love's reversals.

References to other characters known in both Welsh and French versions of romances include several to Enid, the heroine of *Gereint vab Erbin* and Chrétien's *Erec et Enide*; single mentions of Gwen-hwyfar and Melwas; several to Luned and Cai, from *Owein* and *Yvain*; and one to Trystan, where the poet compares himself to Trystan and his beloved to Esyllt (GDG 33). In all cases, the intention of these references is to evoke a courtly atmosphere of romantic love, to emphasize the poet's emotion and the beauty and virtue of his beloved, whether the context is serious, ironical, or humorous. In this way, Dafydd suggests an analogy between the love he is describing and the courtly love of French romance.

However, a great number of the characters named by Dafydd belong to native sources that were not always accessible to French story-tellers. These include some Arthurian names, particularly Uthr and Eigr, the putative parents of Arthur;[13] names from the *Pedeir Keinc y Mabinogi* such as Math, Branwen, Pryderi, Gwawl fab Clud, and Llwyd fab Cel Coed; Menw and Cai from *Culhwch ac Olwen*; and some legendary and unknown names from Welsh tales which have not been preserved or are known only from the Triads.[14] There is also a reference to Derdri (GDG 139.21), the heroine of the Irish tale *Longes mac n-Uislenn*, and finally a small group of names from classical legends—Paris, Helen, and the famous classical beauties listed in 'Rhagoriaeth ei Gariad' (GDG 51). In this group also fall the two references to Virgil (Fferyll) which indicate that Dafydd shared the common medieval conception of him as a magician.[15]

The range of these references to story material show that Dafydd was in touch with a wide variety of romances and tales of the kind generally classified as the Matters of Britain, Rome, and France. In other words, he was aware of a strong popular tradition of romance which was shared by both British and European story-tellers and poets. However, Dafydd's references to this story material are very much from the Welsh point of view. His allusion to native characters go well beyond the content of French romance to encompass tales which never passed into general European currency. In contrast to this wealth of native Celtic material are the few references to classical and biblical figures, such as Paris and Pilatus. Three names are grouped together in a single poem (GDG 51) for a particular purpose, and even these names occur in the Triads, suggesting a long-standing story tradition in Wales.

Though Dafydd largely confines himself to native popular material, the supply of stories and legends on which he draws has evidently expanded since the time of the *gogynfeirdd*, partly because of the assimilation of French material and partly because of the increase in written sources in Welsh.[16] *Gogynfeirdd* references to native heroes and heroines are of an epic rather than romantic nature, though many of the names in Dafydd's poetry are also found in the *gogynfeirdd*, for example Gogfran Gawr, the father of Gwenhwyfar, Garwy Hir, and Myrddin. The many references to saints and biblical figures in Dafydd's poetry also reflect a precedent set by the earlier court-poets.

Some names and incidents used by Dafydd, however, are not alluded to by the *gogynfeirdd*, either because they did not know of them or because they chose to omit them as being unsuited to the courtly tone of their compositions. With regard to Gwenhwyfar, Rachel Bromwich says:

> The twelfth-century *Gogynfeirdd* make no allusion to Gwenhwyfar as Arthur's queen, and therefore it is possible that they had no knowledge of her as such—and this supposition gains support from the absence of all allusion to Gwenhwyfar in Pen. 16. Nevertheless Dafydd ap Gwilym knew of her name (GDG no.82, 33: *rwyf Wenhwyfar*) and knew also the story of her abduction by Melwas.[17]

Dafydd's wider knowledge of legends attached to Gwenhwyfar may therefore reflect his exposure to French Arthurian material, as well as his access to popular native poetry of an earlier period.[18]

Dafydd's references to Arthurian tales in particular reveal the growing popularity of the French romance tradition in Wales during the fourteenth century. While on the one hand his references to Cai follow those of the *gogynfeirdd* in presenting Cai in a favourable light (as opposed to the prose tradition of *Culhwch ac Olwen* and later French romance), on the other hand his introduction of names not found in the *gogynfeirdd* suggests an assimilation between native and foreign sources. Rachel Bromwich has commented on this connection between bardic poetry and the romance tradition:

> Throughout the thirteenth and fourteenth centuries it becomes increasingly apparent that the bards are drawing on literary sources for their allusions; and the introduction of this material of predominantly foreign origin coincides with the evident decline in knowledge of the native Welsh tales which, as has been shown, is reflected in the successive manuscripts of TYP. From the mid-thirteenth century, references in poetry include the names of such figures as Peredur, Evrawc, Erbin, Eigr, Lunet, Enid, Drystan, Essyllt—names which are not mentioned by the earlier poets, and whose comparatively late appearance in the field of bardic reference is to be attributed to the increasing popularity of the literary romance material derived from France, although this in turn was superimposed upon older British traditional narrative about these characters.[19]

It is clear, therefore, that compared to the earlier *gogynfeirdd*, Dafydd makes greater use of both native story material and native versions of Continental tales. A closer contact with native and foreign story-tellers is partly responsible for the popular element in Dafydd's bardic poetry, an element which orginates in the work of the *cyfarwyddiaid* rather than the earlier court-poets. With regard to the French material available in Wales, the social contacts between the two countries and the intermediary function of Breton or Welsh interpreters ensured a two-way supply of story material in both literary and non-literary forms. Thus the French treatment of Celtic tales and characters was almost certainly available to Dafydd, even though he gives more prominence to the native traditions and often echoes the references of the earlier court-poets.

Dafydd's use of popular story material is highly selective and seldom sustained: allusions to certain characters are made merely to emphasize the beauty of his beloved, to express his frustrated desire, to reinforce a courtly atmosphere, or ironically to underline the lack of such an atmosphere. His use of nature imagery, however, the second major area of influence from popular literature, has a fundamental bearing on his attitude to love. Like the popular poets of Europe, composing in both the Latin and vernacular traditions, Dafydd creates an idyllic rustic setting as a means of synthesizing physical desire and spiritual obligation. By pursuing love in surroundings suggestive of God's presence on earth, the poet is able to find the physical and spiritual communion necessary for a rewarding union.

The close relationship between nature imagery and popular forms of literature is well attested in both Welsh and European traditions, particularly in poetry. The nature *topoi* which would have been familiar to Dafydd from his own native poetic tradition occur in gnomic verse, in heroic verse such as that of the Llywarch Hen cycle, in court-poetry and, hypothetically, in oral popular verse which has not survived.[20]

From Europe came the convention of the nature opening, either to reinforce or contrast with the poet's mood; the connection between springtime and the season for loving; and the personification of birds as intermediaries and commentators. Dafydd makes use of all these precedents to some extent, together with their native equivalents and innovations which are associated particularly with his poetry, though they also appear in the works of other *cywyddwyr*. These include the devices of extended metaphor, and *dyfalu* description of one particular natural phenomenon. The main purpose of Dafydd's nature imagery is to create an appropriate context for the pursuit of love. Both physical union and spiritual harmony are shown to be synthesized in a natural setting presided over by God as the creator. Through his images of the natural world, Dafydd aspires to the same transcendence over physical passion as that sought by the troubadours.

Conversely, Dafydd also illustrates the failure of physical love alone, isolated from an accompanying spiritual communion. When the love that is sought is merely lust, then the lover remains fixed in his worldly place, trapped by physical desire and unable to rise above it to experience a higher sense of joy, both physical and spiritual. There is thus a strong moral basis to Dafydd's love-poetry which is not dissimilar from that of the troubadours. Far from advocating free and promiscuous love, Dafydd consistently demonstrates that love based on physical desire alone is inferior and leads to loss of dignity and self-worth.

The woodland is therefore invested with a number of positive values in order to become the appropriate context for a rewarding love-pursuit. It epitomizes beauty, freedom, growth, sensual and aesthetic satisfaction, and above all, it provides abundant and enduring evidence of God's creative presence, bestowing a blessing on all true lovers. In such a context, physical passion becomes ennobled and worthwhile.

But Dafydd's use of nature imagery moves beyond mere poetic convention to acquire a particular relevance for his audience. For the positive values of the woodland are the same values held by his audience of *uchelwyr*. Love in the woodland becomes a symbol of courtly behaviour—specifically marriage—in the context of a courtly and noble society. By celebrating love in the woodland, Dafydd is in fact confirming the nobility and refinement of his audience.

Ownership of hereditary lands was a major component of *uchelwyr* status, which was based on birth. Land was significant not only as a means of income but as a symbol of noble descent, testifying to the status of the owner as a freeborn Welshman. It is not surprising then that Dafydd, in common with other Welsh court-poets before and after him, implicitly celebrates land ownership through his idealized descriptions of the countryside. But Dafydd goes further: in creating an ideal woodland setting for courtly trysts, he is constructing a metaphor of court life which affirms the nobility of his audience.[21] He transfers to the woodland all the values and material sophistications of the court—beauty, abundance, richness, noble buildings—to create a place where love, the true synthesis of physical and spiritual desires, represents not freedom but courtly marriage with all its ritual as well as its social and political importance. Thus the portrayal of the woodland in Dafydd's poems functions in a similar way to the code of chivalry in troubadour song. It allows the lover to become ennobled through his pursuit of a worthy love and it offers a suitably courtly metaphor to mask the social reality of the love pursuit – that is, as a courtship ritual leading to a socially advantageous marriage.

Dafydd's vision of the woodland as a noble context supporting a true and rewarding love is demonstrated particularly in a poem to Dyddgu, 'I Wahodd Dyddgu' (GDG 119). In this poem, Dafydd paints a picture of their rural meeting-place which harmonizes with the kind of pure and noble relationship to which he constantly aspires. He adopts here the persona of Dyddgu's noble young lover, and his invitation to a woodland tryst is a conscious evocation of the delights of nature for the purpose of reinforcing Dyddgu's refinement and the quality of his own love. The first series of lines, using *cymeriad* to link a set of negative statements, present images of non-courtly celebrations which will be specifically lacking; in contrast, the bird-song, representing the music and song of court feasts, will create a mood of refinement appropriate to Dyddgu's status:

> Nid tam o ginio amaeth,
> Nid fal ynyd ciglyd caeth.
> Nid gofwy Sais â'i gyfaillt,
> Nid neithior arf barf mab aillt.

> Nid addawaf, da ddiwedd,
> I'm aur ond eos a medd;
> Eos gefnllwyd ysgafnllef
> A bronfraith ddigrifiaith gref. (GDG 119, 9–16)

(Not a portion of a farm labourer's dinner, not like Shrove Tuesday's meaty restriction, not an Englishman entertaining his friend, not the feast of the shaving-tool of a churl's son. I promise nothing, fine finish, to my golden one except a nightingale and mead, a grey-backed nightingale with soft cry and a thrush of strong pleasant language.)

In his negative statements, the poet rejects the rustic and boorish aspects of the countryside and goes on to paint an idyllic picture of the grove of nine birch trees which will provide a home for himself and Dyddgu. By presenting the grove metaphorically as a building— 'ystafell o fedw ir' (a room of fresh birches), 'lloft i'r adar i chwarae' (a loft for the birds to play), 'newydd adeilwydd da' (a fine new tree-house)—Dafydd is further imposing the world of civilization upon the world of nature. On the one hand the poet rejoices in the beauty of nature as a fitting context for his love, but on the other, as Dafydd ironically shows, this appropriation of the woodland denies its inherently rustic and non-courtly atmosphere.

Dafydd's poem to Morfudd, 'Breichiau Morfudd' (GDG 53), is in many ways a physical realization of the idealized tryst envisaged in 'I Wahodd Dyddgu'. The natural environment is not set up as an idyllic, pastoral setting for a courtly meeting, but is instead infused with a wealth of imagery conveying Morfudd's physical presence. This allows the lovers as well as the natural setting to possess a validity in contrast to the courtly artifice of the previous poem. While Dyddgu symbolized an idealized courtly love object, and the grove repres-ented a *locus amoenus* appropriate to the pursuit of a refined and idyllic love, Morfudd epitomizes the delights of a love relationship which is none the less refined for its physical consummation. Both the love object and the natural surroundings are enjoyed for their own inherent beauties, so that each confers value on the other:

> Amau bwyll, y mae bellach,
> Dawn fu, a rhoi Duw yn fach,
> Rhyw gwlm serch, cyd rhygelwyf,
> Rhôm, od gwn, rhwymedig wyf.
> Manodliw fraich mynudloyw
> Morfudd huan ddeurudd hoyw
> A'm daliawdd, bu hawdd bai hy,
> Daldal yng nghongl y deildy. (GDG 53, 13–20)

(Discretion in doubt, there is now, a gift it was, and God gives a surety, a kind of love-knot, though I hide it too well, between us—indeed, I am in bondage. An arm the colour of fine snow, gracious and bright, of lively Morfudd, with cheeks like the sun, held me, bold crime was easy, brow to brow in the corner of the house of leaves.)

The mood of the poem implies that in the woodland social restraint can be abandoned and the passion of the lovers satisfied. Nevertheless, the implicit harmony of love and nature is undermined by the central image of the poem, that of bondage and imprisonment. A familiar metaphor from European court-poetry, Dafydd has here presented it as an actual captivity: the wit of the poem depends on this single image of Morfudd's arms clasping the poet's neck so that he is bound to her, almost too tightly, literally as well as figuratively. The image is presented in the form of *dyfalu* description of Morfudd's embrace, focusing on this one gesture as a symbol of their physical and emotional relationship.

A similar fusion of sensual and natural imagery, where each intensifies the other, can be found in the short poem 'Taeru' (GDG 55). The point of the poem depends on the initial refusal by the girl to meet the poet in the woodland, and her implied 'no' is strongly rejected by the poet with his repeated *do, do*, 'yes, yes'. The physical beauties of the girl are described in relation to the woodland, for example 'do ddwyfron dan fedw fron fad' (yes, her breast beneath a fine birch hill), with the play on 'ddwyfron' and 'fron'. The poem clearly implies that the woodland creates a sense of natural beauty that perfectly enhances that of the girl, and only her refusal spoils the poet's hopes. No matter how much he insists, his passion, based only on physical desire, remains unsatisfied.

As in his courtly eulogies, Dafydd makes a distinction between Dyddgu and Morfudd regarding the emotions they arouse in him. Dyddgu is an idealized, unattainable figure, symbolic of the native Welsh aristocracy, and an appropriate object of eulogy. Morfudd, however, is given a physical presence in the poems as someone potentially attainable, even if frustratingly elusive. The motif of bondage symbolizes the lover's struggle to release himself from the captivity of physical desire, a captivity which is by no means unpleasing but which must be overcome if a truly spiritual, rather than merely sensual, experience of love is to be achieved. Morfudd is therefore a focus of this struggle between the spiritual and the sensual which the lover-poet must resolve.

Morfudd's importance as a means of focusing on an active love relationship, rather than mere eulogy, is demonstrated by another poem, 'Llw Morfudd' (GDG 43). This describes a pact made between the poet and Morfudd who exchange oaths of loyalty in the woodland, vows made binding by the presence of God:

> Doniog fu'r gredaduniaeth,
> Da y gwn i, a Duw a'i gwnaeth.
> Rhy wnaeth bun â llun ei llaw
> Rhoi dyrnaid, a rhad arnaw.
> Rheidlw perffeithdeg rhadlawn,
> Rhinwedd y wirionedd iawn.
> Llw i Dduw â'i llaw ddeau,
> Llyna, od gwn, llw nid gau;
> Llawendwf balch, lliw Indeg,
> Llw da ar hyd ei llaw deg.   (GDG 43, 35–44)

(Gifted was the agreement, and God has made it, well I know it. With the shape of her hand the maiden has given a handful, and a blessing on it. A willing oath of need, perfect and fair, the virtue of very truth. An oath to God with her right hand, there it is, of course, an oath which is not empty; merry proud person, Indeg's form, a fine oath across her fair hand.)

The formal ritual of a legally binding oath is described in terms of God's blessing on their love, in a manner deliberately evocative of a marriage ceremony. The combination of physical desire and spiritual communion, which is the key to a rewarding love, ideally is ratified by the marriage ceremony. But since Morfudd, on the evidence of other poems, is already married, she and the poet go through their own version of a marriage ceremony by exchanging vows in the woodland. Dafydd is here demonstrating the need to regulate desire with spiritual commitment in order to achieve an acceptable relationship. By acknowledging this, he also implies the value of courtly marriage as a social ritual which governs individual passions.

The significance of marriage is stated more explicitly in 'Y Llw' (GDG 86), where the poet laments the fact that his (unnamed) girl is marrying another man. He swears that if he cannot have her, he will not marry anyone at all. The point of the poem is to describe the poet's despair and sense of betrayal, but it also indicates his helplessness against the power of a noble family and an important social ritual:

> Ei chenedl feilch, gweilch Gwynedd,
> Gorau i'n gwlad, gwerin gwledd,

A'm lladdai am ei lluddias
Briodi'r gŵr, brwydr o gas.   (GDG 86, 15–18)

(Her proud race, hawks of Gwynedd, best in our land, feast-giving
people, would kill me for preventing her from marrying the man, a
conflict of hatred.)

The girl herself is associated with the natural world—'deune'r haf'
(summer's colour), 'unlliw blodau'r drain' (same colour as the thorn
blossoms)—to emphasize her beauty and purity, and the poet's noble
love for her.

In these poems, the natural imagery acts as a displacement of
courtly surroundings. It suggests the ideal of a mutually rewarding
love in association with the freedom and beauty of nature. In the
woodland, the poet is apparently removed from courtly restrictions,
both social and literary, and can explore the true meaning of love. But
in reality, the woodland is a carefully constructed metaphor of
courtly society and provides an appropriate context to explore
uchelwyr concerns. Dafydd is not seriously advocating that his
listeners should go out and seek free love in the woodland. More
persuasively, he describes the woodland in terms of a familiar social
context—that of courtly life—and shows that love can only prosper
within this context. In other words, passion must be contained within
acceptable social rituals, in particular those of marriage and of
religious doctrine.

The equation between woodland and court becomes more obvious
in two poems to unnamed girls, 'Merch ac Aderyn' (GDG 120) and
'Y Deildy' (GDG 121), both of which use the grove as a metaphor for
a building or dwelling-place in which to keep a tryst. In 'Merch ac
Aderyn', the poet, a more youthful and rustic figure here, describing
himself as 'serchogwas golas gŵyl' (a loving lad, quite young and
bashful), is waiting in vain for his girl. While waiting he observes, in
the form of *dyfalu* descriptions, a bird and a birch-tree which
epitomize the beauty and freedom of the woods. More profoundly,
the bird also symbolizes the quality of the poet's love, sweet and yet
painful. The poet calls him 'y gwiw latai gwyllt' (the fitting love-
messenger of the trees), and describes his ambivalent feelings on
hearing the bird-song:

> Digrif, peis gatai'r dagrau
> A red, oedd glywed yn glau
> Dyrain mawr ederyn Mai
> Dan irfedw y dyn erfai.
> Eirian farchog doniog dôn
> Urddol aur ar ddail irion,

>
> Hoyw erddigan a ganai
> Awr by awr, poen fawr pan fai.   (GDG 120, 21–8)

(It was pleasant, if the tears which flow would allow it, to hear out loud the great joy of the bird of May beneath the green birches of the faultless girl. Brilliant knight of gifted tune, noble and golden on green leaves, lively music he sang from hour to hour, great pain when it happened.)

The song of the bird represents the love which the girl inspires in the poet, at once pleasant and painful, a two-sided love which is familiar from court-poetry. The birch-tree, however, is a symbol of the poet himself, of solitary and enduring masculinity, and the combination of bird and tree thus represents the poet's desired union with his girl:

> Da y gweddai 'medwendai mwyn,
> Or delai'r edn i'r deilwyn,
> Corfedw diddos eu hosan,
> Cyweithas gawell glas glân.
> Teg fedwen, to gyfoedwallt,
> Twr diwael ar ael yr allt.
> Tyfiad heb naddiad neddyf,
> Tŷ, ar un piler y tyf.   (GDG 120, 33–40)

(It would suit well, in gentle birch-tree houses, if the bird would come to the leafy grove, dwarf-birches, water-tight their hose, companionship of a cradle, green and lovely. Fair birch, with roof of evenly-grown hair, excellent tower on the brow of the hill-side. Growth without being hewn by an axe, a house, on one pillar it grows.)

Thus the implied nobility of the natural surroundings justifies the lover's pursuit of passion.

The metaphor of the birch-grove as a house is developed in more detail in 'Y Deildy' (GDG 121), where Dafydd uses a wealth of imagery to translate the natural scenery into the language of man-made structures:

> Gwir ddodrefn o'r gaer ddidryf,
> Gwell yw ystafell os tyf.
> O daw meinwar fy nghariad
> I dŷ dail a wnaeth Duw Dad,
> Dyhuddiant fydd y gwŷdd gwiw,
> Dihuddygl o dŷ heddiw.
> Nid gwaith gormodd dan gronglwyd,
> Nid gwaeth deiliadaeth Duw lwyd.   (GDG 121, 7–14)

(True furnishings of the deserted fortress, a room is better if it is growing. If the maiden of my love comes to a house of leaves which God the Father made, the handsome trees will be a solace, a soot-free house today. Not too much work beneath its vaulted roof, no worse is the abode of holy God.)

Not content with presenting God as a heavenly landlord, Dafydd brings the grove's natural inhabitants into the metaphor, transforming them into man's representatives: the nightingale is a carpenter's square, the birds are clerics of the wood, the young animals are musicians of the oak fortress. It is as though the whole of God's creation has been taken over by the poet, ruthlessly co-opted to make a dwelling fit for his lady. Only in these surroundings, accessible to man and yet not man-made, can a satisfying love be found.

The holly-grove functions in the same way, as a metaphorical house or place suitable for the pursuit of courtly love, in 'Y Llwyn Celyn' (GDG 29). The wonder of the holly-grove is that it is green and leafy even in winter, offering year-round comfort and seclusion for lovers. The poet's celebration of the holly-tree emphasizes its noble proportions—'cadrblas uwch piler glas glân' (mighty mansion above a fine green pillar)—and its status as part of God's created world—'pentis, llaw Dduw a'i peintiawdd' (a high chamber, the hand of God painted it). He also explicitly denies any trace of rusticity—'nid fal henfwth, lle glwth glaw' (not like an old hut, a glutton for rain)—and instead represents it as a fortress with towers and steel-tipped defences.

Thus Dafydd creates in the woodland a microcosmic replica of a court, complete with craftsmen, clerics and musicians. The woodland context, far from being a celebration of rustic life, explicitly rejected in 'I Wahodd Dyddgu', is in fact a reinforcement of the sophisticated courtly refinements of the *uchelwyr* and of their identity with the landowning class which sets the standard of court life. The woodland is presented as a civilized place—not deserted or wild—and to be civilized, as Dafydd and his audience understood the term, is to be courtly.

The whole point about Dafydd's portrayal of nature is that it is not 'natural'. Instead, it is the world of nature interpreted through the value-system of a sophisticated courtly culture. What are valued in the woodland are not the inherent qualities of the natural world itself—wildness, varieties of vegetation and animal life, the ecological system, food-producing land—but the things which have a particular cultural value, such as beauty, tranquility, symmetry, colour, music, richness of texture.

The apparently 'realistic' qualities of the woodland which provide the basis of Dafydd's imagery—trees, birds, groves—are in fact transmitted to his audience in the form of objects or concepts already existing within courtly society. Trees are mansions, birds are preachers or musicians, and so on. It is this 'socialized' form of the woodland, not the 'real' countryside (with all its unfortunate rusticity) that Dafydd invokes to confer a positive value on physical passion. The force of the woodland metaphor is to locate physical passion firmly within a socialized context, to legitimate it as part of existing courtly social structures, in particular that of marriage. The effect of Dafydd's woodland poetry is to defuse the threat of physical passion, shown to be disruptive and anti-social in the poems of the troubadours. Dafydd's subtextual message is that passion can be integrated safely and constructively into the existing social structure. It can indeed be a productive and positive life-force when it is properly regulated by the terms of a divinely-ordered institution, namely marriage.

We see this affirmation being made particularly in 'Y Serch Lledrad' (GDG 74), where the lovers live out their secret passion in the safety of the woodland. The apparent motivation of the poem is that the lovers must flee from a hostile and judgmental society to the freedom of the 'natural' countryside. But what they are escaping from is not the courtly society of Dafydd's audience, but an environment which is unable to assimilate courtly love and is, therefore, by definition, non-courtly. This negative environment is represented (as in troubadour poetry) by the slanderer—'un drygdafod' (he of the wicked tongue). What the lovers are escaping to is not the 'natural' woodland, where passion can also be 'natural', but to a positive environment whose contrived beauty and divinely-ordered rituals are the perfect equivalents of the socialized human world as it is perceived by the nobility.

If we consider Dafydd's description of the lovers' retreat in 'Y Serch Lledrad', it is clear that the overt intention of the description is to emphasize the sense of isolation, of separateness, experienced by lovers, whether alone or in a crowd. The technique of *cymeriad* with the repetition of *cyd* (together), as a verbal prefix, draws attention to this undeniable aspect of passion which is a delightful and appropriate poetic *topos*. But at the same time, the nature imagery undermines the lovers' isolation by reconstructing all around them the objects and values of the courtly society from which they have supposedly hidden themselves. Dafydd describes them living together in the birch grove as if it were a woodland court: 'cydblannu bedw, gwaith dedwydd' (together planting birches, happy task), implying the work of the noble landowner; 'cydblethu gweddeiddblu gwŷdd' (together plaiting the beautiful tree-plumage), implying courtly tastes in hand-worked jewellery and ornaments; 'cydyfed medd' (drinking mead together) as if it were a courtly feast. Even their gazing together at 'caeau didrain' (lonely fields) implies the cultivated lands of the noble estate.

Thus the exile of the lovers, which is the apparent topic of the poem, in fact demonstrates the need for passion to be socialized, brought within the sphere of courtly rituals, in order to become acceptable and non-threatening. The lovers identify themselves with the countryside, not because of its rustic atmosphere, but because of its courtly qualities of beauty, order, and wealth. Only the nobility have access to the countryside as a place of beauty and leisure pursuits, rather than as the place for hard labour and food-production. Far from escaping 'back to nature', the lovers are in fact placed in a context which firmly reinforces the nobility and refinement of their love.

This socialization of passion, through imagery of the natural world, is also demonstrated in some of the *cywyddau* which use a sustained metaphor or *dyfalu* description. Five poems which depend on a metaphor drawn from the natural world are 'Hwsmonaeth Cariad' (GDG 87), 'Anwadalrwydd' (GDG 60), 'Yr Adarwr' (GDG 30), 'Serch Dirgel' (GDG 78), and 'Serch fel Ysgyfarnog' (GDG 46). These poems have in common the theme of the lover's helplessness and powerlessness, set in the context of the natural world with all its inevitable and immutable cycles. But the underlying message of the poems is that instinctive passion, unrestrained by social forces, has a potential for the unthinking cruelty and dangerous unpredictability of the natural world.

In 'Hwsmonaeth Cariad', the poet compares his love to a seed which is sown to produce a harvest: the image of the growing seed, in need of nurture and husbandry, implies that love is as essential as sustenance (*gosymaith*). Just as the harvest can be destroyed by the arbitrary elements, however carefully it has been tended, so love can be blighted by indifference and betrayal. The analogy draws together the two contexts, of nature and love, suggesting a common bond of dependence on unreliable physical elements.

'Anwadalrwydd' similarly finds a parallel between the cruelties of nature and of love. The poet describes the hare, the squirrel, and the roebuck as wild animals who desert the countryside which nurtured them. In the same way, his beloved has rejected him after his efforts to nurture and tame her. The poignancy of the image arises from the sense of inevitability, of instinctive behaviour that cannot be controlled by will or desire. His beloved epitomizes the paradox of the wild animals, who are beautiful and free in the wild but who must of necessity resist being tamed in order to preserve their essential qualities.

The next poem, 'Yr Adarwr' makes a similar statement about the ruthlessness of love. In this, a bird-catcher trapping birds beside the lake becomes a metaphor of the poet's enslavement by his girl's eyes, an emphasis which recalls the European poetic convention of the eye being pierced by a shaft of love. The motif of the bird ensnared by lime-coated sticks has a direct precedent in a classical Latin love-poem from the Codex Salmasianus:

> Ut visco capiuntur aves, ut retibus apri,
> Sic ego nunc, Dulcis, diro sum captus amore.[22]

> (As birds are caught by lime, and wild boars by nets, so am I now, sweet one, caught by an ill-omened love.)

Dafydd is here continuing the theme of captivity found in many of his love-poems, and which was also an important part of *fin' amors* convention. Though the lover seeks a spiritually ennobling union, he is inevitably imprisoned by his own desires.

The strength of the metaphor depends on the analogy between the bird and the poet, who are both helpless in the face of treachery and strength. The same analogy occurs in 'Serch Dirgel' where the poet says that love makes a nest in his heart like birds weaving twigs together in a quiet place. The metaphor is cleverly developed to emphasize the identification between poet and birds: the birds are 'adar claear clod' (bright birds of praise), and the poet says 'a'm calon fyth yw nyth nwyf' (and my heart is ever a nest of desire). Like the fragile bird's eggs in the nest, the poet's love is vulnerable to the boorish Eiddig (appearing in a familiar role as destroyer of nature) but he is determined to protect his love by keeping it hidden within him, just as birds conceal their nests. This suggests the same negative and non-courtly context as in 'Y Serch Lledrad' (GDG 74), from which the lovers have to 'escape' into the woodland court. The poet in 'Serch Dirgel' also has to keep his love secret from Eiddig, even while the love retains its essentially noble and courtly quality, piercing him like an arrow.

Finally, the lover's helplessness is conveyed through the extended image in 'Serch fel Ysgyfarnog'. Here, a vivid picture of a hare on the run from a pack of hounds is compared to the poet, weakened and exhausted from his search for refuge against the torments of love. These analogies between the lover and helpless animals suggest the state of mind induced by love—the lover becomes weak, unable to act rationally, and hence vulnerable to social forces aiming to control and contain passion.

Perhaps the most significant of the poems exploiting metaphor is the dream-vision poem, 'Y Breuddwyd' (GDG 39), which clearly belongs, in terms of its genre, to the wider poetic tradition of Europe, with parallels in French and Middle English.[23] Dafydd's lyric version of the theme is obviously less well developed than longer narrative poems, but it does provide a significant indication of foreign influence. The use of a white hind as a symbol of the lady, and the otherworldly pack of hounds have Celtic precedents, however,[24] and Dafydd's interpretation of the genre is not merely an imitation of French or English models.

In this poem, the woodland setting is not presented as a concrete reality but as part of a dream. The poet dreams of setting his pack of hounds on the track of a white hind which runs to the poet for protection. This dream is then interpreted by an old woman as the poet's quest for his beloved, using love-messengers, and she assures him that the dream presages his success in winning his beloved. The dream setting of the woodland suggests its metaphorical function, while the activity of hunting, using hounds to chase a white hind, is a familiar courtly ritual.

The type of love represented by the dream is therefore implicitly a courtly and noble pursuit. But the lover's success is only a wish-fulfilment dream and not a reality. The woodland, as a metaphorical court, provides a context for the desire or vision of love, and an endorsement of physical passion. But this courtly love in the woodland cannot be fully realized unless it is related to a social context, the world of court life. The dream represents a world isolated from social reality, where love remains locked in a vision, unable to be realized.

The woodland setting is used in another way in the *dyfalu* poems, describing a single aspect of nature to which the theme of love is merely incidental. In these poems, Dafydd goes beyond the popular use of nature imagery and combines something of the native gnomic tradition with the keen observation of clerical poetry composed in both Irish and Latin. These poems still exploit metaphor, particularly personification, but the emphasis is on the spiritual harmony which the poet receives in the woodland setting, rather than on the courtly nature of his love. The function of these poems is to convey the need for spiritual commitment in love, as well as physical desire. By appropriating God's creations to pursue physical love, the poet achieves the necessary synthesis of the sensual and the spiritual. Dafydd's appreciation of the woodland as a place to worship God as well as pursue love is particularly obvious in 'Offeren y Llwyn' (GDG 122). Here the grove is described as a church, with the birds officiating at a holy mass. That the mass-service praises love as well as God is made clear in the poem, a blending of spiritual worship and courtly love-worship made possible through an ancient and traditional social ritual.

The significance of the woodland as a focus for spiritual and earthly pursuits is also made clear in 'Y Ceiliog Bronfraith' (GDG 28), where the thrush is described as 'pregethwr a llywr llên' (preacher and reader of doctrine), and as 'prydydd cerdd Ofydd ddifai' (faultless chief poet of the song of Ovid). This juxtaposition of personifications suggests the dual function of the bird, as an echo of God's voice in the woodland and also as the singer of secular love-songs. The implicit equation between the two types of song, secular and religious, is an idea which Dafydd pursues in other poems to reinforce his vision of the woodland as a place where secular and religious aspirations can be assimilated.

In his *llatai* or love-messenger poems, Dafydd goes further in appropriating God's creations to the advantage of the lover. In the woodland he can envisage a reconciliation between earthly desire and spiritual communion, the conflict which so frequently occupied the European courtly love-poets. The key factor in achieving such a reconciliation, and achieving the best of both worlds, is for Dafydd to enlist the moral support of God and the practical assistance of God's natural creations. If the persona of the poem feels in harmony with God and nature then a true and satisfying earthly love is also possible. Moreover, the participation of God's creatures presupposes God's approval of the poet's activities.

This assumption is presented in several of Dafydd's *llatai* poems which acknowledge the natural beauty and divine function of individual aspects of the countryside, while at the same time diverting them towards a more earthly purpose. Two of Dafydd's bird poems, 'Yr Ehedydd' (GDG 114) and 'Y Ceiliog Bronfraith' (GDG 123) use the *llatai* motif combined with a *dyfalu* description of the birds. In both, the birds are personified as preachers and love-poets, suggesting a religion of love which is encouraged by God. The lark in fact combines the functions of religious and secular praise-poet:

> Moled pob mad greadur
> Ei Greawdr, pefr lywiawdr pur.

> Moli Duw mal y dywaid,
> Mil a'i clyw, hoff yw, na phaid.
> Modd awdur serch, mae'dd ydwyd?   (GDG 114, 19–23)

(May every fortunate creature praise his Creator, radiant immaculate ruler. Praising God as it was decreed, thousands hear it, it is valued, do not cease. Author of the ways of love, where are you?)

The thrush is personified mainly by means of legal and political terminology, a source of metaphor employed by Dafydd in several of his poems. The bird is called sheriff, magistrate, steward, and linguist, establishing the personification of someone learned and authoritative and therefore well-qualified to present the poet's credentials to his lady. The legal metaphor continues during the poem as the bird is described as having 'lythr gwarant' (a letter of guarantee), reading from a roll, and collecting fines. At the end of the poem, the poet asks God to arrange 'amod rhwydd' (generous terms) for the bird to argue his case, thereby implying God's complicity in this pursuit of love.

Dafydd's description of the thrush as a preacher is an example of his frequent references to birds as poets and clerics. This personification, and the occasional appearance of a bird in a dialogue with the poet, is doubtless of popular origin, but is not necessarily a conscious European borrowing.[25] Another popular motif is the appearance of Eiddig in 'Yr Ehedydd', presented as a violent and angry man whose attempts to shoot the lark with an arrow are futile and clumsy. This scene at the end of the poem contrasts with the previous description of the sweet-voiced lark singing God's praises, and it is likely that Dafydd identifies himself with the bird, as a singer of love-poetry, in opposition to his boorish rival who wants to kill the bird-poet.

The references to Eiddig in this poem and in 'Y Carw' (GDG 116) seem to confirm the use of a popular folk tradition rather than a conscious borrowing from Continental literary tradition. Eiddig represents a non-courtly figure who is therefore out of harmony with the woodland context, an urbanized interloper who has no appreciation of the woodland and all that it signifies. He appears in a similar role in 'Yr Eos' (GDG 25), where the nightingale complains that he is cutting down all the trees in the forest, and in 'Serch Dirgel' (GDG 78), where he is described as 'arwnoeth ŵr' (coarse unclothed man), who destroys birds' nests.[26]

The *llatai* poem to the seagull, 'Yr Wylan' (GDG 118), evokes a courtly rather than natural setting, with references to 'caer a chastell' (fortress and castle) and to the poem's function as a eulogy. The final statement that the poet will die if he does not receive a response from the lady recalls the stylized convention of bardic love. Here, then, the *llatai* motif has been set in an explicitly courtly context, somewhat comparable to Cynddelw's 'gorvynawc drythyll' (eager mettlesome steed), while the images of the bird, all linked to the sea, form an unconventional nature opening.

Two other *llatai* poems, 'Y Carw' (GDG 116) and 'Y Gwynt' (GDG 117) are similarly courtly in tone, with a longer *dyfalu* of the stag and the wind. The poet promises to be the stag's protector against hounds and other pursuers, in return for a love-errand performed by the stag. The natural imagery evokes the noble world of hunting and ownership of extensive lands, while references to 'teuluaidd' (retinues), 'hardd farwn hir' (beautiful tall baron), and Dyddgu in her father's house reinforce the courtly context of the poem. As in 'Yr Ehedydd' (GDG 114), there is a reference to Eiddig as one of the stag's hunters foiled of his prey, and the stag is also called Dyddgu's love-poet, another equation between Dafydd and the subject of his *dyfalu*.

In his description of the wind, Dafydd emphasizes its properties of freedom and autonomy from the laws governing society:

> Nythod ddwyn, cyd nithud ddail,
> Ni'th dditia neb, ni'th etail
> Na llu rhugl, na llaw rhaglaw,
> Na llafn glas na llif na glaw.
> Ni'th ddeil swyddog na theulu
> I'th ddydd, nithydd blaenwydd blu.   (GDG 117, 13–18)

(Though you scatter leaves, stealing nests, no one accuses you, neither a swift host nor a governor's hand holds you back, not a grey blade nor flood nor rain. A sheriff or his band will not arrest you in your life-time, scatterer of treetops' plumage.)

Having praised the wind for its independence, however, the poet then tries to capture the elusive element and direct it towards his girl to take a message. Though the poet is exiled from the girl's region because of Bwa Bach's angry jealousy, the wind is free to travel and therefore makes an ideal messenger.

Two more *dyfalu* poems illustrate Dafydd's ability to interpret the world of nature according to his earthly preoccupation as a lover. In 'Y Seren' (GDG 67), the poet praises the star which lights his way at night to meet Morfudd. In his description, the star is not only a sign of God's heavenly presence, and thus immune from theft and treachery by man, but also symbolizes God's approval of the poet's night-time excursion:

> Mi a gaf heb warafun
> Rhag didro heno fy hun
> Canhwyllau'r Gŵr biau'r byd
> I'm hebrwng at em hoywbryd.   (GDG 67, 15–18)

(I will take for myself without restraint, lest I stray tonight, candles of the Lord who rules the world to guide me to a gem of bright beauty.)

By contrast, in 'Y Don ar Afon Dyfi' (GDG 71) the wave on the river is an obstacle rather than an aid to the poet's love-mission. In order to persuade the waters to stay calm and allow the poet to cross and keep his tryst, he eulogizes the wave in terms of its mighty strength, greater than wind or battle or horse or man, and its sound, more eloquent than organ or harp or poetry. Once more, a natural element is described through the world of the nobility and its courtly preoccupations of love, warfare, and song, but the poet enlists it as his accomplice without denying its own natural qualities.

Dafydd's eulogies to the summer season also draw noticeably on courtly diction and imagery in order to describe the quality of love which can be achieved in the woodland. Many of his love-poems assume a close connection between the summer, or May-time, and the pursuit of love, which is familiar from popular poetry. The holly-tree is praised because it provides summer greenery as a shelter for lovers even in winter. The lover who tries to win his girl like a fool chasing a shadow pursues her for the whole summer. Birch-tree garlands are the product of May. Morfudd is the merchant of May, dealing in brightness and warmth.

Brief allusions such as these are abundant in the love-poems, particularly those located in a woodland setting. But there are also *cywyddau* in which the association of summer and winter imagery with the joys and sufferings of love is more fully developed—for example, 'Mis Mai' (GDG 23), 'Yr Haf' (GDG 24), 'Mawl i'r Haf' (GDG 27), and 'Mis Mai a Mis Ionawr' (GDG 69). Here the seasons symbolize not only the traditional relationship between the flourishing of love and the regeneration of spring, but also a complete way of life in which natural beauty and growth is equated with emotional serenity and physical contentment.

In each of these poems, May and summer are celebrated in terms of conventional imagery, with references to bird-song, green foliage, sunny weather, and a general burgeoning of the natural landscape.

Dafydd once more assumes the persona of a praise-poet, but the object of praise is no longer a courtly maiden but the summer itself:

> Paradwys, iddo prydaf,
> Pwy ni chwardd pan fo hardd haf?
> Glud anianol y'i molaf,
> Glwysfodd, wi o'r rhodd yw'r haf!   (GDG 24, 15–18)

(Paradise, I compose verse to it, who does not rejoice when summer is pretty? With extreme diligence I praise it, in a pleasant manner, oh what a gift is summer!)

Summer is personified in 'Mis Mai' as 'harddwas teg' (a fair handsome youth) and 'tadmaeth beirdd' (foster-father of poets), but in 'Mawl i'r Haf', the season becomes a princely ruler. The praise-poem recalls the rhetorical stateliness of *gogynfeirdd* poetry to the old independent Welsh rulers, and emphasizes the metaphorical equation of court and woodland:

> Aed bendithion beirddion byd
> A'u can hawddamor cennyd.
> Yn iach, frenin yr hinon,
> Yn iach, ein llywiawdr a'n iôn.   (GDG 27, 41–4)

(May the blessings of the world's poets and their hundred welcomes go with you. Farewell, king of fine weather, farewell, our ruler and our lord.)

The *cywydd* to 'Mis Mai a Mis Ionawr' is just as ceremonial and eulogistic in tone, and its personification of May as a chivalric knight also contributes to the metaphor of the woodland court:

> Cadarn farchog serchog sâl,
> Cadwynwyrdd feistr coed anial;
> Cyfaill cariad ac adar,
> Cof y serchogion a'u câr;
> Cennad nawugain cynnadl,
> Caredig urddedig ddadl.   (GDG 69, 3–8)

(A strong knight, reward for a lover, green-armoured lord of wild woods; friend of love and of birds, the lore of lovers and their kinsman; messenger of nine score trysts, affectionate to noble dialogue.)

The attraction of summer therefore lies not merely in its physical beauties but in its opportunities for idyllic woodland love-meetings. The poet describes such meetings, Morfudd is mentioned in 'Mis Mai a Mis Ionawr', and the general mood is one of contentment and optimism. Conversely, winter is evoked through images of cold and gloom as an explicitly hostile agent with regard to love. 'Yr Haf' begins and ends with a rhetorical emphasis on summer's brevity and the encroachment of winter like a manifestation of evil on an otherwise unalloyed Paradise enjoyed by 'hil eiddil Addaf' (frail offspring of Adam). In 'Mis Mai a Mis Ionawr' winter is portrayed by means of *dyfalu*, emphasizing its cold and dampness and darkness, in opposition to the glowing celebration of summer. The contrast between summer and winter is thus extended to represent a division between good and bad, between a fruitful love which enjoys God's endorsement, and a purely physical love which deteriorates with the decay of beauty.

In terms of style and theme the seasonal poems display a tight fusion of popular and courtly elements. Stylistically, with their rhetorical flourishes, traces of archaic diction, and eulogistic attitude, the poems belong to the native tradition of court-poetry and exemplify Dafydd's skills as a professional bard. For his central premise, however, and for the means to illustrate it, Dafydd has drawn heavily on popular poetry and romance. The celebration of May-time with the song of the cuckoo and the nightingale, and the woodland meetings of a lover and his girl, are fundamental to the whole tradition of popular love-poetry. The intrusion of winter and its associations of despair and failure in love are also familiar from Latin popular verse as well as the European courtly love-poets.

In addition, the chivalric tone of 'Mis Mai a Mis Ionawr' echoes French romance, while Dafydd's soubriquet of 'dyn Ofydd' (Ovid's man) in 'Yr Haf' alludes to the Latin tradition of love-poetry. In 'Mawl i'r Haf', the references to 'pair dadeni' (the cauldron of rebirth) and Annwfn, the Welsh Otherworld, recall native popular stories, and finally, in 'Yr Haf', Dafydd uses the figure of Eiddig, the jealous husband, to represent an old man who belongs to winter, while young lovers enjoy the summer.

In all these woodland poems, then, we can see that Dafydd's appreciation of the natural world is closely related to his philosophy of love, in which physical desire regulated by spiritual communion must inevitably produce a rewarding and socially acceptable union. His portrayal of the woodland and its inhabitants depends strongly on metaphor and personification in order to make comments about human society and behaviour, and thus relate courtly love to a social context.

Most importantly, his view of the woodland represents that of his *uchelwyr* audiences. The thrush who is a sheriff and steward is an amusing reminder of English officialdom, controlled by the *uchelwyr* themselves, while the seagull on the castle wall and the stag in the forest symbolize the courtly world of the Welsh nobility. May's riches are like the florins and fleur-de-lis of the wealthy rulers,[27] and the woodland groves are their mansions, palaces, chambers, and towered fortresses. Courtly activities such as hunting, entertaining, singing, and warfare are also mentioned, so that the whole woodland context serves to epitomize and capture the noble structures of the *uchelwyr*. In such a context, love itself is inevitably courtly and noble, and ultimately successful if governed according to the appropriate social practices, the rituals of religion and courtly marriage.

In the poems discussed so far, Dafydd is referring to a love which is defined as courtly and noble by means of natural imagery epitomizing the courtly aesthetics and lifestyle of the *uchelwyr*. Despite the apparently 'natural' and 'free' surroundings of the woodland, the love pursued within it is highly conventional and ritualized, and is defined in terms of church and court, the primary organizing principles of the medieval nobility.

In other poems, Dafydd draws more extensively on a distinctively rustic, rather than courtly, culture to celebrate his vision of love. The emphasis is on the sensual rather than spiritual aspect of love, which is now defined in terms of seasonal change, folk customs, and rustic beliefs, the organizing principles of the peasantry. However, this rustic culture is processed and evoked through the perceptions of an *uchelwr* poet, and is addressed to members of the same class. Inevitably then, it is a comparatively romanticized and selective view of country life, conjured up to divert and entertain a sophisticated audience.

The poem 'Taith i Garu' (GDG 83) describes the poet's customary journeys across country to meet his girl in 'ein gwâl dan wial da' (our lair beneath fine twigs). The theme of the poem is that the poet's soul is as weary as his body, because his love is unrequited despite all the miles he walked to seek it. But its real appeal lies in its detailed mapping-out of the route taken by the lover-poet, using place-names and landmarks from Dafydd's own home territory around Bro Gynin. His method of incorporating familiar and existing places into his description of unrequited love brings the poem alive as a convincing evocation of the countryside:

> I Fwlch yr awn, yn falch rydd,
> Mau boen dwfn, Meibion Dafydd.

Ac ymaith draw i'r Gamallt,
Ac i'r rhiw er gwiw ei gwallt.   (GDG 83, 19–22)

(To Bwlch Meibion Dafydd I would go, proud and free—mine is a
deep pain. And away over there to Y Gamallt, and to the hill for the
fine-haired one.)

The poem builds up a contrast between the enduring and permanent
qualities of the countryside, and the transience of his worldly
relationship with Morfudd.

Dafydd uses the same structure of a journey in 'Pererindod Merch'
(GDG 99). This time, it is the poet's mistress making the journey,
from Môn in the north to Mynyw (St David's) in the south. It is
evidently a metaphorical rather than literal journey—the poet wants
her to go to St David's to seek forgiveness for her cruelty to him. He
demands *galanas* (compensation), as if he has been the victim of a
murder, yet his description of himself as 'gwas gwawdferw' (the lad
bubbling with poetry), humorously asserts that he is still very much
alive. The poem combines legal and religious terminology with the
geographical description of the journey, and again a very vivid and
concrete image of the Welsh landscape provides a strong context for a
light-hearted account of love's reversals.

The theme of the poet murdered by love is developed in 'Erfyn am
ei Fywyd' (GDG 82). The poet's mistress has rejected him, and he
describes this metaphorically as a death sentence which he begs her to
revise. The legal language,[28] such as 'dirwy' (fine), 'tor heddwch'
(breach of the peace), and 'dienyddu' (execution), is a humorously
exaggerated way of describing the poet's rejection, and echoes the
same kind of imagery in Gruffudd ap Dafydd ap Tudur's poem
accusing his girl of murder. Dafydd also says that he has no hope of
'tir rhydd' (freehold land) in his girl's country, as if he is guilty of a
crime and has to become an exile who will be put to death if captured.
His failure in love has made him a social outcast. At the end of the
poem he uses the same pair of place-names, Mynyw and Môn, as in
'Pererindod Merch', to indicate the full extent of his persecution from
one end of the country to the other.

Dafydd adopts the persona of a victim and law-breaker while
addressing his poem to those in charge of administering the laws. His
use of legal imagery, and its obvious appeal to the *uchelwyr*,
corresponds to his personification of birds and animals as sheriffs,
stewards, governors, and other kinds of officials. Through this type
of imagery he constructs a world of social structures very familiar to

the *uchelwyr*, presenting it from the viewpoint of those who are affected by these structures.

In a number of poems, Dafydd specifically refers to folk-customs and beliefs to help him define love and its effects. Thus in the poem 'Gwadu' (GDG 107), expressing the sadness of the rejected love-poet, we find this image at the end:

> Ni fyn merch er ei pherchi,
> Loywed oedd, fy ngweled i
> Mwy no phe rhoid mewn ffair haf
> Barf a chyrn byrfwch arnaf.   (GDG 107, 19–22)

(Though she is honoured—how bright she was—the girl does not want to see me any more than if I were given, at a summer fair, the beard and horns of a he-goat.)

This self-mockery emphasizes the poet's resentment at his fall from grace after all his efforts as a lover and praise-poet. The reference to the beard and horns of a he-goat contains specifically masculine images suggesting lustiness and virility, and this is placed in the context of the summer fair where folk-customs were likely to be observed. The girl is therefore rejecting the poet as if he were a foolish country boy, and also rejecting him as a lover. Similarly, in 'Y Llwyn Celyn' (GDG 29), whilst extolling the virtues of the holly-tree as a meeting-place for lovers, he describes how impenetrable are its spiky leaves:

> Ni chny gafr hyd yn Hafren
> Un baich o hwn, na bwch hen.   (GDG 29, 35–6)

(No goat from here to the Severn can chew one mouthful of this, nor an old buck.)

The words goat and buck again imply male virility, in terms of fairly coarse and obvious symbols. By denying them access to the holly grove, the poet is perhaps saying that the love to be shared there is not of a merely crude and sexual kind, but is suitably courtly for such beautiful surroundings.

A rustic belief provides the final image in 'Disgwyl yn Ofer' (GDG 146), where the poet refers to the popular notion of the man in the moon as 'gŵr . . . â'r baich gwiail' (the man with the load of sticks).[29] This image marks the end of the poet's fruitless wait for a girl who does not keep her promise to come to a tryst. The wit of the poem lies in its repetition of the times of day—'o'r borau . . . hyd anterth, o anterth . . . hyd hanner' (from morning until the zenith, from the zenith until midday)—and so on. The whole span of time spent in waiting is laid out in the course of the poem, thus emphasizing the poet's prolonged anticipation and ultimate disappointment. He gloomily concludes that if he stayed in the grove all night, until the moon came out, he still would not see her.

The folk-custom of making a wreath or hat from flowers or twigs, to give to a lover, is referred to several times by Dafydd. This custom is exploited most fully in 'Yr Het Fedw' (GDG 59) where a coronet of birch twigs is celebrated as a symbol of Morfudd's love for the poet, and his consequent triumph over Eiddig, the jealous husband:

> Yr het fedw, da y'th gedwir,
> Ys gwae i Eiddig os gwir.
> Ysbail gwŷdd, cynnydd cannoed,
> Ysgythrlen brig cangen coed.   (GDG 59, 1–4)

(The birch hat, well you are kept, there is woe for Eiddig if it is true. Spoils of the wood, booty of a hundred trysts, engraved lid from the tip of a tree branch).

The image of the birch wreath is used more positively in 'Cae Bedw Madog' (GDG 31). Here it is a genuine symbol of love and gratitude bestowed upon the poet Madog Benfras in exchange for his songs. Like Dafydd, Madog is content with love as his only reward, and this attitude is contrasted with that of Iorwerth who prefers payment in gold or silver. The birch wreath, despite its lack of material value, represents genuine sentiments and is therefore worth more than money to whoever receives it.

The motif is given a slight twist in 'Gerlant o Blu Paun' (GDG 32), which also rejects material reward in favour of a genuine token of love. The rustic element of the lover's garland is placed in the context of other popular motifs, the woodland tryst and the love-debate. When the poet asks his girl to make him a garland of birch-leaves, she refuses to pull the leaves off the trees and instead makes him a garland of peacock feathers. Their rich colours provide the material for a *dyfalu* description, with images such as 'glân wead gloywon wiail' (bright weaving of shining twigs), 'gloynnau Duw, gleiniau dail' (butterflies of God, leafy jewels). The finished result not only symbolizes the girl's love but is also a token more permanent than the birch-leaf garland and is representative of the natural glories of God. In addition, it is a worthy reward for the poet's love-song, so that the lover and his girl each offer and receive a love-token marking the harmony and equality of their relationship.

While the birch garland was traditionally a token of shared love, twigs of hazel and willow were the signs of rejected love. Willow hats or head-dresses could also symbolize the death of a lover or spouse. Dafydd refers to this symbolism in his poem 'Siom' (GDG 85), which expresses his anger and pain at Morfudd's betrayal. Friends give him hazel twigs to carry and a willow hat to wear as visible signs of the loss of his beloved. However, since Morfudd is (apparently) the legal wife of another man, the poet's wearing of such tokens seems humorously excessive and ironical, for Morfudd was never his in the first place.

The essentially rustic custom of the garland or wreath is treated in the manner of courtly imagery in 'Yr Euryches' (GDG 38), so that the birch crown described in the poem becomes a token of courtly rather than rustic love. Morfudd, who makes a clasp or coronet from birch twigs for the poet, is described as a goldsmith working 'i efail o ddail' (in a smithy of leaves), and the whole poem becomes an extended metaphor of goldworking. Thus Morfudd's task, essentially simple using natural materials, is made to seem highly skilled and sophisticated and therefore a significant token of the quality of their love. There is a nice contrast between these poems describing a birch wreath, and the *cywydd* 'Penwisg Merch' (GDG 44) which describes a real and magnificent head-dress made of gold. The language is appropriately stately and elevated, and there is constant emphasis on the material value of the crown—'aur bwrw o gaer Baris' (cast gold from the city of Paris). Yet despite this display of external wealth, the girl who wears it is cold and ungenerous, unlike the rustic lovers who exchange simple tokens of true love.

Morfudd is associated with a different folk ritual in 'Chwarae Cnau i'm Llaw' (GDG 50). The rustic imagery deliberately suggests the simplicity of their love—it is not a courtly love pursuit, with all its implicit frustrations, but an uncomplicated union of shared love. Dafydd envisages Morfudd not only as the proud and noble beauty who rejects him, as in 'Morfudd fel yr Haul', but also as the country girl who participates in his vision of simple rustic love, exchanging tokens of birch twigs instead of gold rings. In the same poem, the poet and a friend play the game of 'nuts in my hand', a folk method of determining whether a suitor is loved or not. The nuts come from Morfudd, and after the poet has played the game to his satisfaction, he finds them a good omen for a tryst in the woods. They are also described as 'ffrwyth y ffridd' (fruit of the pasture), and are thus representative not only of God's abundance but of the possibilities of a fruitful union in the woodland, emphasized by the sexual symbolism of the nuts. The opening of the poem also stresses the physical nature of the poet's love by referring to the ritual of the game in terms of a religious metaphor: the exchange of question and answer is called

'salm . . . o lyfr Ofydd' (a psalm from the book of Ovid), implying a
song that is more secular than religious.

The use of rustic imagery to enhance the courtliness of the poet's
love has already been mentioned in connection with 'I Wahodd
Dyddgu' (GDG 119), 'Yr Adarwr' (GDG 30), and 'Hwsmonaeth
Cariad' (GDG 87). In the first, Dafydd actively denies the rusticity of
his woodland feast, instead asserting its courtliness as a fitting
celebration for Dyddgu. In the second the non-courtly activity of
bird-catching functions as a metaphor for a love of the noblest kind.
Similarly, the third poem draws on rural activities as an analogy for
the poet's courtly love pursuit. Images of sowing, ploughing, and
enclosing the crop are set against the passing seasons, from winter to
spring, and the devastation of such a lovingly tended crop is strongly
evocative of the poet's blighted hopes for his love.

Imagery from rustic life also occurs in poems which are not
primarily love-songs, such as 'Merch yn Ymbincio' (GDG 49) and 'Y
Mwdwl Gwair' (GDG 62). In the first of these, the poet observes
country girls dressing up to go to the fair, adorning themselves with
jewels and bright colours. He goes on to moralize about the
importance of inner worth over external decoration, pointing out that
an old bow or a wall do not become suddenly more valuable or
effective simply by being painted and decorated. He concludes by
saying that his girl has no need to adorn herself with costly clothes or
jewels as she already possesses virtues and qualities which transcend
such materialism.

The second poem, 'Y Mwdwl Gwair', opens humorously with the
poet, trying to linger near his beloved's home, being caught in a
downpour of rain and taking shelter in a haycock. From this position,
he begins to ruminate on the fate of the haycock and the analogy to be
drawn from it for human society. The haycock is personified as
'bwrdais y weirglodd byrdew' (short fat burgess of the meadow), and
the transferring of the haycock to a barn for winter storage is
described as 'dy grogi' (your hanging). The metaphor is reinforced by
the poet's use of religious diction:

> Cymynnaf dy gorff adref
> I'r nen, a'th enaid i'r nef.   (GDG 62, 29–30)

> (I commend your body home to the roof-top and your soul to heaven.)

There is a play on words here between *nen* (roof-top), and *nef*
(heaven), and the image of the haycock being hoisted up to the top of
the barn becomes a perfect allegory for the hanging of a man and the

ascension of his soul to heaven. Dafydd uses this parallel with explicit reference to the nobility:

> Erfai o un y'th luniwyd,
> Un fath, llydan dwynpath llwyd,
> Un dramgwydd ag arglwyddi
> Teg, ac un artaith wyd di.
> Ef a'th las â dur glas glew,
> Bwrdais y weirglodd byrdew.   (GDG 62, 19–24)

(Faultlessly from one thing were you constructed, of the same kind, broad pale mound, of the same downfall as noble lords, and of the same punishment are you. You have been killed with stout grey steel, short fat burgess of the meadow.)

Dafydd is briefly evoking a world of noble warfare to describe the fate of the humble haycock, so that the whole poem can be read as a humorous and mock-epic comparison between the short life-cycle of the haycock and the transience of human life.

The poems discussed in this chapter illustrate Dafydd's stance and skills as a court-poet, applied to a range of motifs taken over from European and native popular literature. His treatment of love is more versatile than in the relatively circumscribed eulogistic court-poems, but retains the idealism of courtly love when compared to his more popular and humorous pieces. In some respects, therefore, these poems correspond to the extended courtly love-poems of Europe, with their association of popular motifs and a courtly context as a means of presenting a love which is as noble as *fin' amors* while being more easily realized according to acceptable social rituals.

The actual process of combining courtly and popular elements is not original to Dafydd's poetry, but can be observed also in the work of earlier European poets. Many of the German *Minnesingers*, particularly Walther von der Vogelweide, evoke the woodland and the countryside as joyful surroundings in which to pursue love, an extension of the stylized and deliberate nature-openings in the poetry of the troubadours. The goliards also used learned Latin diction, rhetorical devices, and classical allusions to celebrate a rustic setting for love. French minstrels, such as Colin Muset and Adam de la Halle, employ the conventions of *amour courtois* within an implicitly non-courtly, often rural, context.

Dafydd's European predecessors were composing under the more or less direct impetus of courtly love in its two major literary forms, *fin' amors* and *amour courtois*, whereas Dafydd is an inheritor of the

Welsh bardic tradition of court-poetry and of the kind of extended courtly love filtered through French romance and minstrel song. The combined courtly and popular motifs which may have been accessible to him from European poetry can be exemplified by these stanzas from the poem 'En ceste note dirai' by Colin Muset:

> Hé! bele et blonde et avenant,
> Cortoise et sage et bien parlant,
> A vous me doig, a vous me rent
> Et tout sui vostres sanz faillir.
> Hé! bele, un besier vous demant,
> Et se je l'ai, je vous creant
> Nul mal ne m'en porroit venir.
>
> Ma bele douce amie,
> La rose est espanie;
> Desouz l'ente florie
> La vostre conpaignie
> M'i fet mult grant aïe.
> Vos serez bien servie
> De crasse oe rostie
> Et bevrons vin sus lie,
> Si merrons bone vie.[30]

(Alas, beautiful and fair and comely one, courtly and wise and eloquent, to you I give myself, to you I give myself up and I am all yours without fail. Alas, beautiful one, a kiss I ask of you, and if I get it, I promise you no harm could come to me because of it.

My beautiful sweet lover, the rose is full-blown; beneath the flowering fruit-tree your company greatly eases me. You will be well served with a fat roast goose and we will drink clear wine: thus will we lead the good life.)

In this poem, Colin Muset adopts the stance of a courtly lover seeking a kiss as his reward. The references to the rose and the fruit-tree are popular motifs which serve here as reminders that the season is favourable for lovers and that the countryside offers rich opportunity for pursuing love.

There are similarities between these stanzas and some of Dafydd's imagery in his woodland love-poems, particularly 'I Wahodd Dyddgu' (GDG 119). The eulogistic terms of description, 'bele et blonde et avenant', 'cortoise et sage', correspond to Dafydd's 'dyn cannaid doniog gynneddf' (brilliant girl, gifted by nature), and '(g)wyneb gwynhoyw' (fair lively face). Colin Muset's vision of a rustic feast—roast goose and clear wine—is only slightly more specific than Dafydd's description of his woodland idyll with

Dyddgu, 'nid addawaf i'm aur ond eos a medd' (I promise nothing to my golden one except a nightingale and mead.)

The same motif of the rustic feast also appears in an earlier Latin lyric, one of the Cambridge Songs. This famous poem, beginning 'Iam, dulcis amica, venito', is dated to the tenth century and describes the poet's desire for a tryst with his beloved in a woodland retreat. The Latin poet creates an imaginary room for his beloved, complete with couches, curtains, food, wine and music:

> Iam, dulcis amica, venito,
> quam sicut cor meum diligo;
> Intra in cubiculum meum,
> ornamentis cunctis onustum.
>
> Ibi sunt sedilia strata
> et domus velis ornata,
> Floresque in domo sparguntur
> herbeque fragrantes miscentur.
>
> Est ibi mensa apposita
> universis cibis onusta:
> Ibi clarum vinum abundat
> et quidquid te, cara, delectat.[31]

(Come now, sweet love, whom I prize as much as my own heart; come into my chamber, laden with furnishings.

Here there are couches spread out and a dwelling with embroidered curtains. Flowers are scattered through the house, and sweet-smelling herbs mingle together.

Here is a table laid with all kinds of food; here the clear wine is plentiful, and whatever delights you, beloved.)

The common theme in these poems is that of *mener bone vie* (leading a good life), stated explicitly in Colin's poem, 'si merrons bone vie'. Paul Zumthor categorizes this notion as a register characterized by an abundance of descriptive elements, the rustic meal, and the presence of a willing girl, and finds that this register appears in a more or less coherent form throughout the medieval lyric.[32] Other poems by Dafydd which celebrate the joy of life through nature description, such as 'Merch ac Aderyn' (GDG 120), 'Y Deildy' (GDG 121), and 'Breichiau Morfudd' (GDG 53), contain elements of *la bonne vie* but do not correspond completely to Zumthor's definition.

Though Dafydd shares certain motifs with Colin Muset, as well as the assimilation of courtly and popular elements, his poems are generally more profound and richer in technical detail than the minstrel songs of Colin. By presenting love in a rural context, Dafydd equates a worldly love, controlled by the rules and conventions of courtly society, with a 'natural' love which appears to find simple and honest expression out of reach of social codes and restrictions. For Colin Muset, however, the definition and accepted notion of love has already been fixed and agreed upon by previous poets and story-tellers, and Colin merely has to draw on a range of motifs and key terms, of the kind isolated by Paul Zumthor, in order to create a context which is immediately comprehensible to his audience.

These themes and expressions common to the whole body of European love-lyric cannot always be exactly duplicated in Dafydd's poems, since he is working with a different set of literary traditions and a different set of assumptions about the relationships between courtly society and ideal love, physical love and spiritual harmony. Colin Muset describes his girl as 'cortoise' and says in the last stanza that their rustic idyll will be unspoiled 'si ferez cortoisie'. The whole set of connotations attached to the Provençal and French words related to *cortoisie* are absent from Dafydd's poems. The Welsh word 'cwrteis' appears in the thirteenth century as a borrowing from English in a Welsh version of a Middle English romance. However, it is found only once in Dafydd's poetry, as a part of the phrase 'ystôr gwrteisrym' (powerful store of courtesy) (GDG 59.10), applied to the birch hat, an adornment associated with popular culture.

It seems that Dafydd is using 'cwrteis' deliberately here as an English borrowing, so that its connotations of courtliness have already been processed through Middle English literary conventions, which are largely of a popular kind. Middle English romances and poetry such as the Harley Lyrics represent the literary expression of a non-courtly culture, since French was the language of the nobility. The word 'ystôr' in the same phrase is also a Middle English borrowing.

In fact, the location of courtly love in a rustic setting which is characteristic of many Middle English secular lyrics may have been more influential for Dafydd than the European models. The Harley Lyrics, the most important of the surviving English lyrics before the fourteenth century, were also strongly dependent on French borrowings and influences, and could have provided a channel by which these influences were transmitted to Welsh poets. Certainly the Middle English lyrics resemble Dafydd's poems in theme and mood, while being noticeably less sophisticated in their style and technique.

A fairly representative example is 'When þe Nyhtegale Singes', whose first and last stanzas are as follows:

> When þe nyhtegale singes þe wodes waxen grene;
> lef ant gras ant blosme springes in Aueryl, y wene,
> ant loue is to myn herte gon wiþ one spere so kene,
> nyht ant day my blod hit drynkes; myn herte deþ me tene . . .
>
> Bituene Lyncolne ant Lyndeseye, Norhamptoun ant Lounde,
> ne wot y non so fayr a may as y go fore ybounde.
> Suete lemmon, y preȝe þe þou louie me a stounde.
>   Y wole mone my song
>   on wham þat hit ys on ylong.[33]

In keeping with French song tradition, the English poet describes his love-suffering like a spear in his heart, and begs for one kiss to release him from torment. The references to place-names in the last stanza, emphasizing the beauty of his beloved, unparalleled throughout the land, and to the poet's ceaseless song of complaint, recall similar motifs in Dafydd's poems. As already mentioned, his conventional use of Mynyw and Môn (GDG 82 and 99) indicates the expanse of countryside over which his love stretches. The motif of the poet spreading his song of love without reward also occurs frequently in Dafydd's poetry, for example in 'Talu Dyled' (GDG 34), 'Hudoliaeth Merch' (GDG 84), and 'Gwadu' (GDG 107).

Dafydd's use of popular themes and his selectiveness with regard to the conventions of *amour courtois* also have a parallel in the Irish *amhráin* and *dánta grá* of the fourteenth to seventeenth centuries. Seán Ó Tuama comments on the influences from northern French poetry which reached Ireland in the wake of the Norman Conquest, and notes some of the differences between the European movement and the later Irish lyrics:

> The principle difference I would say is this: that we find only echoes in our Irish love-poetry of the conscious philosophic background of the original movement. The beloved is still quite often a married woman; but the ennobling idea of desire and the whole technical vocabulary of love, *courtesy, solace, joy, service,* have all but disappeared . . . while the tendency to dramatize, the refusal to deal in abstract concepts, sometimes gives an intermittent breath of life to the more monotonous or conventional compositions.[34]

These comments apply equally well to Dafydd's serious love lyrics, which display a similar tendency towards dramatization, and towards the assimilation of existing traditions and influences of the European courtly love movement. Elsewhere, Ó Tuama discusses themes from early Irish folk-song which are found later in Middle Irish love-poetry, and which correspond to some of the conventions of *fin' amors*: for example, the idealization of love, love bringing sleeplessness and causing illness, love coming in a vision or dream.[35] The paucity of surviving popular poetry from Ireland and Wales before the Norman Conquest inhibits precise conclusions, but it seems likely that native popular traditions exerted at least as much influence on the formal love-lyrics of these countries as European popular themes.

Taking this popular element into account, the impact of European courtly love-poetry on Welsh and Irish verse has evidently been moderated and tempered by the pre-existing literary forms. The Irish poems of the *dánta grá* are similar to Dafydd's serious love-poems in that they use European influences to give colour and connotation to lyrics which are native in spirit and intention.[36] Some of the themes shared by Dafydd's poetry and the *dánta grá* include the use of a love-messenger (a book and a letter in *Dánta Grádha* no.1 and no.27), the poet's contempt for the jealous husband (no.77), the notion of the poet being killed by his beloved (no.27), and the lament of the poet who is too old for love (no.100). The occurrence of this last motif in the Llywarch Hen cycle[37] suggests it may have a popular origin. In other ways, the Irish songs differ from Dafydd's poetry such as in their praise of married life, and in the songs of husbands addressed to wives (for example, no.58), and these may reflect the influence of French romance.

The *dánta grá* share with Dafydd's poetry an assimilation of European and native traditions, a close analysis of the effects of love, and an often witty or ironic tone. The irony is not directed against the extremes of *fin' amors*, as it often is in Dafydd's poems, but may take the form of an argument or play on words within the poem, for example:

> Uaimse ag inghin an iarla
> truagh gan iasacht mo chroidhe,
> go dtuigeadh féin nách bhféadar
> bréagadh croidhe i mbí toirse.

> Cuirfead iomchar mo chroidhe
> ar dhuine oile i mbliadhna;
> gidh eadh, dá gcleachta a iomchar,
> biaidh sí diomdhach don iasacht.

> Biaidh sí tinn, biaidh sí corrach,
> biaidh sí gan chodladh choidhche,

> biaidh sí ciamhair cumhach,
> biaidh sí dubhach gach n-oidhche.
> (*Dánta Grádha* no.49, 11.5–16)

(Sad that the earl's daughter has not borrowed my heart from me, so that she may understand that it is not possible to soothe a heart in which there is a flame.

I will invite another person to carry my heart for a year; but even if she carries it habitually, she will be disappointed by the loan.

She will be sick, she will be unsteady, she will have scarcely any sleep. She will be sad with grief, she will be mournful every night.)

Here, the bitter lover transfers the symptoms of love's sickness from himself to his lady, as a punishment for not returning his love. The theme of the heart as a symbol for love and possession runs through the poem: in the final couplet, the poet implies that since he owns his lady's heart but she will not take his, he owns two but she has none and is therefore heartless and cruel.

In another poem, the lover defiantly refuses to conform to the convention of dying for love, while torturing himself by remembering his beloved's beauty:

> Ní bhfuighe mise bás duit,
>   a bhean úd an chuirp mar ghéis;
> daoine leamha ar mharbhais riamh,
>   ní hionann iad is mé féin.
>
> Créad umá rachainnse d'éag
>   don bhéal dearg, don déad mar bhláth?
> an crobh míolla, an t-ucht mar aol,
>   an dáibh do-gheabhainn féin bás?
>   (*Dánta Grádha* no.99, 11.1–8)

(I shall not die because of you, oh you woman with body like a swan; ever have you slain insipid people, I myself am not the same as they.

Why should I go to death for red lips, for teeth like flowers? The soft hand, the breast like lime, should I commit myself to death for these?)

Many of the love-lyrics echo the intensity of emotion and the concentration on the physical signs of love which are found in troubadour poetry, for example:

> Atáid dias is tigh-se a-nocht
>   ar nách ceileann rosg a rún;
> gion go bhfuilid béal re béal,
>   is géar géar silleadh a súl . . .

Uch, ní léigid lucht na mbréag
smid tar mo bhéal, a rosg mall;
tuig an ní-se adeir mo shúil
agus tú insan chúil úd thall.
(*Dánta Grádha*, no.38 11.5–8 and 13–16)

(There are two in the house tonight whose eyes do not hide their secret; though lip may not meet lip, their eyes are glancing sharply . . .

Alas, the liars will not let a syllable pass my lips, o gentle eye; take the meaning from my eye and you stay in your corner yonder.)

The importance of the eyes as messengers and receivers of love, and the reference to 'lucht na mbréag' (liars), recall troubadour conventions, but in this poem the love appears to be felt by both the poet and his lady, in contrast to the unrequited love usually sought by the European poets. Dafydd also exploits this theme of mutual, but secret, love in 'Serch Dirgel' (GDG 78) and 'Y Serch Lledrad' (GDG 74), where the reference to 'slanderer' parallels the 'liars' of the Irish poem.

Though the Irish love-poems are courtly in technique and context, while drawing on themes which appear to have come from popular literature, there is a clear distinction between the courtly *dánta grá* and the popular folk-song or *amhráin grá* which only emerged as a literary form well after the medieval period.[38] This popular song seems to correspond to the popular and extended courtly love verse of northern France, with its natural imagery (largely absent from the *dánta grá*), references to marriage, traditional descriptions of a girl's beauty, and greater emphasis on the equal status of poet and beloved. The same kind of popular song, emerging in the later *canu rhydd*, was available to Dafydd in Wales, and has been incorporated into his courtly lyrics. So while the two traditions—courtly and popular—remained fairly distinct in the Irish lyric tradition, Dafydd's poetry exemplifies an amalgamation of the two in Welsh poetry.

The result of such a fusion is Dafydd's definition of courtly love in the context of *uchelwyr* society. He interprets a courtly love as one which achieves an assimilation of physical desire and spiritual obligation. The woodland is the ideal setting for such an assimilation since it represents physical beauty created and maintained by the benign presence of God. Yet love in the woodland cannot be entirely free from social restraints. The noble and refining values of the court must be transferred to the countryside in order to avoid a boorish rusticity which devalues the quality of love sought by the poet.

By pursuing love in the woodland, Dafydd can introduce, at the level of metaphor and symbol, the notion of consummation which is inseparable from a perfect and mutually rewarding love. The grove of tall straight birches, the enclosing ring of twigs, the imagery of imprisonment, embrace, and encirclement, all suggest Dafydd's awareness of physical union as integral to the pursuit of love. At the same time, the suggestions of bondage and captivity implicit in the same imagery are indicative of the social pressures exerted by the court which must be transferred to the woodland. Physical desire must be regulated by spiritual commitment and social ritual if it is to lead to individual ennoblement and collective stability.

Dafydd's extended courtly love-poetry presents a view of love which is consensual rather than based on conflict. The ideal fusion between physical and spiritual values is possible in the context of the woodland court, and the pursuit of one without the other is shown to be unsatisfying and ultimately barren. The notion of a love based on physical consummation and blessed by the presence of God, to which the poet aspires in the woodland, is in fact a symbol of marriage in its socially recognized form.

Thus Dafydd's blending of popular motifs with a courtly tradition of poetry rises above the level of mere literary convention. With his introduction of nature imagery and an extra-courtly context, he shows that bardic love as it is presented in eulogy, where physical desire is suppressed and finds no real expression, is inevitably grounded in conflicting obligations. The metaphor of the woodland, which introduces the validity of physical union in a courtly love relationship, offers a means of revitalizing the sterility of eulogistic love, while at the same time endorsing the social value of an enduring relationship.

CHAPTER 7

Dafydd's Poems of Humour and Irony

WHILE sharing the same degree of bardic proficiency as the formal love-lyrics, Dafydd's humorous poems use the themes of love and nature to make some important comments about the pursuit of love as a social occupation. In his court-poems, declarations of love are a form of eulogy, defining Dafydd's role as an official bard. The more popular poems seek a socially acceptable form of love which is seen to be of divine inspiration and in which physical desire is ratified by God's approval. The humorous and ironical poems, however, describe the debasement of such a love into mere lust, an impulse which is both anti-social and discordant with the divine order of the created world.

The distinction between the courtly and popular poems can be seen mainly in terms of their function. As the composer of courtly songs for noble audiences, Dafydd's court-poetry fulfils a recognized and long-standing function of reinforcing, through eulogy, the political and social significance of the ruling class. Just as the court-poetry of the troubadours attributed the qualities of *cortezia* to the knightly class, thereby acknowledging their entry into the upper nobility, so Dafydd's court-poetry reaffirms the existence and continued importance of the native Welsh aristocracy in the century following the loss of Welsh independence. However, Dafydd composes poetry not only as a *prydydd*, but also as a representative of the *clêr*, a lower grade of poets whose duties specifically included the composition of satirical verse.[1] Thus Dafydd's popular poetry is marked by the use of motifs and genres from Continental poetry, both Latin and vernacular, expressed through the register of satire as a significant native poetic form.

Like the poetry of humour and satire in the Continental tradition,

Dafydd's popular poems still serve to reinforce the élitism of the aristocracy. The objects of satire are not the nobility themselves but the Church and the emergent bourgeoisie, both of whom seek social advancement, the former through patronage and the latter through marriage and the possession of wealth. The Latin poems of the goliards express the antagonism between the regular and secular clergies, with the goliards rejecting the blatant materialism of established Church members and embracing instead a hedonistic enjoyment of secular pleasures. Vernacular poems such as the *chansons à personnages, chansons de mal mariées,* and the fabliaux recognize the economic importance of the socially mobile middle classes while also exploiting their possibilities for satire. These kinds of concerns are very relevant to Dafydd's poetry, which is determined not only by his bardic role but also by the contemporary social context. In the wake of the English defeat of the last of the independent Welsh kings, the *uchelwyr* were concerned to maintain their position as the established élite, descendants of the old independent nobility.

The integration of the Welsh, themselves already assimilated with the earlier Norman invaders, and the English occupiers after 1284 was achieved through intermarriage and the acquisition of property, resulting in a certain amount of jostling for position among the Welsh and English landowners. The rise of the *uchelwyr* class, to which Dafydd belonged, based primarily on a tradition of service to the English Crown, marked the political acceptance of English rule. Socially however, the presence of English borough towns, methods of government, and castles to ward off Welsh uprisings, were constant reminders of the subjugation of the Welsh.[2]

Dafydd's poetry inevitably recognizes this social and political context, and his own involvement as a poet of the native nobility. His verse does not simply express an absolute rejection of all things English and a fervent embracing of everything Welsh. Even if such a dichotomy were possible in fourteenth-century Wales, after three centuries of Anglo-Norman infiltration, Dafydd's family connections with the English Crown would have led to divided loyalties. The primary feeling was one of ambivalence, of a selective acceptance of English customs coupled with a desire to preserve the native culture of Wales and the traditional status of bards.

The *uchelwyr* attitude towards the emerging bourgeoisie and the 'new rich' among the heterogeneous society of fourteenth-century Wales is clearly conveyed through humour and irony in Dafydd's poems. His poetry confirms the solidarity of the ruling class and the exclusiveness of the nobility by satirizing those who seek to join it. In particular, Dafydd's humorous poems expose the materialism of those who use marriage for social or economic advantage. This kind of contract has little to do with the love he celebrates in the woodland as a symbol of noble union among members of the *uchelwyr*. The popular French poetic tradition of marriage being incompatible with love arises from this same context of upwardly mobile classes of merchants and officials seeking to enter the nobility through marriage. The more courtly genre of romance, both French and English, in fact asserts and confirms the compatibility of love and marriage as an essential part of social practice among the true nobility.

Dafydd makes the same assertion in his serious love-poems celebrating noble courtship. The social reality may have been rather different—noble marriages were more likely to be contracted for political or economic reasons rather than for love—but the literary illusion was that courtly love was the essential prerequisite of a noble marriage union. This promotion of courtly love, through poetry and romance, acted as a convenient endorsement of noble marriage practice which masked its essentially political and expedient nature. By the same token, marriages apparently contracted without the ennobling influence of courtly love were presented in literature as base, venal, and materialistic. This is the difference between Chaucer's presentation of the marriage of Dorigen and Arveragus in *The Franklin's Tale*, and the marriage of Januarie and May in *The Merchant's Tale*. It is also the difference between Dafydd's presentation of Morfudd's union with her love-poet, and her marriage to Eiddig.

In order to satirize non-courtly marriage, Dafydd sometimes adopts for himself the persona of a boorish seeker of sensual pleasures. This persona, which has affinities with the character of Eiddig, pursues physical gratification in isolation from the refinements and restrictions of courtly love, a pursuit which represents the desire for material advantage through marriage without the moral commitment to a system of courtly values. The distinction between a noble love which has a social value, and a corrupting and ignoble lust which is socially sterile, and perhaps threatening, is therefore a primary function of Dafydd's humorous poems.

Another obvious, and traditional, target of Dafydd's satire is the established Church, with its rigid doctrine and denial of earthly pleasure, its inflexibility and hypocrisy. The narrow-minded preacher of doctrine stubbornly denies that there are ways of worshipping God outside the confines of the orthodox Church, a view which Dafydd undermines by his satire of the Church and his praise of God through nature and love.

In the humorous poems, then, Dafydd aims at the emergent bourgeoisie and the hidebound Church establishment, and strikes both by dramatizing the effects of lust unrestrained by truly spiritual concerns. These poems fall into several groups, representing ways in which Dafydd explores this issue and ultimately reinforces the importance of marriage. In a group of clerical poems,[3] which imitate the genres of goliardic and *clêr* poetry or which introduce clerical personae, Dafydd rejects the notion of spiritual communion devoid of physical passion, and hence rejects the restrictive preachings of the orthodox Church.

In a second group of poems describing hindrances to love,[4] Dafydd makes a distinction between the world of nature and the physical and material world of humanity in order to show the limitations of the latter. His poetic persona, the failed lover, cannot rise above his earthly desires and thus cannot achieve a socially acceptable love. The intrusions of the natural world are a reminder of God's presence in the human world and an indication of the spiritual barrenness of lust. Oppositions between light and darkness, summer and winter, are symbolic reinforcements of the differences between love and lust.

In a series of love-debates,[5] Dafydd enables the poetic persona to examine his own consciousness and admit to his earthly motives in pursuing love. The birds who often appear in these debates represent the voice of God, condemning the poet's commitment to physical love and reminding him of his spiritual obligations. The poet's rejection of their advice, and his general hostility towards anything which hinders his love-pursuit, indicate his confinement within the boundaries of the physical world and his inability to transcend these. The same persona of the failed lover appears in the fabliau poems,[6] where he is associated with the non-courtly settings of urban tavern and rustic farmyard. Love is devalued to the desire for consummation, which is itself the reward for material favours.

The poems describing adulterous love provide a continuing role for the figure of Eiddig, the jealous husband, which is an extension of his function in Continental popular poetry. The Continental tradition of *le jaloux* depends largely on the characterization given in the *Roman de la Rose*, where the function of the jealous husband is to deliver a bitter condemnation of marriage in order to reinforce the doctrine of Ami that love must be free and not constrained by marriage. Dafydd appears to be subscribing to this viewpoint in some of his courtly poems, where Eiddig is shown to be aggressive and out of harmony with nature, symbol of noble and courtly love. However, in some of the humorous poems, the persona of the lover is as unsympathetic as the husband, and the two of them are described as participants in an ignoble battle for physical possession.

Since the figure of the lover is also cast in an unflattering light, Dafydd is clearly not advocating courtly love as an alternative to marriage. Instead his humorous and satirical presentation of adulterous love is specifically composed to support the conservative attitude of the *uchelwyr* towards marriage. Socially appropriate marriage among members of their own class, or with members of the established Norman aristocracy, was a significant method of elevating and maintaining *uchelwyr* prestige and exclusiveness.

Thus Dafydd would not be serving his audience's interests by undermining the institution of marriage. Instead he is implicitly affirming the nobility of *uchelwyr* marriage practices by satirizing those of the bourgeoisie. The jealous husband, as he appears in the courtly poems, is the low-born and unworthy possessor of a noble girl loved by the poet, suggesting scorn of the social pretensions of the bourgeoisie who marry above themselves. In the humorous poems, lover and husband alike exemplify the materialism and sensuality which are apparently the primary motives for bourgeois marriage.[7]

Turning first to the clerical poems, it is clear that Dafydd's role as a *clerwr* is crucial to the context of his popular poems, since many of their motifs and images belong to a tradition disseminated by the *clêr*, an amorphous group of wandering entertainers.[8] The role of the *clêr* was undoubtedly of great significance in bringing together native and foreign popular traditions in a form which would have been accessible to Dafydd. Exactly who these people were is a matter of debate, but it seems safe to assume that they were part of a body of wandering entertainers disseminating an oral tradition of popular verse and story material. Though the word *clêr* is ultimately derived from the Latin *clerus*, the Welsh *clêr* probably included lay entertainers as well as members of the secular clergy.

However, the clerical connections of the *clêr* meant that, while being native Welsh poets, they also shared characteristics with the *clerici vagantes* of Europe, such as their type of secular songs, their inferior status, their rejection by, and of, the established Church, and their itinerant way of life. It is quite likely, therefore, that popular influences from goliardic poetry, such as the debate between clerk and knight, may have reached Dafydd through the *clêr*, not directly from Latin but through the medium of French and possibly English as well.

A striking example of this influence is found in the drinking-song, 'Cyfeddach' (GDG 132), where the poet exults in his capacity for strong drink as an adjunct to his activities as a lover. The tradition of the drinking-song is well developed in goliardic poetry and is also found in northern French poetry.[9] In Dafydd's popular songs, the tavern and the Church are both presented as centres of social activity for the non-courtly population, symbolizing the necessity for material as well as spiritual well-being despite the apparent polarization of the two activities.

Dafydd's drinking-song also suggests the significance of Anglo-Norman poetry as a means of channelling Continental influences into Wales.[10] The poem contains some striking borrowings from English, such as 'gildiais' (I paid), 'gild' (payment), and 'gildwin' (guild-wine), all from Middle English *gild* or *guild*; also *golden*, straight from English 'golden', and *ladin* from Old English 'laden' (to put liquor into a vessel).[11] Similarly, the *cywydd* 'Y Gainc' (GDG 142), describing the poet in the process of composing and singing his song, uses the musical term 'solffeais' (I sang in sol-fa), an English expression derived from the Latin notes of the musical scale; 'sawtring' (psaltery), ultimately from French *sauterie*, a kind of stringed instrument; and 'siffancainc' (symphony-tune), ultimately from late Latin *symphonia* compounded with the native Welsh *cainc*.

The same orders of friars which established themselves in Wales, the Cistercians, Dominicans, and Franciscans, had already settled in England during the thirteenth century, and their song-books, the friars' miscellanies, illustrate the significance of their contribution to vernacular religious song.[12] Didactic and exemplary material, mainly in English and Anglo-Norman, was gathered together as the basis for sermons and preaching to various kinds of audiences. Both the regular clergy and the friars also collected secular lyrics and narrative verse of a popular kind, and it seems likely that the Harley Lyrics were part of a miscellany compiled by a cleric.

The affiliation between the monastic orders in Wales and in England and the support given by the Welsh friars to English rule may well account for Dafydd's antipathy towards the friars, as much as their disapproval of the secular clergy and profane song.[13] However, the activities of regular and secular clerics in England, both as scribes and as composers, are likely to have provided a means by which popular French material, along with that of the lay minstrels, could have reached the *clêr* in Wales. The most significant foreign influences in the Harley Lyrics, such as the *reverdie* opening and the pursuit of a love which is neither courtly nor eulogistic, also appear in Dafydd's verse. The didactic and moralistic tone which pervades many of the Middle English lyrics, mainly the religious ones, is entirely absent from Dafydd's poetry, however, indicating that he was not preaching the doctrine of the established Church.

Though Dafydd occasionally affects to belong to the *clêr*, and was evidently influenced by their poetry, his family links with the *uchelwyr* and his attachment to courts in south Wales make it unlikely that he was always an itinerant minstrel dependent on random favours in quite the same way as the *clêr*. It is not even certain whether he himself was a member of the secular clergy or merely a non-clerical supporter who sympathized with the hedonistic ideals of the *clêr* as opposed to the inflexible principles of the established Church.

The evidence of the poems suggests that Dafydd's concern with the opposition between secular and spiritual demands was from the point of view of a layman rather than that of a cleric. Many of his references to the *clêr* suggest that they had a lay function of minstrels, while his hostility towards the established Church makes it doubtful that he was connected with it in any formal way. His concern seems to be that of a secular poet attempting to minimize the distinction between secular and religious songs in order to de-mystify religious doctrine.

Thus in the poem 'Y Gainc' (GDG 142), Dafydd describes himself composing and playing a love-song intended for Dyddgu, which he describes as 'salm rwydd' (a fluent psalm). This conflation of religious diction and secular meaning is a deliberate piece of irony, emphasizing the congruence between secular and religious song. The poem also includes a number of technical terms associated with the bardic craft, such as 'cainc' (song), 'cildant' (top string of the harp), 'cwlm' (tune), and 'tant' (string of an instrument). The poet praises his song by comparing it to that of professional musicians, calling it 'cwlm y glêr' (a tune of the *clêr*), 'prydyddgainc' (a chief poet's song), and superior to anything of 'pibydd ffraeth o Ffrainc na phencerdd' (a fluent piper from France or a chief poet). This range of bardic allusions suggests that the poet is a secular composer who can rival the professional bards, both courtly and popular.

In the *cywydd* 'Gwadu Iddo Fod yn Fynach' (GDG 35) Dafydd explicitly denies being a monk, that is, a member of the regular clergy. Morfudd has mocked the poet for wearing a tonsure, and he reproaches her for scorning his natural tendency to baldness, asserting that it would make no difference to her if she truly loved him. He frames his denial in an emphatic series of negatives:

> Ni bydd dy Ofydd difai,
> Ni bûm nofis un mis Mai;
> Ni wisgais, dileais lid,
> Na gwiwben gwfl nac abid;
> Ni ddysgais, gwbl drais o drin,
> Ar wiw ledr air o Ladin.   (GDG 35, 43–8)

(Your Ovid will not be without blemish, I have not been a novice for a single month of May; I have not worn, I have driven away anger, a head-fitting cowl nor a habit; I have not learnt, with all the force of scolding, on fitting parchment, a word of Latin.)

The poet's reference to himself as Ovid is wittily juxtaposed to his denial that he knows any Latin, implying that it is Ovid's skills as a poet, and as a lover, which he emulates. He also calls himself 'prydydd hoyw Forfudd hael' (chief poet of bright generous Morfudd), and it is evidently in the role of Morfudd's praise-poet and lover that he is singing, not as a newly-ordained monk.

The *cywydd* 'Merch yn Edliw ei Lyfrdra' (GDG 58) is a humorous version of the medieval convention of a debate concerning the rival merits of a clerk and a knight.[14] An early Latin poem, from the *Carmina Burana*, the 'Altercatio Phyllidis et Florae', presents two girls debating the merits of their two lovers, with the final decision in favour of the clerk, a conclusion which is repeated in most of the later examples.[15] Dafydd's poem is in the form of a humorous argument between the poet and his girl, with the poet presented as a clerk who warns against the ferocity and cruelty of a man dedicated to warfare. Dafydd is here supporting the way of life of a clerk who studies '[g]waith llyfr Ofydd' (the work of Ovid's book), but, as with his other references to Ovid, the implications of the pursuit of love rather than of classical learning are present.

Because of the traditional topic of the poem, the persona of the poet is assumed to be a clerk, but Dafydd is actually exploiting a conventional form in order to press his own suit as a lover. The argument concerning the rival merits of clerk and knight is directed mainly towards an attack on the savagery of the fighting man. The debate form of the poem is reduced to a short interpolation by the girl in the midst of a lengthy piece of rhetoric from the poet, who appropriates the forensic character of debate in order to declare his love-suit. The clerical nature of the original *topos*, with its consideration of religious and secular ideals and the opposition between the active and contemplative way of life, has been diluted to the point where secular and lay pursuits predominate throughout the poem.[16]

In three of his *cywyddau*,[17] Dafydd expresses an antipathy towards moralistic friars which recalls, not the goliardic and troubadour satires against corrupt churchmen, but rather the longstanding opposition of the established Church, including the monastic orders, to profane vernacular song.[18] These poems present advice given to the poet by friars, generally advocating a return to religious devotion, and the poet's defence of his secular songs in praise of women and love. The poet not only scorns the advice of the friars, to abandon the pursuit of love in the woods, to think of death and the afterlife, but is extremely unflattering about the friars themselves. The Black Friar is referred to in these terms:

> Yna y cefais druth atgas
> Gan y brawd â'r genau bras,
> Yn ceisio, nid cyswllt rhwydd,
> Fy llygru â'i haerllugrwydd.   (GDG 138, 9–12)

(Then I received odious nonsense from the friar with the thick lips, trying, not an easy touch, to contaminate me with his impudence.)

To the friar in 'Cyngor gan Frawd Llwyd' (GDG 136), the poet openly mocks his measured words of reproof by declaring hyperbolically his sufferings from the wounds of love.

The pointed references to the Grey Friar's old age, pessimism, and begging, as well as the poet's blatant adoption of Church rhetoric to present his argument, make 'Y Bardd a'r Brawd Llwyd' (GDG 137) a clever piece of satire endorsing secular song. This poem presents a direct confrontation between secular pursuits and the religious obligations demanded by the Church, and the poet shows that music and song are ways in which the worship of love and of religion can be reconciled:

> Cerdd a bair yn llawenach
> Hen ac ieuanc, claf ac iach.
> Cyn rheitied i mi brydu
> Ag i tithau bregethu,
> A chyn iawned ym glera
> Ag i tithau gardota.
> Pand englynion ac odlau
> Yw'r hymnau a'r segwensiau?   (GDG 137, 51–8)

(Song brings greater happiness to old and young, sick and well. It is as necessary for me to compose verse as for you to preach, and as right for me to wander as a minstrel as for you to beg. What are hymns and sequences, if not englyns and odes?)

The poet draws a parallel between himself and the friar as itinerant performers who aim to bring relief and entertainment to the people. Even their messages are delivered in the same medium, through music and song, so that the difference between their secular and religious functions is minimized.

Dafydd's contempt for the monastic way of life, as an extreme form of rejection of the secular world, is expressed in 'Cyrchu Lleian' (GDG 113). This is a mock love-messenger poem in which the poet sends a bird to a convent to bring one of the nuns to a tryst in the wood. The nuns are admired for their physical, rather than spiritual, virtues, and described as 'chwiorydd bedydd bob un i Forfudd' (god-sisters, every one, to Morfudd). The references to the jailer indicate the poet's frustration at the inaccessibility of the nuns, and his final command, 'cais frad ar yr abades' (try a trick on the abbess), indicates his lack of respect for those in holy orders.

Dafydd's cavalier attitude to the established Church is shown in those poems which exploit the language and ritual of the Church for different purposes, such as the woodland mass in 'Offeren y Llwyn' (GDG 122) and his witty rhetoric in 'Y Bardd a'r Brawd Llwyd' (GDG 137). In two other poems, the function of prayer is diverted from spiritual salvation to earthly fulfilment. Thus in 'Pererindod Merch' (GDG 99), the poet prays for the safety of his beloved undertaking a journey into exile because she has killed him through love. Despite his apparent piety, such as his reference to the girl as a nun, the poem is a witty parody of prayers for safety on a pilgrimage, which in this case are necessitated by a secular rather than religious reason. The appeals to various rivers and waterways to hold back so that the girl can pass across recall not only the parting of the Red Sea but more immediately the poem to the wave on the River Dyfi (GDG 71), where Dafydd makes the same appeal for a different reason.

In 'Galw ar Ddwynwen' (GDG 94), Dafydd subverts an orthodox plea to a saint from its religious purpose to his own secular interests. St Dwynwen was traditionally regarded as the patron saint of lovers, so that Dafydd's address to her is appropriate. However, within the rhetorical framework of the prayer, characterized by eulogy, direct address, and the final emphatic plea, Dafydd expresses the concerns of his secular love-poetry. St Dwynwen is not merely to intercede for him with Morfudd, she is to go to Cwm-y-glo as a love-messenger, a role normally fulfilled by creatures from the natural world. More than that, she is charged with the task of restraining Eiddig from inflicting violence on the poet and Morfudd as they go to their tryst. The mood of rustic love pursuit is thus combined with a respectful petition to St Dwynwen reminiscent of folk rituals connected with religious festivals and saints' days.

In 'Merched Llanbadarn' (GDG 48), attendance at a church service is presented as essentially the occupation of a rural community, and its function is social rather than spiritual.[19] The setting of the poem in the parish church suggests social interaction of a non-courtly kind which places the love-pursuit at a popular level where physical union is more important than spiritual fulfilment. The poet's explosive opening words, and his lament that he cannot find love, display a concern with secular affairs which overrides any thoughts of religious communion:

> Plygu rhag llid yr ydwyf,
> Pla ar holl ferched y plwyf!
> Am na chefais, drais drawsoed,
> Onaddun' yr un erioed,
> Na morwyn fwyn ofynaig,
> Na merch fach, na gwrach, na gwraig.   (GDG 48, 1–6)

(I am bent over from passion, a plague on all the girls in the parish. Because I have never won a single one of them, violence of oppressions, neither a gentle desirable maiden, nor a young girl, nor an old hag, nor a wife.)

The poet's activities in church, where he spends more time craning round to look at the girls and imagining what they might be saying about him, than in praying, also underline the social function of the Church. The verbs 'plygu' (bending over) and 'pengamu' (head bowed), at the beginning and end of the poem have overtones of religious worship, in the form of genuflexion and bowing to pray, but in both cases the poet is expressing the entirely secular connotations of rage and defeat caused by his lack of love.

A similar tone is used in 'Y Drych' (GDG 105), where the persona expresses bitter dissatisfaction with his appearance, as reflected in a mirror. His unflattering description of himself, which he blames on the girl who rejects him, is humorous in its hyperbolic intensity, but Dafydd is making a serious comment on superficial appearances compared to inner worth. The lover assumes that if he is really ugly, then his soul is evil as well, and hopes instead that his appearance has been distorted by the mirror. He describes the mirror as a magical vehicle for deceiving people, which implies that outward and physical appearances may not be a reliable guide to spiritual worth.

In these poems, the teachings of the orthodox Church, and church buildings themselves, are rejected by the poetic persona who consistently, and misguidedly, relies on the external physical world. In Dafydd's courtly love-poems, the woodland is seen as a metaphor of the court where a noble but earthly love can receive the spiritual blessing of God which, in social terms, constitutes marriage. In Dafydd's bardic eulogies, as in the courtly love-poetry of the Continent, an excessive awareness of moral and spiritual obligations causes conflict with physical desires so that love remains an unfulfilled ideal. In the tradition of popular poetry, however, the opposite is shown to be true: the overriding importance of physical pleasure denies the spiritual fulfilment which is equally necessary to a permanent and socially effective relationship.

In the group of poems describing hindrances to the poet's love-pursuit, the world of nature, as a symbol of God's presence on earth, is shown to be hostile to those who ignore the spiritual aspect of love. The would-be lover, attempting to keep a tryst, is shown to be out of harmony with nature and therefore with God. Dafydd is thus reinforcing the need for both physical and spiritual communion as the basis of an ennobling love. In describing a lover motivated primarily by lust whose love-pursuit is hindered by the intrusion of the natural world, Dafydd gives nature the role of representing God's divine wrath against sinners whose anti-social activities bring down forces of chaos and darkness.

The *cywydd* to the mist, 'Y Niwl' (GDG 68), is in the form of a *dyfalu* description similar to that used in 'Y Gwynt' (GDG 117). The evocation of the mist is preceded by a short narrative introduction explaining that the poet is on his way to meet his girl, and is followed by the bald accusation that the sudden rising of the mist prevented him from keeping the appointment. The imagery used to describe the mist alternates between the mystical and the unflattering:

> Cnu tewlwyd gwynllwyd gwanllaes
> Cyfliw â mwg, cwfl y maes.
> Coetgae glaw er lluddiaw lles,
> Codarmur cawad ormes.
> Twyllai wŷr, tywyll o wedd,
> Toron gwrddonig tiredd.
> Tyrau uchel eu helynt,
> Tylwyth Gwyn, talaith y gwynt.   (GDG 68, 25–32)

(Thick grey fleece, pale and white, weak and trailing, the same colour as smoke, a cowl of the plain. A hedge of rain which hinders achievement, the coat-armour of the oppressive shower. It would deceive men, dark in form, boorish cloak over lands. Towers of Gwyn's family coursing on high, province of the wind.)

The poet is torn between wonder at the magnificent sight of the mist rolling over the fields, and annoyance at the resulting disruption of his personal plans. Unlike the love-messenger poems, nature is no longer under the poet's control but represents an independent force expressing the power of darkness. The contrast between darkness and light is made explicit at the end of the poem, when the poet says:

> Y sêr a ddaw o'r awyr
> Fal fflamau canhwyllau cwyr,
> Ac ni ddaw, poen addaw pŵl,
> Lloer na sêr Nêr ar nïwl.   (GDG 68, 49–52)

(The stars come from the sky like the flames of wax candles, but neither moon nor stars of the Lord come, pain of a blunt promise, with a mist.)

The light of the sun, moon and stars is the light of God, representing God's approval of the poet's earthly pursuits, whereas the primitive fear of darkness expresses a fear of the withdrawal of God's support, and the exposure to Otherworldly forces, represented by Gwyn ap Nudd and the witches of Annwn.[20]

The same sort of superstitious fear is implied in the poet's aggressive hostility towards the owl in 'Y Dylluan' (GDG 26). The owl's only crime is to keep the poet awake at night with her loud screech, for which she is abused as 'budrog' (a slut), 'lygodwraig hen' (an old mouse-woman), 'ystig, ddielwig, ddiliw' (over-industrious, worthless, colourless). The references to the night-time activities of the owl, to the hounds of the night, and to Gwyn ap Nudd, associate the owl with the Otherworld and with the popular tradition of the owl as a malevolent and Otherworldly creature whose cry is a portent of doom and evil.[21] The poet's solution, to set fire to all the ivy-trees, indicates the traditional home of the owl, in an ivy-clad tree, and also the purifying, exorcizing power of fire. Such a drastic plan suggests more than mere annoyance, but irrational fear as well.

The fox is also represented as a creature from the Otherworld in 'Y Llwynog' (GDG 22).[22] The poem describes the poet's attempt to shoot the fox with an arrow and the subsequent flight of the fox to its lair:

> Taradr daeargadr dorgau,
> Tanllestr ar gwr ffenestr gau.

> Bwa latwm di-drwm draed,
> Gefel unwedd gylfinwaed.
> Nid hawdd ymy ddilid hwn,
> A'i dŷ annedd hyd Annwn.   (GDG 22, 37–42)

(Piercer of the mighty earth's hollow belly, a lantern in the corner of a closed window. Copper bow, light-footed, like pincers his bloody snout. It is not easy for me to follow him, with his dwelling-place as far as Annwfn.)

The poet feels the same ambivalence towards the fox as towards the mist. The flight of the fox makes an impressive flash of colour through the woodland, but the poet's failure to kill it with his arrow inspires in him the same feeling of impotent rage that he felt with regard to the mist.

A similar mood is invoked by the eerie presence of an echo-stone which frightens away the poet's girl in 'Y Garreg Ateb' (GDG 130). Here again, the stone is described and reviled as a source of supernatural fear apparently determined to spoil the love-meeting. The stone is compared to Myrddin, the legendary magician, and there are implications of Otherworldly forces present in the rock:

> Mae naill i mewn ai ellyll
> Ynddi, hen almari hyll,
> Ai cŵn yn y garreg gau
> Sain cogor, ai sŵn cawgiau.   (GDG 130, 33–6)

(There is either a ghost inside it, ugly old cupboard, or hounds in the hollow stone of croaking sound, or the noise of basins.)

The reference to hounds recalls the tales of 'cŵn Annwfn', the Otherworld pack of hounds, and 'sŵn cawgiau' (the noise of basins) perhaps refers to the motif of the basin attached to a stone slab marking the entrance to the Otherworld, as in the tales of *Owein* and *Manawydan*. These suggestions of the supernatural powers of the stone emphasize its function as a warning to the poet not to neglect his spiritual duties in his eagerness to pursue earthly love.

In four other poems, 'Y Cyffylog' (GDG 61), 'Y Fiaren' (GDG 65), 'Y Rhew' (GDG 91), and 'Y Pwll Mawn' (GDG 127), the intrusive presence of the natural world as a hindrance to love is represented by the wood-cock, a thorny briar, a heavy frost, and a cold peat-bog. Each of these poems combines a narrative account of the poet's amatory hopes with a graphic description of his tribulations: the wood-cock frightens away his girl, the briar ensnares him with its thorns and scratches him, the frost causes him to fall into an ice-covered pool full of freezing water, and the peat-bog trips him up in the darkness. The contrast between the expectation and the actual outcome is reinforced by the poet's anger and his determination to destroy the offending object, by shooting, burning, melting and cursing, just as the poet planned to take revenge on the owl.

These four poems in particular take up a theme already found in the courtly poems, the preference of lovers for the summer season instead of winter. While Dafydd extolled the beauties of May in the courtly poems, he is here exemplifying the difficulties of pursuing love in the depths of winter. 'Y Cyffylog' begins:

> A fu ddim, ddamwain breiddfyw,
> Mor elyn i serchddyn syw
> Â'r gaeaf, oeraf eiroed,
> Hirddu cas yn hyrddio coed? (GDG 61, 1–4)

(Was there anything, life-endangering state, so hostile to a fine lover-lad as the winter, coldest snow-tryst, a long black hatefulness hurling the trees?)

The woodcock is reviled as a winter bird, as distinct from the cuckoo and nightingale of the summer. The opposition between summer and winter, one offering help and the other only hindrance to lovers, corresponds to the distinction in 'Y Niwl' between light and darkness. There is thus a polarization of social and anti-social forces, with the poet's pursuit of a physical love seen as threatening and in need of curtailment.

The negative aspects of seeking love in the wintertime are emphasized in 'Caru yn y Gaeaf' (GDG 145), in which the poet tells of an unsuccessful attempt to see his girl, after drinking at the tavern. Not only is the poet attacked by an icicle but he is also chased away by the husband who thinks he is a thief. The humorous indignities suffered by the poet and his derogatory references to the icicle and the husband are balanced by a wistful contrast between the birch-grove in summer and in winter. When the poet runs to his old refuge, he finds it an alien place in its winter appearance:

> Tybiaswn fod, clod cludreg,
> Y tyno dail a'r to'n deg,
> A mwyn adar a'm carai,
> A merch a welswn ym Mai.
> Yno nid oedd le unoed,
> Llyna gawdd, eithr llwyn o goed;
> Nac arwydd serch nac arail,
> Na'r dyn a welswn na'r dail. (GDG 145, 53–60)

(I supposed that there would be, blessed praise, the home of leaves with the lovely roof, and gentle birds who loved me, and the girl I used to see in May. There was no place there for a single tryst, behold sadness, except a grove of trees. No portent of love or caring, no girl I had seen, no leaves.)

The grove in summer is the poet's refuge and a reinforcement of his belief in a noble and true love. The winter landscape, the physical entity of the house, and the presence of the churlish husband, are all hostile forces which drive the lover away from his quest for consummation and back to the physical and spiritual harmony of the woodland. The birch-grove stripped of its foliage in winter symbolizes the 'dark' side of love, shorn of its moral and spiritual refinements to reveal the starkness and barrenness of lust.

'Noson Olau' (GDG 70) is another hindrance poem in which contrasts between light and darkness are used to reinforce the immorality of the poet's adulterous love. Whereas the *cywydd* to the star, 'Y Seren' (GDG 67), praised the light provided by God in heaven to guide the way to a love-meeting, this poem curses the brightness of the moon which will expose the predatory lover to the danger of discovery. As in 'Y Niwl' (GDG 68), a large part of the poem consists of a *dyfalu* description of the moon which reveals the poet's ambivalence towards it:

> Ei threfn fydd bob pythefnos
> (Ei thref dan nef ydyw nos)
> I ddwyn ei chwrs odd yna,
> Myfyr oedd, mwyfwy yr â
> Hon, oni fo dau hanner,
> Huan, nos eirian, y sêr.
> Hyrddia lanw, hardd oleuni,
> Haul yr ellyllon yw hi.   (GDG 70, 25–32)

(Its system is every fortnight (the night is its home beneath the heavens) to take its course thence, there was careful thought, more and more it goes until there are two halves, radiant night, of the sun of the stars. It hurls the tide, beautiful brightness, it is the sun of the ghosts.)

The beauty of the moon and its wondrous waxing and waning impress the poet but, because of its association with night, he calls it 'haul yr ellyllon' (sun of the ghosts), illumination for the eerie creatures of the night. It therefore has a sense of mystery and power as well as beauty, but it is also seen as a symbol of God's goodness whose light vanquishes the evil forces of darkness. The poet himself is one of these, a thief of the night whose adulterous intention is exposed by the all-encompassing light of the moon:

> A fu ddim waeth, rygaeth reg,
> I leidr no nos oleudeg? (GDG 70, 21–2)

(Was there anything worse, a gift too restricted, for a thief than a bright fair night?)

The poem ends with a plea that in order to help lovers, God should save light for the daytime only, and keep the nights completely dark. Love during the night-time would therefore be completely devoid of any spiritual illumination and would be concerned only with deceiving the jealous husband and stealing away his wife.

The weather also has a symbolic function in 'Dan y Bargod' (GDG 89), where the poet is prevented from seeing Morfudd by being locked out of her house.[23] She does not appear, despite a pre-arranged tryst, and the poet has to wait outside in the rain, sheltering uncomfortably under the eaves. The bad weather signifies a condemnation of his adulterous motive in seeking Morfudd, and also a cleansing of his soul by means of physical discomfort. The poet describes his vigil in the rain as a means of supporting his declarations of love, but the absurdity of his situation, with 'rhëydr o'r bargawd . . . ar y mau gnawd' (waterfalls from the eaves upon my skin), and his criticisms of Morfudd, 'geirffug ferch' (lying girl), 'gorffwyll, myn Mair, a bair bai' (her fault, by Mary, drives me mad), detract from the supposedly noble nature of his love. Though he says towards the end of the poem that he forgives Morfudd for not keeping the tryst, he makes a contrast between his discomfort and her presence in the house:

> Yma ydd wyf drwy annwyd,
> Tau ddawn, yn y tŷ ydd wyd.
> Yna y mae f'enaid glân,
> A'm ellyll yma allan.   (GDG 89, 37–40)

(I am out here getting cold, yours the prize, you are in the house. In there is my pure soul, and my ghost is here outside.)

The association of 'ellyll' (ghost) with the darkness and rain outside the house implies that the poet is a lost soul condemned to purgatory, a meaning reinforced by the use of 'enaid' (soul), for his girl inside.

In three poems, 'Y Ffenestr' (GDG 64), 'Y Cloc' (GDG 66), and 'Y Rhugl Groen' (GDG 125), the poet is foiled not by natural elements but by specifically man-made objects, a window, a clock, and a rattle-bag. These represent intrusions of the external physical world to thwart the poet and cause anger and frustration. They can also be seen, within the medieval context, as elements of contemporary technology, symbols of the relatively sophisticated *uchelwyr* culture.

In these poems, the lover feels threatened by the concrete reality of his environment, which discourages the pursuit of physical gratification. Social constraint and active sexuality are both suggested by the imagery of 'Y Ffenestr' (GDG 64) where the poet tries to kiss his girl through a window but is hampered by the narrowness of the frame.[24] The poet's invocation to the devil to smash the window suggests that he is driven by an ungodly desire in his pursuit of love.

The opposition between earthly lust and a spiritually elevating love is made clear in 'Y Cloc' (GDG 66), where the poet is woken from a dream of his beloved by the chiming of the monastery clock.[25] The dream, though sensual, also implies a spiritual communion between the lovers, as the poet suggests when he sends the dream as a love-messenger to his girl:

> Eto rhed ati ar hynt,
> Freuddwyd, ni'th ddwg afrwyddynt.
> Gofyn i'r dyn dan aur do
> A ddaw hun iddi heno
> I roi golwg, aur galon,
> Nith yr haul, unwaith ar hon.   (GDG 66, 45–50)

(Run to her again along your way, dream, it will not cause you any difficulty. Ask the girl beneath golden hair if sleep will come to her tonight to give a glance, golden heart, niece of the sun, upon her once.)

The intrusion of the clock, however, brings the poet back to the physical world, a transition which is emphasized by the imagery used to describe the clock. The machinery of the clock itself is listed, as well as the farmyard noises set off by it:

> Difwyn fo'i ben a'i dafod
> A'i ddwy raff iddo a'i rod,
> A'i bwysau, pelennau pŵl,
> A'i fuarthau a'i fwrthwl,
> A'i hwyaid yn tybiaid dydd,
> A'i felinau aflonydd.   (GDG 66, 23–8)

(May its head and its tongue be disagreeable, with its two ropes and its wheel, and its weights, stupid balls, and its yards and its hammer, and its ducks thinking it is day, and its restless mill-wheels.)

In addition, the clock is compared to animate characters such as 'cenau ci yn cnöi cawg' (whelp of a dog chewing a bowl), 'sadler' (saddler), and 'deiler' (tailor), thereby linking the clock with domestic reality as opposed to the dream. The juxtaposition of *hwyneb*, referring to the girl's face in the dream, and *ffriw* referring to the clock face, also emphasizes the distance between the two worlds, and the humorous contrast between dream and mundane reality.

In 'Y Rhugl Groen' (GDG 125), the poet berates the rattle-bag which frightened away his girl, in the form of an energetic and vindictive *dyfalu*. The *reverdie* opening of the poem, describing the setting of the love-tryst under trees between mountain and meadow, is set in complete contrast to the *dyfalu*, with the abrupt change of pace and diction capturing the sudden intrusion of the noisy rattle-bag. Though the poet refers to the bag as 'cloch ddiawl' (the devil's bell), it clearly represents the imposition of the material world of man upon an idyllic natural scene. The rattle-bag, whose function was to frighten animals, acts here to discourage physical love beyond the constraints imposed by civilized (that is, courtly) society.

These rustic and non-courtly love-poems, relying on humour and bathos, as well as nature description, present a very different view of nature from that of the courtly poems. The world of nature is no longer an idealized metaphor of the court, but rather a representation of socialized reality, with its failures, disappointments, discomforts and reminders of moral obligations. The pursuit of love is merely a device to introduce the theme of malevolent nature, but the poems also show how this pursuit can be undermined by the earthly limitations of human lovers. Nature is not kind to lovers who attempt to practise a non-courtly love.

A rustic setting is also used for a group of poems in the form of love-debates, a genre widespread throughout Europe. In three of these poems, 'Digalondid' (GDG 36), 'Cyngor y Biogen' (GDG 63), and 'Y Cyffylog' (GDG 115), the poet's interlocutor is a bird.[26] In 'Digalondid', when the poet complains he is half-dead from love, 'ceiliog bronfraith cyweithas' (the sociable cockthrush) reminds him of the consolation offered by God's woodland. Despite the bird's advice, the lovesick poet insists he would rather die than live without love. The bird evidently represents the presence of God and is urging the poet to turn to spiritual contemplation, but the poet is committed to the active pursuit of earthly love.

The poem 'Cyngor y Biogen' (GDG 63) opens with a woodland scene that comes as close to a *reverdie* as anything in Dafydd's poetry, with its rich imagery of spring and the busy nest-building of the birds so at variance with the poet's own despair:[27]

> A mi'n glaf er mwyn gloywferch,
> Mewn llwyn yn prydu swyn serch,

> Ddiwrnawd, pybyrwawd pill,
> Ddichwerw wybr, ddechrau Ebrill,
> A'r eos ar ir wiail,
> A'r fwyalch deg ar fwlch dail –
> Bardd coed mewn trefngoed y trig –
> A bronfraith ar ir brenfrig
> Cyn y glaw yn canu'n glau
> Ar las bancr eurlais bynciau.   (GDG 63, 1–10)

(I was in a grove, sick because of a bright girl, composing a love-spell one day, a snatch of powerful praise-poetry, under a soft sky, at the beginning of April, and the nightingale on green twigs, and the fair blackbird on a leafy notch—the poet of the wood dwells in a woodland home—and a thrush on a fresh tree-top singing loudly before the rain, golden-voiced notes on the green leaf-covering.)

However, the very length and syntactic complexity of the opening description, with its absence of finite verbs, undermines the conventional prettiness of the scene and suggests a tendency towards parody. This tendency becomes more developed in the dialogue between the poet and the magpie which concerns, not the intricacies of love, but the exchange of insults and the magpie's scorn of the poet's old age:

> 'Ofer i ti, gweini gwŷd,
> Llwyd anfalch gleirch lled ynfyd,
> Ys mul arwydd am swydd serch,
> Ymleferydd am loywferch'.   (GDG 63, 45–8)

('It is pointless for you, waiting on passion, grey, worthless, decrepit person, almost senile—it is a foolish symptom of love's task—to rave about a bright girl.')

Thus the *reverdie* opening sets up the expectation of a young rustic suitor, while the dialogue exposes the reality of a bad-tempered ageing lover who vows to break any magpie eggs which he finds in future, in revenge for the bird's unpalatable home-truths.[28] Such an action recalls the destructive attitude of Eiddig in the courtly poems and suggests that Dafydd is deliberately assuming a non-courtly persona for the sake of humour.

Advice of a different kind is provided by the woodcock in 'Y Cyffylog' (GDG 115), where again a bathetic effect is achieved by the contrast between the poet's exuberant address to the bird and the bird's crusty reply. As in the other poem to the woodcock (GDG 61), the bird is associated with the discomforts of winter, but in this case it is the bird itself which complains of the cold. The poet recommends that it find shelter in the home of his beloved where it can make itself useful by watching over his girl. However, this attempt to manipulate the creatures of the woodland, as in the love-messenger poems, is doomed to failure. Far from allowing itself to become part of the poet's scheme, the bird announces, with grumpy satisfaction, that the girl has already gone off with another man. The poet is left, completely deflated, to muse on the truth of the old proverb 'Pren yng nghoed . . . arall â bwyall biau' (a tree in the wood belongs to the one with the axe.)

The effect of this image is enhanced by its occurrence in one of the courtly poems, 'Y Deildy' (GDG 121), where a different persona and tone are used. Here the voice of the noble young lover, describing the dwelling-place fashioned by the trees for himself and his beloved, calls himself 'bwyall' (1.30), the axe which hews the trees. Thus in both poems, the axe is a symbol of masculine power and possession.

Some of the debate-poems involve the poet and his beloved, but the outcome is just as unsatisfactory in each case. In 'Y Bardd yn Onest' (GDG 33), the eager young suitor has to convince his girl that he is not courting her merely because of her money. Since this was in reality the motive behind many of the marriages of the Welsh *uchelwyr*, as well as among the European aristocracy, the poem can be read as a satire on the idealization of love which tried to deny the economic significance of marriage. This satirical intention is activated more clearly in 'Bargeinio' (GDG 47), describing the debasement of love when viewed purely in material terms. The poet contemplates how much money to pay his girl and gradually decreases the amount from six pounds to nothing.

'Merch Gyndyn' (GDG 41) is in a form very like that of the *pastourelle*, beginning with the characteristic opening, 'fal yr oeddwn' (as I was), and describing the poet's unsuccessful attempt to make a love-tryst with his girl. The diction of the poem is specifically non-courtly, with the girl's coy havering contrasting with the ardency of the poet as she replies:

> 'Ni chai, fab o ael y fro,
> Un ateb; na wn eto.
> Down i Lanbadarn Ddyw Sul,
> Neu i'r dafarn, ŵr diful;
> Ac yno yn yr irgoed
> Neu'n y nef ni a wnawn oed.
> Ni fynnwn, rhag cael gogan,
> Wybod fy mod mewn bedw mân.'   (GDG 41, 19–26)

('You will not get, boy from the brow of the hill, an answer; I still do not know. Let us go to Llanbadarn on Sunday, or to the tavern, cunning man; and there we will make a tryst, in the green-wood or even in heaven. I would not like, for fear of being mocked, my presence in the birch-grove to be known.')

The token resistance offered by the girl and her suggestions for future meetings in the church or tavern reinforce the non-courtly environment of the poem and its presentation of a rustic love.

The same effect is achieved in 'Y Wawr' (GDG 129) which is a clever parody of the courtly genre of the *aube*, or dawn-song, an obvious example of foreign influence in Dafydd's work. Whereas the courtly genre typically relies on noble declarations of love and references to the signs of the coming dawn, such as the rising sun and the beauty of the morning light, Dafydd's poem relies on bathos. Here he denies the coming of the dawn:

> 'Hirfun dda hwyr fain ddiell,
> Hyn nid gwir; hynny neud gwell.
> Lleuad a roes Duw Llywydd,
> A sêr yn ei chylch y sydd.
> Hyn o dodaf henw didyb,
> Honno y sydd dydd o dyb.'
> 'Gair honnaid, pei gwir hynny,
> Paham y cân y frân fry?'
> 'Pryfed y sydd yn profi,
> Lluddio ei hun, ei lladd hi.' (GDG 129, 19–28)

('Tall maiden, good and calm, slim and pure, that is not true; this is something better. It is the moon which God the Ruler gave and the stars all around it. If I put a name on it without any doubt, it is this which appears to be day.' 'A likely story—if that is true, why is the crow singing aloft?' 'It is the fleas which are trying, hindering her sleep, to kill her.')

This lowering of the poetic register sets the tone of the encounter, and deliberately parodies the format of the *aube*, where the lover tries to pretend the dawn has not yet come. The final references to the lover escaping without being caught stress the conventionally illicit nature of the meeting and undermine the poet's aspirations to courtliness. Similarly, the phrases 'fardd diwyd da' (fine faithful poet), and 'mi yw dy eos' (I am your nightingale), give a spurious air of legitimacy to the love-meeting, as though the lover is there merely in the capacity of praise-poet.

Among the dialogue poems is one to Morfudd, 'Amau ar Gam' (GDG 77), in which Morfudd swears devotion to the poet in preference to her own husband, Eiddig, a theme which is similar to that of the *chanson de mal mariée*. The existence of the husband undercuts the protestations of true love voiced by the two speakers, and there is deliberate irony in the fact that the poet has fears of losing Morfudd's love but thinks it is quite proper for her to scorn Eiddig and ignore his claims on her. The poem thus seems to suggest a confrontation between love and marriage, with an endorsement of the former, but the case is weakened by the nature of the love which is not as noble and uplifting as the poem pretends.

The final dialogue poem, 'Ei Gysgod' (GDG 141), resembles the debates between body and soul found in both Latin and vernacular literatures, but here expressed in the form of an exchange of insults. While waiting in the rain for his girl, the poet is confronted by his shadow which is the voice of his conscience accusing the poet of many crimes. The poet reacts with abuse and anger, protesting his innocence, but fails to appease his conscience. There is thus a mixture of rustic diction, such as 'heusor mewn secr yn cecru' (bickering herdsman wearing motley), 'bwbach ar lun mynach moel' (scarecrow in the shape of a bald monk), and the sinister, threatening voice of the shadow:

> 'Myfy wyf, gad d'ymofyn,
> Dy gysgod hynod dy hun.
> Taw, er Mair, na lestair les,
> Ym fynegi fy neges.
> Dyfod ydd wyf, defod dda,
> I'th ymyl yn noeth yma,
> I ddangos, em addwyn-gwyn,
> Rhyw beth wyd; mae rhaib i'th ddwyn.'
>
> (GDG 141, 13–20)

('I am—leave off your asking—your own strange shadow. Be silent, for Mary's sake, don't hinder a good work, while I state my business. I have come, a good habit, to your side here all naked, to show, jewel of gentle complaint, what kind of thing you are; there is a spell taking over you.')

In most of these debate-poems, the poet's interlocutor offers negative criticism about the persona who is so obviously out of harmony with the natural world. The birds represent the voice of social order and of God's law, reminding the poet of his duty as a member of a social and religious community, while the poet's shadow is a more direct link between his physical and his spiritual selves.

The same non-courtly persona is used to demonstrate the failure of
a love based only on physical and material values in a number of
humorous poems and fabliaux. The lover who desires only physical
possession is doomed to failure and, worse, characterized as part of
the non-courtly world of the money-based bourgeoisie. This world is
constantly satirized by Dafydd in order to stress the distance of the
uchelwyr from such a context and their right to align themselves with
the Norman aristocracy.[29]

Dafydd's attitude to the urban bourgeoisie is illustrated most
pungently in his ironic eulogy to 'Niwbwrch' (GDG 134). The
opening lines begin with a ceremonial greeting which is immediately
undermined by the references to wine and beer:

> Hawddamawr, mireinwawr maith,
> Tref Niwbwrch, trefn iawn obaith,
> A'i glwysteg deml a'i glastyr,
> A'i gwin a'i gwerin a'i gwŷr,
> A'i chwrw a'i medd a'i chariad,
> A'i dynion rhwydd a'i da'n rhad.   (GDG 134, 1–6)

(Greetings to the town of Newborough, long since of noble aspect,
home of true hope, with its fine handsome temple and its grey towers,
with its wine and its people and its men, and its beer and its mead and
its love, with its generous people and its goods for free.)

It soon becomes clear that the whole poem is in fact a celebration of
the easy money to be earned in a town, and the pleasures that money
can buy. The use of a Welsh form of the English name, Newborough,
as well as the native name of Rhosyr, is a way of making a joke at the
expense of the town's English inhabitants.[30]

A similar context of convivial drinking is evoked in order to
describe a love encounter in 'Lladrata Merch' (GDG 135). The lover
appears to be bold and successful, but the nature of his love is
undermined by the circumstances in which he steals her away from
home after a drunken revel. The descriptions of the drunkenness and
the secret tryst, expressed in terms of a theft, create an impression of
physical abuse and violence which counteracts the poet's references
to his girl in courtly terms—'gwen em addwyn' (fine fair gem), 'Mai
degwch' (May's beauty). Indeed, the very passivity of the girl, who
functions mainly as an object of the poet's desire for physical victory,
also undermines the quality of the poet's love.

The ultimate failure and indignity of any love based primarily on
sexual conquest is made clear in those poems comparable to the
European genre of fabliau, where humour and satire are the main

poetic tools. The persona of these poems is held up to ridicule and mockery and shown to be inadequate to the task of achieving physical possession. Failure in love thus involves loss of personal dignity and honour, making an equation between earthly love and social values.

Two of these fabliau poems, 'Tri Phorthor Eiddig' (GDG 80) and 'Y Cwt Gwyddau' (GDG 126) are on the theme of the rivalry between husband and lover. In these comic narratives, however, the lover has no claims of superiority over the husband but is shown to be as ridiculous and cowardly as the husband is boorish and aggressive. The settings of the poems are explicitly domestic, and the imagery of courtly love-poetry is applied to a manifestly non-courtly love-pursuit with great comic effect. Thus in 'Tri Phorthor Eiddig' (GDG 80), Dafydd employs the Ovidian motif of the old hag protecting the chaste maiden, but places it in the context of the jealous husband's household. A squeaking door and barking dog are the other two 'porters' who prevent the lover from meeting his girl. The ignominious flight of the lover is described in a sequence which combines courtly and domestic imagery:

> Ciliais yn swrth i'm gwrthol
> I'r drws, a'r ci mws i'm ôl.
> Rhedais, ni hir sefais i,
> Gan y mur, gwn ym oeri,
> I am y gaer loywglaer lân,
> I ymarail â gem eirian.
> Saethais drwy'r mur, gur gywain,
> Saethau serch at y ferch fain.
> Saethodd hon o'i gloywfron glau
> Serch ymannerch â minnau.   (GDG 80, 45–54)

(I fled backwards suddenly to the door, with the stinking dog after me. I ran, I did not stay long, by the wall, I know I got cold, around the fair fortress, clear and bright, watching for the brilliant gem. Through the wall, a skilful striking, I shot arrows of love to the slender girl. From her bright breast swiftly she shot her love to greet mine.)

The courtly motif of the arrows of love, with all that this implies of a noble and spiritual love pursuit, is humorously inappropriate to the course of events already described, and the figure of the retreating lover is far removed from the knightly persona of courtly love-songs. References to cold and darkness imply the anti-social nature of the poet's activities, and the closing image of his refuge in the wood emphasizes the contrast between the physical world of humanity

where love is reduced to lust, and the natural world of God where love
is ennobled:

> Rhydd y mae Duw yn rhoddi
> Coed briglaes a maes i mi.   (GDG 80, 63–4)

(Freely does God give a branchy wood and field to me.)

The same humorous contrast between courtly and domestic
imagery is exploited in 'Y Cwt Gwyddau' (GDG 126), where the lover
is frightened off by the jealous husband and seeks refuge in a goose-
pen. The poet and his girl are exchanging sweet pleasantries when the
husband approaches and interrupts the courtly mood with his
aggressive threats. The lover's loss of dignity is completed by his
maltreatment in the goose-pen by a hostile mother-goose, who
represents yet another antagonist keeping watch over his girl. The
domestic setting of the smallholding and its farmyard is thus overtly
unsympathetic to the lover's pursuit of an adulterous physical love.

The last two poems, 'Athrodi Ei Was' (GDG 128) and 'Trafferth
mewn Tafarn' (GDG 124), are again placed in the world of the tavern
and urban social mores of a non-courtly kind. The persona in both
poems is a young squire, representing the urban population of the
Welsh boroughs, with aspirations to nobility, and his loss of dignity
represents the nobility's reluctance to accept these pretensions.

In 'Athrodi Ei Was' (GDG 128), the poet admires a girl at the fair
in Rhosyr (the bourgeois Newborough) and sends his servant to her
with a gift of wine. The courtly motif of the *llatai* is thus given a more
popular form, with the servant offering wine as a symbol of the poet's
declaration of love. The girl responds by pouring the wine over the
servant's head, which the poet takes as a personal insult, and his final
abuse of the girl is ironically contrasted to the courtly imagery used to
express his initial admiration:

> Yno'dd oedd, haul Wynedd yw,
> Yn danrhwysg, Enid unrhyw,
> Gwanddyn mynyglgrwn gwynddoeth,
> A gwych oedd a gwiw a choeth . . .
>
> . . . Amorth Mair i'm hoywgrair hy.
> Os o brudd y'm gwarthruddiawdd
> Yngod, cyfadnabod cawdd,
> Asur a chadas gasul,
> Eisiau gwin ar ei min mul.   (GDG 128, 5–8, 52–6)

(There was there, Gwynedd's sun is she, in glowing display, another Enid, a frail maiden with round neck, pale and wise, and she was splendid and fitting and refined . . .

. . . Mary's curse on my bold flighty treasure. If she deliberately shamed me there, acquaintance of anger, in blue braided cloak, may she lack wine on her foolish mouth.)

The drastic response of the girl, the poet's complete change of attitude, and the non-courtly setting undermine the refinement of the love-pursuit, so that the lover, despite his outward appearance of social position, is shown to be as venal as the girl and her other suitors at the fair.

This contrast between outward show and inner lack of worth is also made in 'Trafferth mewn Tafarn'. The young squire, who arrives at the tavern full of arrogance and confidently makes an assignation with a girl at the inn, is reduced to a trembling penitent at the end of the poem, terrified of discovery. His assignation fails because of his clumsiness in the darkened inn, tripping over furniture and other objects (which are superfluous and intrusive, unlike the trees in the birch grove) in his efforts to find the girl's room. For this description, Dafydd uses a wealth of domestic imagery, as well as a fast-moving style which makes use of *sangiadau* and *tor-ymadroddion*. This increased movement, which arises from the interrupted syntax and the extension of meaning beyond the usual boundary of the couplet, is characteristic of Dafydd's humorous narrative descriptions:

> Trewais, ni neidiais yn iach,
> Y grimog, a gwae'r omach,
> Wrth ystlys, ar waith ostler,
> Ystôl groch ffôl, goruwch ffêr.
> Dyfod, bu chwedl edifar,
> I fyny, Cymry a'm câr,
> Trewais, drwg fydd tra awydd,
> Lle y'm rhoed, heb un llam rhwydd,
> Mynych dwyll amwyll ymwrdd,
> Fy nhalcen wrth ben y bwrdd,
> Lle'dd oedd gawg yrhawg yn rhydd
> A llafar badell efydd.   (GDG 124, 29–40)

(I struck—I did not jump up uninjured—my shin (and woe to my leg) against the side of a stupid noisy stool, above the ankle, because of an ostler. Getting up, it was a sorry tale, Welshmen who love me, I struck —evil is too much lust—(where I was given, without a single easy step, many a trap of foolish blows) my forehead against a table-top, where a basin long remained loose, and the noise of a brass pan.)

The detailed depiction of the course of events, with its emphasis on physical contact between the poet and an assortment of mundane domestic appliances, underlines the non-courtly nature of his love-pursuit which is motivated purely by physical desire. It is only when he is safely back in his room, having roused the entire household, that he thankfully prays to God for forgiveness, a blatantly expedient use of religious support. The lover's loss of dignity during the course of his adventures, including the waking of the 'drisais mewn gwely drewsawr' (three Englishmen in a stinking bed), is a judgement on his social pretensions and his uncourtly lust.

The fabliau poems are an extreme expression of Dafydd's attitude towards a love based merely on physical desire which results in the lover's loss of social acceptance. The object of ridicule in most of Dafydd's humorous poems is the lover who loses face, and is exposed as a lustful and hence anti-social individual who has to be reminded of the obligations and restrictions imposed by religion and society. These reminders are in the form of natural elements such as birds and the woodland environment, or manifestations of the material and technological human world. At the same time, Dafydd is making a clear distinction between noble society, which is that of his audience, and the bourgeois environment of the borough towns and settlements. This distinction is made through the opposition of a spiritually ennobling love and one that is based merely on physical lust, demonstrating the superficial values of material possessiveness. The satire is even more effective because it neatly disguises the fact that *uchelwyr* status owed a lot to the conspicuous consumption of material goods, the clothes, jewels, houses and furnishings mentioned in the courtly poems, items produced and sold in the burgess towns which Dafydd so much deplored.

The persona of the lover is not viewed entirely in negative terms however in Dafydd's humorous and ironic poems. The triangle of husband, lover and mistress which is exploited by European popular poets, particularly in the fabliaux, is also used by Dafydd to portray the persona of a brash, often aggressive, lover competing with a churlish and detestable husband. The battle for possession and the sexual jealousy between husband and lover illustrate a number of themes common throughout the whole corpus: firstly, the spiritual emptiness of those who value material possessions above intrinsic worth; secondly, the corruptness of a desire based only on lust; and, finally, the inferiority of non-courtly marriage practices. All these themes are directed towards the growing middle classes who were emerging, with the help of the urban cash economy and expedient marriage alliances, into the nobility and who were therefore perceived as a threat by the *uchelwyr*.

The confrontation between love and marriage—the one representing everything that is noble and ennobling, the other representing only materialistic and bourgeois values — is made explicit in a poem of truly Ovidian connections, 'Trech a Gais nog a Geidw' (GDG 72). Here the poet, as the brash and aggressive lover, confidently asserts his superiority over the jealous watchful husband. Despite being morally in the wrong, as an adulterer, which he acknowledges by calling himself 'un orchwyl . . . â lleidr' (of the same occupation . . . as a thief), the poet openly scorns the husband who has to keep guard over his wife to maintain possession:

> Ceisio yn lew heb dewi
> Beunydd fyth bun ydd wyf fi.
> Cadw y mae Eiddig hydwyll
> Ei hoywddyn bach hyddawn bwyll.
> Traws y gwŷl treisig olwg,
> Trech a gais trwy awch a gwg
> Nog a geidw rhag direidwas
> Ei ddyn gwyn ar ael glyn glas. (GDG 72, 1–8)

(Constantly and always am I seeking a maiden, valiantly and without silence. Gullible Eiddig guards his lively little girl, gifted of thought. Perversely he watches, oppressive look, stronger is he who seeks, through ardour and resentment, than he who guards, for fear of a mischievous lad, his fair girl on the brow of a fresh valley.)

The opposition between the lover who seeks and the husband who guards is set up at the beginning of the poem and continued throughout, with a final declaration of the poet's intention to keep pursuing his beloved despite the efforts of the husband to prevent him. The poet says confidently:

> Mwy blyg ni bydd mablygad
> Ym mhen gwledig, unben gwlad.   (GDG 72, 33–4)

(No more askance will be the pupil in the eye of a chieftain's head, lord of a land.)

In other words, Eiddig guards his humble possessions far more assiduously than any great chieftain watches over his vast and wealthy acreages. This jealous possessiveness makes the gullible

Eiddig appear paranoid and foolish—and there is an analogy here, as in many of the 'triangle' poems, with the great Welsh landowners confident of their inheritance and the English occupiers who need towns and castles to watch over and contain the native population.

The point of the poem, and again it has a specific relevance to the *uchelwyr*, the native ruling class, is that legal possession—of a woman, of land, of a country—does not necessarily displace those who are the real owners in historical or physical terms. To make this point, Dafydd draws on the Ovidian tradition of the watchful husband, which also appears in French poetry, most notably the *Roman de la Rose*. In Ovid's *Amores* and *Ars Amatoria*, difficulties such as a jealous husband, dutiful doorkeeper, or bolted door, are necessary to make the pursuit of love more exciting. At one point in the *Amores*, Ovid actually urges the husband to be more watchful so that his own pursuit, as lover, is made more challenging:

> Si tibi non opus est seruata, stulte, puella,
> at mihi fac serues, quo magis ipse uelim.
> quod licet, ingratum est; quod non licet, acrius urit:
> ferreus est, si quis, quod sinit alter, amat.[31]

> (If you, fool, do not need the girl to be watched over, then have her watched for me, so that I might desire her even more. Whatever is allowed is not worth having; what is not allowed burns more fiercely: he who loves what another allows him is as hard as iron.)

This conveys something of Dafydd's attitude to love-pursuit and certainly suggests the same kind of contempt and cynicism towards legal owners.

Aggressive hostility towards the figure of the jealous husband is also expressed in the two poems 'I Ddymuno boddi'r Gŵr Eiddig' (GDG 75) and 'Y Cleddyf' (GDG 143). In the first of these, Eiddig sails away to war and the persona of the lover-poet uncharitably hopes that he will drown on the way or be killed by the enemy in France.[32] This wish is formulated amidst a tirade of abuse in the best traditions of Welsh poetic satire, such as 'yn elyn dianwylyd i fardd bun' (an enemy detested by the girl's poet), 'ffroen eiddig wenwynig' (poisonous jealous muzzle), 'ffriw ddifwyn' (unpleasant face). Again, the husband is abused for being alive while the poet feels that his love gives him the right of possession.

This poem, like 'Trech a Gais nog a Geidw', implies that the poet has to outwit the watchful husband constantly in order to meet his beloved, and that his attempts are not always successful. He says:

> Y sawl gwaith rhag trymlaith trwch
> Y ffoais gynt, coffëwch,
> Rhagddaw'r cawell ysgaw cau,
> A'i dylwyth fal medelau.   (GDG 75, 17–20)

(Many times before have I fled, you remember, from a wretched and wicked death, before him—the hollow basket of elder-wood—and his retainers like reapers.)

This scenario of the lover and the husband engaged in a constant battle of wits which also involves physical violence is supported by the poem 'Y Cleddyf' (GDG 143). Here the poet gloats over his possession of a sharp sword with which to protect himself against Eiddig or his men, an image which also suggests the lover's greater sexual prowess. The eulogy of the sword recalls *cynfeirdd* diction which imparts a mock-heroic tone:

> Catgno i gilio gelyn,
> Cyrseus, cneifiwr dwyweus dyn.
> Coethaf cledren adaf wyd;
> Collaist rwd, callestr ydwyd.
> Coelfain brain brwydr treiglgrwydr trin;
> Cilied Deifr; caled deufin.   (GDG 143, 23–8)

(A stab to rout the enemy, Cyrseus, a man's shearer with two lips. A hand's most refined stave are you. Rust you have lost, you are flint. Good omen of battle-crows in the tumult of war; let Deira flee, hard the two edges.)

The reference to Deira is an echo of the struggle of the British against the Saxons in the world of Aneirin's epic, *Y Gododdin*. There is an unmistakably contemporary analogy here, the inference that the English have stormed Wales by force just as the Saxons took over the Old North in the sixth and seventh centuries. Nevertheless, there is a suggestion of passivity in the poem that belies the aggressive stance. Though the poet seems to be prepared to fight, he actually chooses the refuge of the woods and the pacific occupation of loving:

> Ar herw byddaf ar hirwyl
> Dan y gwŷdd, mi a'm dyn gŵyl.
> Nid ansyberw ym herwa,
> Os eirch dyn, nid o serch da.
> Talm o'r tylwyth a'm diaur;
> Tew fy ôl ger tai fy aur.
> Ciliawdr nid wyf, wyf Ofydd,
> Calon serchog syberw fydd.   (GDG 143, 45–52)

(I will be outlawed for a long feast beneath the trees, I and my modest girl. It is not ignoble for me to be an outlaw, if a girl asks, not from love of wealth. Some of my family will excuse me; thick my track near the house of my golden one. I am not one who retreats, I am Ovid, a loving heart will be noble.)

The repetition of 'syberw' (noble), and 'nid ansyberw' (not ignoble), implies a general moral that a peaceful union is preferable to open aggression.

The poet's hostility towards the figure of the husband is comple- mented by his attitude in two poems which reinforce his own skills as a lover. In 'Rhagoriaeth y Bardd ar Arall' (GDG 54), the poet expresses jealousy of a rival and reminds his girl of all the things he has suffered for her. The persona of the poet here is not the confident and aggressive lover of the previous poems, but 'mab dewrfalch mebyd erfai' (a valiant proud lad, splendid in youth), who sincerely presses his case on the basis of his loyalty and poetic skills.

In 'Amnaid' (GDG 40), the image of the lover peering in at the window of his beloved's house is deliberately ridiculous. The lover is outside, 'gar llys Eiddig a'i briod' (near the court of Eiddig and his wife), and can only exchange a hurried greeting through the window. There is a humorous contrast between the lyrical description of the girl's beauty and the reality of the poet's adulterous pursuit which keeps him lurking outside her window. Nevertheless, sympathy is with the devoted lover rather than with the legal owner in his 'court'.

The opposition between lover and husband is developed particu- larly in poems describing Morfudd's fickleness, a theme which I have discussed previously in relation to the court-poems. Not only does Morfudd's fickleness symbolize the insecurity of the court-poets in fourteenth-century Wales, it also reinforces the attitude of the ruling élite to non-courtly marriage. I have already referred to the poem 'Y Cariad a Wrthodwyd' (GDG 93), in which the poet reproaches Morfudd for alternating between her lover and her husband. Dafydd uses a series of non-courtly images to describe the poet's chagrin at being only one of Morfudd's two lovers. Thus Morfudd is said to be:

> Megis y gŵr, gyflwr gau,
> Ag iddo dan y gweddau
> Deubar o ychen diball
> Dan yr un aradr cadr call.   (GDG 93, 19–22)

(Like the man, vain situation, who has beneath the yoke two pairs of perfect oxen beneath the same strong sensible plough.)

In conclusion, the lover complains that he has been pushed aside like an empty cask, because Morfudd has no more use for him in the birchwood. The perspective of the poem shows the lover in the right—he describes himself as 'dirprwyo dy ŵr priawd' (deputizing for your legal husband)—while the husband is portrayed as the unlawful interloper.

Another poem, 'Siom' (GDG 85), expresses the same bitterness of failure and the pain of Morfudd's fickleness. The poet's attitude is that of the wronged party who denies the husband any rights at all. His despair in this poem arises specifically from Morfudd's pregnancy, which he sees as an act of betrayal. It is the lover who thinks of himself as a cuckold, and who describes himself wearing a willow hat, the folk-custom signifying betrayal or abandonment as a lover.

In two other poems, 'Gwallt Morfudd' (GDG 73) and 'Llychwino Pryd y Ferch' (GDG 81), the obtrusive and unwelcome presence of the husband is made clear by a contrast between the girl's beauty and the husband's lack of physical attractions. Thus 'Gwallt Morfudd' (GDG 73) is concerned mainly with a *dyfalu* description of Morfudd's hair, which seems to make it a pair with 'Breichiau Morfudd' (GDG 53) describing an idyllic love meeting. Morfudd's hair is extolled with courtly diction, in a long series of lines joined by *cymeriad*:

> Llonaid teg o fewn llinyn,
> Llaes dwf yn lleasu dyn.
> Llin merch oreuserch rasawl,
> Llwyn aur mâl, llinynnau'r mawl.   (GDG 73, 11–14)

(Fair fullness enclosed by a band, trailing growth slaying a man. Flax of a best-loving welcoming girl, grove of wrought gold, strings of praise.)

Towards the end of this *cywydd*, however, the poet compares the luxurious fullness and length of Morfudd's hair to the balding crown of her husband, whom he calls Cynfrig Cynin:[33]

> Llwdn anghynnil gwegilgrach,
> Llwm yw ei iad lle y mae iach,
> Lledfeddw, rheidus, anlladfegr,
> Lletpen chwysigen chwys egr.   (GDG 73, 29–32)

(A coarse animal with a scabby neck, bare is his skull where it is healthy, half drunk, needy, wanton beggar, cheek blistered with sour sweat.)

The difference in appearance between Morfudd and her husband is marked not only by the change in diction, from the language of praise to the language of abuse, but also by the repetition of the *cymeriad* in 'll' to link the two contrasting descriptions.

The notion that the husband's unattractive presence can diminish the beauty of his wife is made explicit in 'Llychwino Pryd y Ferch' (GDG 81). Here the poet claims that his beloved (referred to as Enid) has had her complexion ruined by the foul breath of her husband:

> Meddylio'r wyf, mau ddolur,
> Myfi a'i gwn, mau fwy gur,
> Y chwaen gyda'r ychwaneg
> A ludd ei deurudd yn deg.
> Enid leddf, anadl Eiddig
> O'i enau du a wna dig,
> Gwedy gollyngo, tro trwch
> Y gŵr dygn, bu Eigr degwch,
> Anadl fal mwg y fawnen
> Yn ei chylch (pam nas gylch gwen?)   (GDG 81, 13–22)

(I am thinking, pain is mine, that I know, more care is mine, the repeated breathing which spoils her two fair cheeks. Modest Enid, Eiddig's breath from his black mouth does harm, when he may have let forth—a wicked turn, the gross man—she was of Eigr's beauty—a breath like smoke from a peat-bog around her. Why did the fair one not wash it?)

As a comparison to this spoiling of beauty, Dafydd refers to 'saerwaith Sais' (an Englishman's wood-work), with the loan-word 'fernais' from English 'varnish', being blackened by a smoky lamp; and 'pân Seisnig' (English fur), being soiled by peat smoke. Valuable material objects, explicitly connected with the wealthy English, are equated with the woman's physical beauty, all of them representing the husband's material possessions. This reinforces the poet's view of non-courtly marriage as a type of commercial contract based on considerations of profit and personal gain.

The poet's attitude to physical beauty, as merely an external adornment unrelated to intrinsic worth, is made explicit in the lament for Morfudd's old age, 'Morfudd yn Hen' (GDG 139). This poem begins with a description of a black friar, elsewhere reviled by the poet, but now given the status of a prophet, ennobled by his poverty and wild demeanour. His external appearance, 'noeth droed' (bare-footed), and 'unwallt nyth drain' (hair like a nest of thorns), is no guide to his actual nature, which is wise and articulate. Such a change of attitude to the friar marks the poet's realization of the temporal nature of his love for Morfudd. With old age, Morfudd has lost her beauty which is now only a dream to the poet. The transience of worldly life, including physical beauty, means that love itself, in the form of sensual joy, is also impermanent and unreliable. The figure of the ancient dishevelled friar is a symbol of passing time ordained by God, and a warning against trusting in earthly things.

A similar mood is expressed in 'Doe' (GDG 131), where the poet himself is now old and is remembering his love for Morfudd as a thing of the past. He justifies his pursuit of Morfudd—'iawn y gwneuthum ei chanmawl' (I did right to praise her)—but acknowledges that he never succeeded in winning her entirely, because she was already the wife of Bwa Bach. Yet his loyalty and commitment to her are more valuable in the long term than the mere physical possession of her enjoyed by Bwa Bach.

The distinction between the material possession of the husband and the true commitment of the lover is clearly set out in 'Rhag Hyderu ar y Byd' (GDG 76). The lover complains that he was once wealthy, but now, thanks to 'Eiddig leidr, Iddew gwladaidd' (Eiddig the thief, boorish Jew), he has lost what he had. This wealth is Morfudd's love, worth more to him than any material possessions. Moreover, the poet finds material reward, not through his pursuit of Morfudd, but in his work as praise-poet to the native *uchelwyr*:

> Ac ni ŵyr Fair, glodair glud,
> Ym wylo deigr am olud,
> Gan nad oes, duunfoes deg,
> Gymroaidd wlad Gymräeg
> Hyd na chaffwyf, bwyf befriaith,
> Durfing was, da er fy ngwaith.   (GDG 76, 35–40)

(And Mary knows, persistent word of praise, that I will not weep a tear for wealth, since there is not—a fine settled custom—a Welsh land of Welsh language where I do not get—may I be an assiduous young man of radiant language—payment for my work.)

In other words, he will never lack money because of his skills as a poet which belong specifically to Wales and the native Welsh culture. This emphasis on nationality implies that the poet sees a distinction between his own culture and that of the English settlers introduced into Wales. As in the references to English woodwork and fur in 'Llychwino Pryd y Ferch' (GDG 81), Dafydd is making a distinction between Eiddig's worldly materialism, desiring only to possess beauty as a valuable object, and the poet's appreciation of beauty as part of his cultural heritage, which he does not need to possess in order to share.

These oppositions between true lover and legal husband, between enduring commitment and worldly possessiveness, between courtly love and commercial marriage, are set up most explicitly in the poems 'Dewis un o Bedair' (GDG 98) and 'Morfudd a Dyddgu' (GDG 79). In both of these, the lover-poet makes a definite choice between a noble and chaste love or an adulterous liaison, and decides he prefers the former. 'Dewis un o Bedair' describes four women loved by the poet, or to whom he has addressed love-songs. These are Morfudd, Dyddgu, the wife of Robin Nordd, and an unnamed beauty, 'gwawr brenhiniaeth' (queen of a kingdom). His love for Morfudd, though true and fulfilling, was bound to end because 'prid oedd i'r priod eiddi' (she was valuable to her husband). The connotation of *prid*, which can also mean ransom or something bought, implies Morfudd's status as a material possession within the terms of her marriage. Similarly, the suggestions of commerce attached to the poet's love for Elen, the wife of Robin Nordd, 'y porthmonyn moel' (the bald merchant), representative of the English bourgeoisie, mark it as a purely business arrangement:

> Ni chymer hon, wiwdon wedd,
> Gerdd yn rhad, gwrdd anrhydedd.
> Hawdd ym gael, gafael gyfa,
> Haws no dim, hosanau da.   (GDG 98, 23–6)

(She would not take, form of a fitting wave, a song for free, stout honour. Easy for me to get an entire load, easier than anything, of fine stockings.)

With regard to Dyddgu, the poet's reward for his praise-songs is worth far more than clothing, being in the form of 'eiriau arwyrain' (words of praise), or even gold. But despite his rewards, the poet concludes that his main task is 'olrhain anwadalrhwydd' (to follow fickleness), for his role as poet does not secure him Dyddgu's loyalty as a lover.

The poet finally directs his allegiance towards the fourth girl, who appears to be a new subject for praise and a challenge to his skills as a lover. He abandons his fruitless pursuit of married women in order to devote himself to the task of winning this girl through praise, an endorsement of the function of eulogy as a metaphor of love-pursuit:

> Nid oes na gwraig benaig nwyf,
> Na gŵr cymin a garwyf
> Â'r forwyn glaer galchgaer gylch;
> Nos da iddi, nis diylch.
> Cair gair o garu'n ddiffrwyth,
> Caf, nid arbedaf fi, bwyth.   (GDG 98, 45–50)

(There is no wife, passion's chief, nor any man, whom I love as much as the bright maiden from the round lime-white fortress; a goodnight to her, she gives no thanks for it. Word gets around about loving fruitlessly, I will get, I will not spare myself, payment.)

The final exclamation, 'gwyn ei fyd a'i medd' (happy is he who possesses her), indicates the true goal of love-pursuit, to possess the desired object both legally and physically. Dafydd thus rejects adulterous love, which is ultimately barren, for a socially legitimate courtship and marriage.

His poetic persona makes the same choice in the poem 'Morfudd a Dyddgu' (GDG 79), which compares these two objects of many of his love-poems. Dyddgu is praised in the manner of eulogy, the poet adopts towards her the stance of the court-poet:

> Yn gariad dianwadal,
> Yn lath aur, yn loyw ei thâl,
> Mal y mae, mawl ehangddeddf,
> Dyddgu â'r ael liwddu leddf.   (GDG 79, 13–16)

(A steadfast lover, a rod of gold, bright her brow, such is, liberal right of praise, Dyddgu with the smooth black-coloured brow.)

Morfudd, on the other hand, is described in the sensual image, 'farworyn rhudd' (glowing ember), and the poet recalls his many assignations with her, by day and night. His love for her is not merely the by-product of eulogy but is based on a physical and emotional union.

However, the poet's love for Morfudd, and even Morfudd herself, are irreparably flawed by the existence of her boorish husband. Whereas the poet sings praises of Dyddgu, the husband loudly publicizes his wife's unfaithfulness, thereby debasing the whole affair. The poet crudely suggests that if he had a wife he could do a swap with Morfudd's husband and then they would all be satisfied. The poet's contempt for the husband lowers the register of the poem, which descends from the opening eulogy of Dyddgu to the closing abuse of 'y gŵr chwerw' (the bitter man). This change in tone reflects the difference between his two loves, and the poet recognizes, in the very last couplet of the poem, that Dyddgu's love, though harder to win, is worth more to him than the immediate gratification of his union with Morfudd which exposes him to the anger of the boorish husband:

> Dewis yr wyf ar ungair
> Dyddgu i'w charu, o chair.   (GDG 79, 53–4)

(In a word I will choose Dyddgu to love, if she can be had.)

Here again, the poet values a true and noble love, however hard to attain, above an adulterous and anti-social union.

In all the poems based on the triangle of husband, wife and lover, Dafydd is exploring the duality of the courtly love tradition. Just as the two parts of the *Roman de la Rose*, by Guillaume de Lorris and Jean de Meun, polarize the literary traditions regarding courtly love, so Dafydd's poems also express both sets of attitudes. His serious love-lyrics convey the significance of courtly love as a defining characteristic of the ruling nobility, in this case the *uchelwyr*. Marriage between the lovers is seldom referred to, because courtly love itself is a metaphor of noble marriage, an idealization of what were primarily political or business contracts.

In his humorous poems, however, and in his regular references to the figure of the jealous husband, Dafydd is participating in the 'bourgeois-realist' tradition of French fabliau, popular song, and Jean de Meun's *Roman*. According to this tradition, love is incompatible with marriage because one is noble and free, and the other is irrevocably based on power-struggling and possessiveness. This is how Jean de Meun describes the contrast between love and marriage, through the character of Ami:

> Amour ne peut durer ne vivre
> S'el n'est en cueur franc e delivre.
> Pour ce reveit l'en ensement
> De touz ceus qui prumierement
> Par amour amer s'entreseulent,
> Quant puis espouser s'entreveulent,
> Enviz peut entr'aus avenir
> Que ja s'i puisse amours tenir,
> Car cil, quant par amour amait,
> Sergent a cele se clamait
> Qui sa maistresse soulait estre,
> Or se claime seigneur e maistre
> Seur li, que sa dame ot clamee
> Quant ele iert par amour amee.[34]

(Love cannot live or endure except within a heart that is noble and free. For you often see it happen thus among all those who begin by loving each other as lovers, that as soon as they wish to marry each other, in spite of themselves it happens that love can never last; for he who declared, when he loved as a lover, that he was a slave to the one who was accustomed to being his mistress, now proclaims himself lord and master over her, which his lady claimed when she was loved as a lover.)

This perception of the incompatibility of love and marriage was commonly expressed in Continental literature of a humorous or non-courtly nature, so that Dafydd's use of the theme primarily as an agent of satire or humour is well within the mainstream of European poetry. As I have been arguing, such a perception of marriage specifically excluded marriage among the nobility, to whom the poems were addressed, but referred instead to bourgeois and commercial marriages as a way of dispersing the threat of the upwardly mobile middle classes. Chaucer, in his courtly *Franklin's Tale*, paraphrases the section of the *Roman de la Rose* which I have just quoted in order to show that it specifically did *not* apply to the noble lovers, Dorigen and Arveragus, whose marriage was a perfect union of social equals and true courtly lovers.

Dafydd's use of the character of the jealous husband is an important part of the theme of incompatibility between love and (non-courtly) marriage. Because love is not to be found in marriage, the husband must jealously guard his wife who seeks love elsewhere. The figure of Eiddig is used most commonly by Dafydd in this role, either as Morfudd's husband or as the husband of an unnamed woman. The name Bwa Bach is twice used for Morfudd's husband (GDG 117.44, 131.40) and there is a possibility that this name belonged to a real person, identified in a legal document as surety for a man convicted of theft.[35] However, as in the case of the names Morfudd and Dyddgu, the poetic references to Bwa Bach do not offer any conclusive evidence about the kind of man he was or his actual relationship to Dafydd ap Gwilym. Because he is named as Morfudd's husband, and therefore associated with Eiddig, who is also named as her husband, we cannot assume that the 'real' Bwa Bach was in fact married to the 'real' Morfudd, or that he was really a jealous husband. The name simply functions as a reminder that Morfudd was married and that the poet therefore had to exercise discretion in his pursuit of her. In fact, both Bwa Bach and Cynfrig Cynin, also named once as Morfudd's husband (GDG 73.27), clearly merge with Eiddig in terms of their function, and the occurrence of several different names for Morfudd's husband makes it unlikely that any one of them refers to a 'real' person who actually was Morfudd's husband.

It is clear that the figure of the jealous husband, as a poetic type, features consistently throughout the poems as a threatening and hostile figure. The lover-poet is constantly evading his wrath, tricking him, foiling his attempts to guard his wife, abusing him and satirizing him. Even when Eiddig is not interacting directly with the lover, he is shown to be churlish, non-courtly, and unsympathetic to the world of nature.

On a literal level, the jealous husband is the obstacle standing between the lover-poet and possession of his beloved, whether it is Morfudd or another married woman. But since I am arguing that Dafydd supports courtly marriage practice, and not adultery, it seems to me that Eiddig must represent a symbolic as well as a literal threat. I have already suggested that Morfudd is representative of Dafydd's *uchelwyr* audiences whom he must praise and flatter but also remind of their duty to be loyal to the native culture. It seems likely, then, that Eiddig epitomizes the threat to the native culture coming primarily from the urbanized Welsh and the introduced English settlers. Morfudd's marriage to 'Eiddig', and the poet's hatred of this union, can be interpreted as *uchelwyr* resentment of the socially mobile bourgeoisie and their attempts to share the power and prestige reserved for the Welsh-Norman nobility. Through his persecution of Eiddig, Dafydd demonstrates very clearly the desire of the *uchelwyr* to close ranks against outsiders.

Dafydd's humorous and satirical poems are clearly contributions to a well-established European tradition of anti-bourgeois satire, and as such offer some insights into the structures of his society. This is not to say, of course, that the primary function or motivation of any of the poems is political. They are clearly intended for entertainment and not for serious social comment. Nevertheless, the objects of humour and satire in Dafydd's poems—lustful lovers, boorish husbands, hypocritical clerics, people motivated by greed and desire—are exaggerated stereotypes of those whom the *uchelwyr* regard as being outside their own native élitist class. To satirize them in such a way both confronts the problem and suggests a resolution—according to the poems, such people are too foolish and uncultured to pose a serious threat to *uchelwyr* status.

Dafydd is not making a simple distinction between the Welsh nobility with its centuries of traditional culture, and the uncivilized English invaders. As I said before, such a distinction was not possible in the context of fourteenth-century Wales when the *uchelwyr* generally co-operated with the existing system of English adminis-tration. Because Dafydd, and poets like him, were concerned with preserving the native culture, which was basically aristocratic, their satire is directed towards those who did not participate in this culture, that is towards members of a non-courtly class, both English and Welsh. Dafydd's verse expresses the *uchelwyr* attitude to culture and politics at this time—culturally they support the native Welsh inheritance, politically they support the English administration.

Nevertheless, there are definite indications of anti-English sentiments in Dafydd's poetry which presage a stronger expression of political discontent in the work of later bards. With the uprising of Owain Glyndŵr in 1400, the *uchelwyr* separation of culture and politics could no longer be sustained and the ruling Welsh families were forced to choose one or the other. Dafydd contents himself with mocking references to boorish Englishmen, such as 'drisais mewn gwely drewsawr' (GDG 124.48) (three Englishmen in a stinking bed), and to their desire for status through material possessions. His mention of 'y pân Seisnig da ddigawn' (GDG 81.29) (the fine enough English fur), is as ironically disparaging as his assurance to the stag that this animal's beautiful coat will not be wasted on an Englishman: 'nid â dy bais am Sais hen' (GDG 116.42) (your coat will not go for an old Englishman [to wear]). At the same time, Dafydd refers elsewhere in his poems to the offices and institutions of the English administration with apparent lack of irony and indeed affectionate familiarity, such as his description of the cock-thrush as a sheriff (GDG 123.9).

The poems of Iolo Goch, a slightly later contemporary of Dafydd, display an even greater sense of loyalty to two cultures. Not only did Iolo Goch compose love-songs in the style of Dafydd's verse, he also sang praise-poems to patrons as diverse as Edward III and Owain Glyndŵr. Eurys Rowlands, who rightly acclaims the fourteenth-century Welsh bards as among the most politically aware sections of the community, sees a particular significance in Iolo Goch's eulogy to Roger Mortimer. Iolo praises him as the descendant of Llywelyn ab Iorwerth, prince of Aberffraw, and hails him as another Arthur— that is, as a hero of the Welsh preparing himself to accept the sovereignty of Britain.[36]

Dafydd ap Gwilym and his contemporaries held to an ideal of separation, the establishment of a Welsh principality separate from England though still subject to the English Crown. This ideal was destroyed forever by the failure of the Glyndŵr uprising. As Eurys Rowlands has said, the Welsh bards of the post-Glyndŵr era cultivated a new kind of Welsh nationalism in which hatred of the English was far more entrenched and overt.[37]

Dafydd ap Gwilym's verse, then, displays a comparatively cooperative and accepting attitude towards the political status quo, an attitude which appears to have been typical of the *uchelwyr* in the fourteenth century. It was not in his interests, or those of his patrons, to challenge the status quo by overt hostility towards the English.[38]

As I have been arguing, his aim is to foster class solidarity, the élitism of the native ruling class rather than a political movement towards nationalism. As part of this aim, Dafydd readily made fun of boorish and non-courtly figures, whether the Englishmen in the pub or the Welsh Eiddig and Bwa Bach.

Perhaps Dafydd displays his loyalty to the native culture most clearly through his parodies of French literary themes. I have already referred, in a previous chapter, to his ironic use of hyperbolic courtly love conventions, as in 'Y Galon' (GDG 108) and 'Yr Uchenaid' (GDG 109). His version of the *aube*, 'Y Wawr' (GDG 129), his use of a *reverdie* motif to introduce an anthropomorphized magpie (GDG 63), his imitation of a *pastourelle* opening in 'Amnaid' (GDG 40), are all examples of ways in which Dafydd turns borrowed conventions to humorous account, and at the same time implies his ironic opinion of their French provenance.

Nevertheless, French borrowings, whether direct or through English or Anglo-Norman, are clearly a crucial factor in Dafydd's poetry. The aristocratic convention of courtly love is used to reinforce the noble status of the *uchelwyr* in relation to their Norman neighbours and lords. More popular themes and genres are used for humorous effect, to satirize the bourgeoisie who cannot share in the cultural traditions of the aristocracy, either Welsh or French. Fundamentally, however, Dafydd is arguing for the superiority of the native poetic tradition and the obligation laid upon the *uchelwyr*, in the wake of 1284, to maintain this tradition as an essential and definitive aspect of Welsh nobility.

Conclusion

D AFYDD'S popular poems support his courtly love-poems in their celebration of a union which assimilates spiritual and earthly desires in the form of a legally binding marriage recognized by both Church and State. His court-poems describe the stalemate reached in a relationship which allows no physical expression, suggesting the conflict of interest which can arise between individual desire and social stability. The poet's pursuit of an idealized bardic love, which has a primarily eulogistic function, masks the role of the court-poems as the literary validation of a socially élitist group.

The same kind of validation is made by the non-eulogistic love-poems in which Dafydd recognizes a love which is socially beneficial while at the same time individually satisfying. The process of courtship and marriage among the members of the Welsh nobility and the Anglo-Norman ruling class was both necessary and desirable as a means of maintaining an élite class structure in the face of a rapidly growing urban bourgeoisie. The woodland tryst becomes a metaphor of this socially acceptable kind of union. The natural world, where God's benediction and human activities are in harmony, represents the world of the courtly ruling class which maintains the same sort of balance and harmony.

The humorous popular poems also serve a consensual and conservative function. Through irony and satire, Dafydd reinforces the position and status of the *uchelwyr* as distinct from the bourgeoisie and from the imported French culture. At the same time he implicitly consents to the significance of courtly marriage as a religious and social institution. Despite the popular motifs and the humorous and ironical tone of these poems, Dafydd is still composing for his own élitist class and its entrenched values.

The social function of Dafydd's poetry as the expression of a court-based élite is clearly analogous to that of Continental court-poetry. The ideals of *fin' amors* formulated by the troubadours related exclusively to a chivalric and aristocratic society. This body of courtly lyric-poetry, arising out of an originally eulogistic purpose, expressed a conflict between social and moral obligations in a society where the two were regarded as compatible. To be a member of the upper nobility was to be defined as possessing the combined virtues of *cortezia*, including the pursuit of *fin' amors*. This pursuit of an apparently adulterous and sensual love raised moral and spiritual problems which were examined by many of the troubadours.

The preoccupation with conflict in troubadour poetry highlights the situation of an élite ruling class forced by political and economic reasons to open its ranks to an emerging social group, that of the knights. The knightly persona of the courtly lover in troubadour and trouvère poetry, attempting to reconcile conflicting loyalties and obligations, is a symbolic representation of the knightly class as a whole, the newly emergent nobility pursuing social status in the form of land and property.

The fact that aristocratic women in Provence and France could own land in their own right made them worthy of pursuit, leading to an expedient and mutually beneficial marriage. This type of union, motivated largely by social and political concerns, was poetically interpreted as an idealized form of love, a hallmark of the *cortezia* or *courtoisie* which the knights sought to possess. The praise of patrons' wives also indicated the need of the knights for influential support for their emergence as a powerful new class.

In terms of the social context, then, *fin' amors* need not be viewed as an adulterous and illicit threat to the sanctity of marriage, but rather as a metaphor masking the upward social mobility of the knights and their desire to merge with the upper ranks of the aristocracy. Marriage was still sought as a means of social and financial advancement, and women were regarded as desirable because of their wealth and prestige.

The assimilation of love and marriage found in the romance genre of northern France demonstrates a literary movement away from the restricted *fin' amors* of the court-poets to a form of courtly love which is extended in its range of conventions, its context, and its audience. Conflicts of duty, of spiritual and chivalric obligations, of individual and social responses, occur within an established social structure where such problems can be resolved in terms of existing institutions such as marriage and the feudal hierarchy. Again, the function of romance and lyric is to reinforce the status of the nobility, and courtly love is legitimated as an acceptable pursuit of the aristocracy by its association with marriage and the acquisition of property.

This movement from a restricted to an extended form of courtly love reflects a social movement from a court-based aristocracy to a structure of urban organization in which a growing class of administrators and merchants aspired towards membership of the nobility. Popular songs and lyrics which imitate the register of court-poetry by using key images and expressions associated with courtly love suggest an identity between their audiences and those of the royal and aristocratic courts. The genre of romance in northern France is particularly significant in supporting the claims of barons and knights to belong to the upper nobility, while the genre of fabliau is often used to satirize the pretensions of the bourgeoisie.

The court-poetry of medieval Wales has a comparable social function as a means of affirming the élitism of the native ruling class in the face of progressive intrusions by the Normans and the English. In the eulogies of the early *gogynfeirdd*, love is a metaphor for praise and has no natural sequel or outcome but remains unrequited as one of its characteristic features. This eulogistic love is as restricted as the troubadour *fin' amors* but lacks the range of motifs and conventions found in the Provençal lyrics because of the different social context. The eulogistic love of the Welsh bards does not define a social group like the knights, but instead ratifies the existence and continued patronage of the poets themselves.

In Dafydd's poetry, the conflict of eulogistic love is resolved in the pursuit of a socially acceptable union, a resolution analogous to that of French romance and lyric. As in the literature of *amour courtois*, Dafydd is asserting the noble status of the *uchelwyr* as the descendants of the Welsh aristocracy and maintaining its exclusiveness from the emergent middle classes. The pursuit of love thus becomes the pursuit of marriage and status, as in European literature, and there is a marked distinction between courtly and non-courtly marriage practices.

Dafydd's poetry is analogous to the European lyric not only in terms of its conservative and consensual social function, but also in its treatment of popular themes. The influence of popular folk-poetry, already glimpsed in troubadour lyrics, was felt more widely in northern French literature, especially in the romance genre. The notion of courtly love as a system of aristocratic values became isolated from its original frame of reference, the courts of southern France, and was attached instead to the world of folk-tale and popular dance-song. Because of this association, popular literary forms became elevated to a more courtly and noble register, and found audiences from a cross-section of society. Whereas the restricted courtly love of the troubadours remained within the province of the aristocratic and educated classes, the extended courtly love of French lyric and romance formed a link between the world of the common people and the upper strata of noble society. The court-poems of German composers such as Walther von der Vogelweide, and the secular Latin verse of the goliards, exemplify the assimilation of popular themes into courtly and learned modes, and the consequent relaxation of the restrictive conventions governing *fin' amors*.

Dafydd's poetry illustrates the same process of assimilation within the native bardic tradition. Though his poems are directed towards an aristocratic audience, and make conscious use of the antecedent tradition of court-poetry, the majority of the poems are grounded firmly in popular literary conventions, both native and Continental. His courtly love is not the restricted *fin' amors* of the troubadours, with its highly specialized social relevance, but is rather the extended courtly love of European popular poetry with its emphasis on the pain of unrequited love divorced from any eulogistic function.

More significant than this European influence is the strong vein of native tradition flowing through the poetry, with the nature imagery, references to Celtic story material, allusions to places and contemporary events, the social context of church, tavern, borough town and woodland, all attesting to Dafydd's native inheritance. The society which supported the *gogynfeirdd* no longer existed when Dafydd was composing, and his immediate literary influences came from the popular culture of Wales rather than from an official bardic class.

Nevertheless, Dafydd performs a role comparable to that of the European court-poets by elevating popular conventions to the level of aristocratic entertainment. His three kinds of verse, the courtly eulogies, the popular love-poems, and the humorous verse, are all directed towards the same kind of audience, despite their varying levels of language and mood. Dafydd is composing for his own class, the *uchelwyr*, and is offering, not the conflicts associated with *fin' amors* and social change, but rather a consensual viewpoint which endorses and justifies the existence of an élitist minority while disguising the materialism by which its status is maintained.

In terms of social function and literary content, Dafydd's poetry clearly forms part of the mainstream of medieval lyric verse. The uniqueness of his contribution arises not only from his flexible and controlled handling of a common stock of themes, but also from the particular social environment in which he was composing. Dafydd's court-poetry is indebted almost exclusively to the native bardic tradition of eulogy, while his love-poems mainly depend on Continental influences disseminated through popular and non-courtly literary channels. Dafydd has taken his stock of themes and transformed them into bardic poetry characterized by its beauty, wit, and clarity of perceptions. Through his assimilation of native and foreign influences, of courtly and popular traditions, the Continental ideal of courtly love is successfully transposed to a different social and literary context to become a fresh celebration of love in all its aspects.

Notes

INTRODUCTION

1 T.M. Chotzen, *Recherches sur la poésie de Dafydd ap Gwilym* (H.J., Paris, Amsterdam, 1927).

2 The five theories are set out in *Recherches*, 11–26.

3 My own discussions of Dafydd's work are based on Thomas Parry's *Gwaith Dafydd ap Gwilym* (Gwasg Prifysgol Cymru, Caerdydd, 1963), abbreviated to GDG and using his numbering.

4 These are *Tradition and Innovation in the Poetry of Dafydd ap Gwilym* (University of Wales Press, Cardiff, 1972); 'Influences upon Dafydd ap Gwilym's Poetry', *Poetry Wales*, 8 (1973), 44–55; and 'Dafydd ap Gwilym: Y Traddodiad Islenyddol', in John Rowlands (ed.), *Dafydd ap Gwilym a Chanu Serch yr Oesoedd Canol* (Gwasg Prifysgol Cymru, Caerdydd, 1975), 43–57.

CHAPTER 1

1 Robert S. Hoyt, *Europe in the Middle Ages* (Rupert Hart-Davis, 1957), 172.

2 Georges Duby, *The Chivalrous Society* (trans. by Cynthia Postan) (Edward Arnold, 1977), 85–6, and 158ff.

3 R.W. Southern, *The Making of the Middle Ages* (Hutchinson University Library, 1953), 112.

4 These interpretations have been conveniently summarized and discussed by Roger Boase in *The Origin and Meaning of Courtly Love* (Manchester University Press, 1977).

5 These are defined by Boase, op. cit., 107 and 109.

6 Peter Dronke, *Medieval Latin and the Rise of European Love-Lyric* (Clarendon Press, Oxford, 1965–6), vol. I, 2.

7 Paul Zumthor, *Essai de poétique médiévale* (Editions du Seuil, Paris, 1972), 82ff.

8   Roger Boase, op. cit., 129.

9   Ibid., 129–30.

10   L.T. Topsfield, *Troubadours and Love* (Cambridge University Press, 1975), 39.

11   Ibid., 136.

12   Georges Duby, op. cit., 122.

13   L.T. Topsfield, op. cit., 288 and 290.

14   Moshé Lazar, *Amour courtois et 'fin' amors' dans la littérature du XIÎ siècle* (Klincksieck, Paris, 1964), 32–3.

15   Maurice Valency, *In Praise of Love* (Macmillan, New York, 1958), 110–13.

16   Raymond T. Hill and Thomas G. Bergin, *Anthology of the Provençal Troubadours* (Yale University Press, 1973), (revised edition), vol. I, p.40 11.49–56. This edition (and volume) is henceforward referred to as Hill and Bergin.

17   L.T. Topsfield, op. cit., 143, 126, 49.

18   M. Lazar, op. cit., 54, Lazar's view has been convincingly challenged by Alan R. Press who points out that in the courtly lyric 'the civil status of the beloved is hardly ever textually specified' ('The Adulterous Nature of Fin' Amors', *Forum for Modern Language Studies*, 6 (1970), 340).

19   George D. Economou recognizes this conflict as the common medieval notion of the 'two Venuses', the good Venus who fosters an earthly love in harmony with natural and divine laws, and an evil Venus who promotes lust. Man thus has to choose between two kinds of earthly loves and invariably opts for the latter because of his fallen condition. The *Roman de la Rose* as well as the troubadour lyrics can be seen as exemplifying this choice. See 'The Two Venuses and Courtly Love', in Joan M. Ferrante and George D. Economou (eds.), *In Pursuit of Perfection: Courtly Love in Medieval Literature* (Kennikat Press, New York, 1975), 17–50.

20   Hill and Bergin, op. cit., nos. 4 and 5.

21   L.T. Topsfield, op. cit., 50–1.

22   From 'Ans que.l terminis verdei', see L.T. Topsfield, op. cit., 56.

23   Ibid., 118.

24   Ibid., 113; and James J. Wilhelm, *Seven Troubadours* (Pennsylvania State University Press, 1970), 113.

25   C.B. West, *Courtoisie in Anglo-Norman Literature* (Haskell House, New York, 1966), 7.

26   James J. Wilhelm, op. cit., 118.

27 Notice, however, that Bernart distinguishes between a noble spiritual love and a base physical lust which is both earthly and sensual in nature; he does not practise the kind of Christian love preached by Marcabru.

28 J.M.L. Dejeanne, *Poésies complètes du troubadour Marcabru* (Librairie Edouard Privat, Toulouse, 1909), no. 36, 174.

29 Ibid., no. 40, 196.

30 L.T. Topsfield, op. cit., 169–70.

31 André Berry, *Florilège des troubadours* (Librairie Firmin-Didot, Paris, 1930), 372–4.

32 Ibid., 206–8.

33 'Doutz brais e critz', 11. 33–8. Text from Alan R. Press, *Anthology of Troubadour Lyric Poetry* (Edinburgh University Press, 1971), 176–8.

34 'Per solatz revelhar', Hill and Bergin, op. cit., no. 50.

35 'Si tuit li dol e.lh plor e.lh marrimen', Hill and Bergin, op. cit., no. 75.

36 On the *pastourelle* form and possible origins, see J. Audiau, *La Pastourelle dans la poésie occitane du moyen-âge* (E.de Boccard, Paris, 1923), and Michael Zink, *La Pastourelle, poésie et folklore au moyen-âge* (Bordas, Paris, 1972).

37 See F.J.E. Raby, *A History of Secular Latin Poetry in the Middle Ages* (Clarendon Press, Oxford, 1957), vol. 2, 333.

38 W.P. Jones, *The Pastourelle* (Octagon Books, New York, 1973), 191.

39 Alfred Jeanroy, *Les origines de la poésie lyrique en France au moyen-âge* (Champion, Paris, 1925), 30.

40 Ibid., 65–8.

41 Erich Koehler, 'Observations historiques et sociologiques sur la poésie des troubadours', *Cahiers de civilisation médiévale*, 7 (1964), 28.

42 Ibid., 29.

CHAPTER 2

1 Peter Dronke, *Medieval Latin and the Rise of European Love Lyric* (Clarendon Press, Oxford, 1965–6), vol.I, 163ff.

2 E.K. Rand, 'The Classics in the Thirteenth Century', *Speculum*, 4 (1929), 249–69. See also Gilbert Highet, *The Classical Tradition* (Clarendon Press, Oxford, 1936).

3 L.P. Wilkinson, *Ovid Recalled* (Cambridge University Press, 1955), 51.

4 The poems have been edited by Karl Strecker in *Die Cambridger Lieder* (Monumenta Germaniae Historica, Weidmann, Berlin, 1966), and numbers refer to this edition.

5   Strecker nos. 14 and 15. For translations of these and others from the Cambridge Songs, see Jack Lindsay, *Medieval Latin Poets* (Elkin Mathews & Marrot Ltd., London, 1934); F. Brittain, *The Medieval Latin and Romance Lyric* (Cambridge University Press, 1937); and Helen Waddell, *Medieval Latin Lyrics* (Constable & Co Ltd, London, 1933).

6   Compare, for example, the thirteenth-century French lyric by Colin Muset, 'En Ceste Note Dirai' (edited by Bédier, *Les Chansons de Colin Muset* (Champion, Paris, 1912) no. 10) and Dafydd ap Gwilym's poem 'I Wahodd Dyddgu' (GDG 119).

7   On the origin of the name 'goliard' see H. Waddell, *The Wandering Scholars* (Constable and Co Ltd, London, 1927), 183, and J.H. Hanford, 'The Progenitors of Golias', *Speculum*, 1 (1926), 38–58.

8   For a description of the manuscript and its contents, see B. Bischoff, *Carmina Burana, Faksimile-Ausgabe der Handschrift Clm 4660 und Clm 4600a* (Institute of Medieval Music Ltd, New York, 1967), 19–31, and P.G. Walsh, *Thirty Poems from the Carmina Burana* (Reading University Medieval and Renaissance Latin Texts, 1976), 1–8. The manuscript has been edited by Hilka and Schumann in 3 volumes, *Carmina Burana* (1930, 1941). Poem numbers refer to this edition. Translations of selected poems appear in Waddell, *Medieval Latin Lyrics*, G.F. Whicher, *The Goliard Poets* (New Directions, New York, 1965), and E.H. Zeydel, *Vagabond Verse, Secular Latin Poems of the Middle Ages* (Wayne State University Press, Detroit, 1966).

9   Waddell, *The Wandering Scholars*, 184–5.

10   The satires are discussed by Jill Mann in *Mittellateinisches Jahrbuch*, 15 (1980), 63–86.

11   W.P. Jones, *The Pastourelle* (Octagon Books, New York, 1973), 143.

12   See Dronke, op. cit., 181ff., for a discussion of the *flos florum* image.

13   See André Moret, *Les Débuts du lyrisme en Allemagne* (Bibliothèque Universitaire, Lille, 1951), 283–5; Roger Dragonetti, *La Technique poétique des trouvères dans la chanson courtoise* (De Tempel, Brugge, 1960), 163ff. The motif of spring in the *Carmina Burana* is discussed by James J. Wilhelm, *The Cruelest Month* (Yale University Press, 1965), 105ff.

14   For the text of this poem, see H. Moser and H. Tervooren, *Des Minnesangs Frühling* (S. Hirzel, Stuttgart, 1977), vol.1, 124. The poem is translated by M.F. Richey in *Medieval German Lyrics* (Oliver and Boyd, London, 1958), 43–4.

15   On the classical *topos* of the invocation to nature, see E. Curtius, *European Literature and the Latin Middle Ages* (Pantheon, New York, 1953), 92ff.

16   Texts and translations of these poems appear in Waddell, *Medieval Latin Lyrics*, 78, 88, 96.

17   Text and translation appear in Dronke, *op. cit.*, vol.2, 380–2. The poem is discussed by him in vol.1, 293ff., where he asserts that this poem is 'closest to troubadour love-lyric'.

18   Ibid., vol.2, 374–6.

19   W.P. Jones, op. cit., 149.

20   Bischoff, op. cit., 27.

21   'Alte Deutsche Volksliedchen', *Zeitschrift für Deutsches Alterthum und Deutsche Litteratur*, 29 (1885), 121–236.

22   Allen, *Medieval Latin Lyrics* (University of Chicago Press, 1931), 312–17.

23   Hilka and Schumann nos. 156 and 135. The poems are translated by Whicher, op. cit., 207, 199.

24   On this poem see Stephen Gaselee, *The Transition from the Late Latin Lyric to the Medieval Love Poem* (Cambridge, 1931), 26ff.

CHAPTER 3

1   The Church's attitude to popular song and dance has been discussed by F.M. Warren, 'The Romance Lyric from the Standpoint of Antecedent Latin Documents', *PMLA*, 26 (1911), 280–314.

2   On the minstrels and their function, see E.K. Chambers, *The Medieval Stage* (Oxford University Press, 1903); G.R. Owst, *Literature and Pulpit in Medieval England* (Cambridge University Press, 1933); M.W. Labarge, *Medieval Travellers* (W.W. Norton & Co., New York, 1982); J.J. Jusserand, *English Wayfaring Life in the Middle Ages* (trans. by L.T. Smith) (T. Fisher Unwin, London, 1897).

3   Gaston Paris, *Mélanges de littérature Française du moyen-âge* (Champion, Paris, 1912), 570. Paris also surmises that the transformation of popular songs into courtly lyrics probably took place in the Poitou-Limousin region of France which lies between the south, home of the *fin' amors* lyric, and the north, breeding ground for both trouvère and *jongleur* song.

4   Joseph Bédier, 'Les Fêtes de Mai et les commencements de la poésie lyrique au moyen âge', *Revue des deux mondes*, 135 (1896), 146–72.

5   See Alfred Jeanroy, *Les origines de la poésie lyrique en France au moyen-âge* (Champion, Paris, 1925), xvii ff.

6   *Popular Culture in Early Modern Europe* (Temple Smith, London, 1978), 28.

7   On the origins of German poetry, see André Moret, *Les Débuts du lyrisme en Allemagne* (Bibliothèque Universitaire, Lille, 1951), 93–7.

8   The theories of origin of the *Natureingang*, or nature opening, are summarized by Dmitri Scheludko under the following headings: folk-song, Arabic poetry, cultural-historical circumstances (such as seasonal festivals), classical Latin poetry, and medieval Latin lyrics. See 'Zur Geschichte des Natureingang bei den Trobadors', *Zeitschrift für Französische Sprache und Litteratur*, 60 (1936–7), 257–334. Given the widespread use of the nature opening, it is likely to have been based on popular rather than learned conventions, since these were more accessible through oral tradition.

9   Text from C.C. Abbott, *Early Medieval French Lyrics* (Constable & Co, London, 1932), 52.

10   Hill and Bergin, *Anthology of the Provençal Troubadours* (Yale University Press, 1973), vol.1, 68.

11   Fridrich Pfaff, *Der Minnesang des 12. bis 14. Jahrhunderts* (Union Deutsche Verlagsgesellschaft, Stuttgart, 1894), vol.2, Minnelieder no.17.

12   Roger Dragonetti gives examples of ways in which the *reverdie* is used by the trouveres in their court-poetry—see *La Technique poétique des trouvères* (De Tempel, Brugge, 1960), 169ff.

13   J. Bédier, *Les Chansons de Colin Muset* (Champion, Paris, 1912), no.1.

14   These terms are used by G.F. Jones in *Walther von der Vogelweide* (Twayne Publishers, New York, 1968), 44.

15   Bédier, *Chansons de Colin Muset*, no.10.

16   See Jeanroy, op. cit., 84ff. and 15ff.

17   See Paris, op. cit., 572ff. and Jeanroy, op. cit., 45--60.

18   Text from Jeanroy, op. cit., 464.

19   H.A. Kelly, *Love and Marriage in the Age of Chaucer* (Cornell University Press,1975), 333.

20   On the different kinds of debate poems, see Charles Oulmont, *Les Débats du clerc et du chevalier dans la littérature poétique du moyen-âge* (Slatkine Reprints, Geneva, 1974) (1st edn. 1911); Edmond Faral, 'Les Débats du Clerc et du Chevalier', *Recherches sur les sources latines des contes et romans courtois du moyen-âge* (Champion, Paris, 1913); W.A. Neilson, *The Origins and Sources of the 'Court of Love'* (Russell and Russell, New York, 1967) (1st edn. 1899); Jacques Lafitte-Houssat, *Troubadours et cours d'amour* (Presses Universitaires de France, Paris, 1971); A.C. Spearing, *Medieval Dream Poetry* (Cambridge University Press, 1976).

21   The French text has been edited by Ernest Langlois in 5 volumes (Librairie de Firmin-Didot, Paris, 1914–24), and has been translated into English by Harry W. Robbins, *The Romance of the Rose* (Dutton, New York, 1962) and into modern French by André Lanly, *Le Roman de la Rose* (Club de Livre, Paris, 1977).

22 Kelly, op. cit., 47.

23 On the fabliau genre, see Per Nykrog, *Les Fabliaux* (Copenhagen, 1957); Charles Muscatine, *Chaucer and the French Tradition* (University of California Press, 1957); and Saul N. Brody, 'The comic rejection of Courtly Love' in Joan M. Ferrante and George D. Economou (eds.), *In Pursuit of Perfection* (Kennikat Press, New York, 1975), 221–57. The whole tradition of anti-bourgeois satire has been thoroughly discussed by Jean V. Alter, *Les Origines de la satire anti-bourgeoise en France* (Librairie Droz, Geneva, 1966).

24 Nykrog, op cit., 187ff.

25 Edited by Jean Rychner, *Contribution à l'étude des fabliaux* (Université de Neuchatel, Geneva, 1960), vol.2, 100–9.

26 The tale is edited by R.C. Johnston and D.D.R. Owen, *Fabliaux* (Basil Blackwell, Oxford, 1965), 78–84.

27 John Speirs, *Medieval English Poetry: The Non-Chaucerian Tradition* (Faber & Faber, London, 1957), 50.

28 Arthur K. Moore, *The Secular Lyric in Middle English* (Greenwood Press, Connecticut, 1970), 41ff.

29 A.K. Moore supports the view that secular poets were mainly responsible for the Harley manuscript (ibid., 43), while Derek Pearsall refers to 'a class of clerical *jongleurs*' as the likely composers (*Old and Middle English Poetry* (Routledge and Kegan Paul, London, 1977), 129).

30 See for example the poems 'Annot and John' and 'The Fair Maid of Ribblesdale' in G.L. Brook, *The Harley Lyrics* (Manchester University Press, 1968), nos. 3 and 7.

31 For example, 'The Three Foes of Man' (Brook, op. cit., no.2) and 'A Winter Song' (ibid., no.17).

CHAPTER 4

1 *The Court Poets of The Welsh Princes* (Sir John Rhŷs Memorial Lecture, British Academy, 1948), 26.

2 Anthony Conran, *Penguin Book of Welsh Verse* (1967), 57. See also J.E. Caerwyn Williams, 'Cerddi'r Gogynfeirdd i Wragedd a Merched', *Llên Cymru*, 13 (1974–9), 40.

3 On the influence of troubadour song on Anglo-Norman and Middle English poetry, see Jean Audiau, *Les Troubadours et l'Angleterre* (Paris, 1927) and H.J. Chaytor, *The Troubadours and England* (Cambridge, 1923).

4 T. Gwynn Jones, *Rhieingerddi'r Gogynfeirdd* (Dinbych, 1915), 4ff.

5   The importance of Irish influence on *gogynfeirdd* poetry has also been stressed by W.J. Gruffydd, 'Rhagarweiniad i Farddoniaeth Cymru cyn Dafydd ap Gwilym', *Transactions of the Honourable Society of Cymmrodorion*, (1937), 257–83.

6   J.E. Caerwyn Williams, 'Cerddi'r Gogynfeirdd i Wragedd a Merched', op. cit.

7   T. Gwynn Jones, 'A "Court of Love" Poem in Welsh', *Aberystwyth Studies*, 4 (1922), 85.

8   Lloyd-Jones, op. cit., and Ifor Williams, 'Dafydd ap Gwilym a'r Glêr, *Transactions of the Honourable Society of Cymmrodorion* (1913–14), 83–204.

9   Text taken from J. Morris-Jones and T.H. Parry-Williams (eds.), *Llawysgrif Hendregadredd* (University of Wales Press, Cardiff, 1971), 122, 124. This edition is henceforward abbreviated to Ll.H.

10 See Ll.H. 289, 40.

11 In my translation I have followed K.A. Evans' reading of *gorwyth* instead of *gorwych* in l.1. ('Cerddi'r Gogynfeirdd i Rianedd a Gwragedd', M.A. Thesis, Aberystwyth, 1972, 260).

12 K.H. Jackson, *Early Welsh Gnomic Poems* (University of Wales Press, Cardiff, 1961), 39.

13 Gerard Murphy, *Early Irish Lyrics* (Clarendon Press, Oxford, 1970), 156.

14 T. Parry, *Oxford Book of Welsh Verse* (Oxford University Press, 1962), no.31.

15 *Rhieingerddi'r Gogynfeirdd*, op. cit., 40ff. On Gruffudd and his poetry, see D. Myrddin Lloyd in A.O.H. Jarman and G.R. Hughes, *A Guide to Welsh Literature* (Christopher Davies, Swansea, 1980), vol.2, 41–2.

16 T. Gwynn Jones, 'A "Court of Love" Poem in Welsh', op. cit., 92ff.

CHAPTER 5

1   E. Cowell, 'Dafydd ap Gwilym', *Y Cymmrodor*, 2 (1878), 110.

2   Ibid., 109.

3   W. Lewis Jones, 'The Literary Relationships of Dafydd ap Gwilym', *Transactions of the Honourable Society of Cymmrodorion* (1907–8), 118–53. See also Theodor Chotzen, *Recherches sur la poésie de Dafydd ap Gwilym* (H.J., Paris, Amsterdam, 1927), 118ff.

4   W. Lewis Jones, op. cit., 134.

5　Gwyn Thomas, *Y Traddodiad Barddol* (Gwasg Prifysgol Cymru, Caerdydd 1976), 156.

6　Gareth Davies, 'The Poetry of the Welsh *Cywydd*', *Proceedings of the Leeds Philosophical and Literary Society*, 14 (1972), 288.

7　Ibid., 290.

8　The group of poems referred to here is GDG 1–21.

9　These are GDG 45, 37, 34, 102, 42, 106, 56, 84, 51.

10　Rachel Bromwich, 'Influences upon Dafydd ap Gwilym's Poetry', *Poetry Wales*, 8 (1973), 51.

11　This can be taken as an example of the rhetorical figure of speech *occupatio*, since Dafydd is denying his ability to compose poetry while in the very act of composing a skilful and beautiful poem to Dyddgu.

12　Dafydd's reference to himself as a *cerddawr*, a non-specific word for any poet, exemplifies the rhetorical figure of thought, *diminutio*, in which the poet deliberately underestimates his status. Compare Raimbaut d'Aurenga's use of a similar device:

> E soy fols cantayre cortes
> Tan c'om m'en apela ioglar.

(Topsfield, *Troubadours and Love* (Cambridge University Press, 1975), 145.) ' And I am such a foolish courtly singer that I am called a *joglar*.'

13　Compare this with the troubadours' custom of referring to themselves by name, to add weight to their argument and underline their official status. See for example Topsfield, op. cit., 182–3.

14　The motif of the lover being like a ship at sea is fairly common in Latin and vernacular love-lyrics. For examples, see James J. Wilhelm, *The Cruelest Month* (Yale University Press, 1975), 273.

15　The cuckoo is mentioned in a number of early Welsh poems, including gnomic verse and pieces from the Llywarch Hen saga, for example 'Claf Abercuawg' (The Sick Man of Abercuawg):

> Yn Aber Cuawc yt ganant gogeu
> Ar gangheu blodeuawc.
> Coc lauar, canet yrawc.

(Ifor Williams, *Canu Llywarch Hen* (Gwasg Prifysgol Cymru, Caerdydd, 1970), 23.) 'Cuckoos sing in Abercuawg on flowering branches. Loud cuckoo, may it sing for a long time to come.'

16　The motif of the cuckoo is also found in Latin secular poetry, so that the comparison with a Latin prayer has some point to it. Compare, for example, Alcuin's famous lament for the cuckoo, 'Heu, cuculus nobis fuerat cantare suetus', and the song from the *Carmina Burana*, 'Musa venit carmine', which contains the lines:

> cuculat et cuculus
> per nemora vernata.

'The cuckoo cries 'cuckoo' throughout the wooded hill.' Both poems are printed in Helen Waddell, *Medieval Latin Lyrics* (Constable & Co., London, 1933), 78ff. and 238ff.

17   In French and Latin dance-song, the seasonal opening is used to reinforce the poet's happiness, whereas in troubadour, Minnesang and learned Latin love-lyrics a description of spring or summer often emphasizes by contrast the poet's suffering. See Roger Dragonetti, *La Technique poétique des trouvères dans la chanson courtoise* (De Tempel, Brugge, 1960), 163ff. In Welsh poetry of the *gogynfeirdd*, the same contrast is also found, for example in the religious poem 'Tristwch ym Mai':

> Ban ganhort cogeu ar blaen guit guiw
> Handid muy vy llauuridet.

(Henry Lewis, *Hen Gerddi Crefyddol* (Gwasg Prifysgol Cymru, Caerdydd, 1974), no.5.) 'When cuckoos sing on the tips of full-grown trees, my melancholy becomes greater.'

18   This technique of *adnominatio* (repetition of a word with variant forms) is a commonplace ornament of Latin rhetoric and is found in Latin secular lyrics as well as more learned and scholarly pieces. Dafydd makes use of it occasionally and also of the similar device, *repetitio*, the repetition of the same word at the beginning of successive phrases, as in this poem.

19   'Morfudd fel yr Haul', *Ysgrifau Beirniadol*, 6 (1966), 26. Rowlands also lists Dafydd's use of sun imagery elsewhere in his poetry (ibid., 25–6).

20   Ibid., 44.

21   Rachel Bromwich says that comparisons with all forms of light, especially the dawn, sun, moon, stars, candles, and lamps were among the most popular images used by the *gogynfeirdd* to describe a girl's beauty. See *Tradition and Innovation in the Poetry of Dafydd ap Gwilym* (University of Wales Press, Cardiff, 1972), 18. Chotzen (op. cit., 207–8) also lists some stock expressions related to light which are used by the *cywyddwyr* as well as the earlier court-poets. Images of light are also found in Continental court-poetry and Latin secular poetry where they often have a specifically symbolic function. Peter Dronke's comments on images of the sun and moon in the poetry of Heinrich von Morungen have some relevance here: 'The dominant use of sun-moon imagery in the Middle Ages was as figura of God and the Virgin Mary . . . The lady bestows joy on her lover; as moon he is filled with her sunlight, as the Virgin was filled with the Sol Invictus.' *Medieval Latin and the Rise of European Love-Lyric*, (Clarendon Press, Oxford, 1965–6), vol.1, 128–9.

22 Topsfield, op. cit., 132.

23 J. Gwenogvryn Evans, *Poetry of the Red Book of Hergest* (Llanbedrog, 1911), 83.

24 As part of his bardic persona, Dafydd usually presents himself as being of comparatively humble status. In reality, of course, his position as a member of the *uchelwyr* made him a social equal of both Morfudd and Dyddgu.

25 The evidence has been discussed in detail by Thomas Parry in his Introduction to GDG, xxiii ff.

26 See especially the Introduction to *Cywyddau Dafydd ap Gwilym a'i Gyfoeswyr* (Gwasg Prifysgol Cymru, Caerdydd, 1935), xxviff. and 'Dafydd ap Gwilym a'r Glêr', *Transactions of the Honourable Society of Cymmrodorion*, (1913–14), 147ff.

27 The list of virtues given by Dafydd in 11.40–8 of this poem corresponds to the instructions in the Bardic Grammar as to how a noblewoman should be praised. See G.J.Williams and E.J. Jones, *Gramadegau'r Penceirddiaid* (Gwasg Prifysgol Cymru, Caerdydd, 1934), 16.

28 See *Trioedd Ynys Prydein* (University of Wales Press, Cardiff, 1978),129–30, where Rachel Bromwich draws attention to Dafydd's poem using the triad; also her article 'Cyfeiriadau Dafydd ap Gwilym at Chwedl a Rhamant', *Ysgrifau Beirniadol*, 12 (1982), 72.

29 Compare the classical rhetorical devices of *effictio* and *notatio*, used to describe physical appearance and moral probity respectively. The need to praise both aspects of a woman's virtue was recognized by Einion Offeiriad in his Grammar. See D.J. Bowen, 'Dafydd ap Gwilym a Datblygiad y Cywydd', *Llên Cymru*, 8 (1964), 25.

30 This group consists of the following poems: GDG 52, 93, 88, 97, 60, 104, 107, 110, 95, 96, 90, 100, 133, 108, 111, 109.

31 Compare this poem to 'Dagrau Serch' (GDG 95) which uses a similar theme of the poet's tears but which is much more conventional and explicitly courtly in its style and setting.

32 These motifs are found in Ovid's works as well as in Latin secular poetry of the medieval period, so it is likely that they were absorbed into vernacular poetry from the classical tradition. For Latin examples, see Dronke's motif index in *Medieval Latin and the Rise of European Love-Lyric*, op. cit., vol.2, 599ff.

33 Arnaut Daniel says, for example:

> e si.l maltraich no.m restaura
> ab un baisar anz d'annou
> mi auci e si enferna.

(Topsfield, op. cit., 209.) 'And if she does not cure my pain with one kiss before the new year, she will kill me and burn in hell herself.' More common forms of reward were to be granted a look, or merely to be in the presence of the beloved.

34   A *cywydd* on the same topic, 'Y Cusan', by Dafydd ab Edmwnd (fl. 1450–90), completely lacks the motif of reward and instead concentrates on the physical act of the kiss itself, the joining of lips and mouths. See Eurys Rowlands, *Poems of the Cywyddwyr* (Dublin Institute for Advanced Studies, 1976), 35–6.

35   Bernart de Ventadorn in particular associates joy and sorrow with the heart, as in the opening lines of this poem:

> La dousa votz ai auzida
> del rosinholet sauvatge,
> et es m'ins el cor salhida
> si que tot lo cosirer
> e.ls mals traihz qu'amors me dona,
> m'adousa e m'asazona.

(Topsfield, op. cit., 124.) 'I have heard the sweet voice of the wild nightingale, and it has pierced the depths of my heart so that all the care and sufferings which love gives me are sweetened and assuaged for me.'

36   Two other poems belong to this group, 'Y Fun o Eithinfynydd' (GDG 57) and 'Merch Fileinaidd' (GDG 101), but I have omitted them from the discussion as Parry considers their authenticity to be doubtful. The first is a simple love-poem to Morfudd and the second is a praise-poem to an unnamed girl in which praise turns to abuse when she continues to resist the poet's courtship.

37   Parry suggests it is very likely that the Angharad referred to here is the same as the one in 'Marwnad Angharad' (GDG 16). See GDG xxxviii–ix.

CHAPTER 6

1   On Dafydd's references to native prose tales, see Rachel Bromwich, 'Cyfeiriadau Dafydd ap Gwilym at Chwedl a Rhamant', *Ysgrifau Beirniadol*, 12 (1982), 57–76.

2   See D.J. Bowen, 'Bardd Glyn Teifi', *Y Traethodydd*, 131 (1976), 139.

3   Ibid., 136–7.

4   On Dafydd's French influences and the importance of oral traditions see R. Bromwich, *Tradition and Innovation in the Poetry of Dafydd ap Gwilym* (University of Wales Press, 1972) and 'Dafydd ap Gwilym: Y Traddodiad Islenyddol', in John Rowlands (ed.), *Dafydd ap Gwilym a Chanu Serch yr Oesoedd Canol* (Gwasg Prifysgol Cymru, Caerdydd, 1975), 43–57.

5   Dafydd's references to Ovid are summarized by Theodor Chotzen, *Recherches sur la poésie de Dafydd ap Gwilym* (H.J., Paris, Amsterdam, 1927), 142–4. Parry maintains that the works of Ovid were not

necessarily known to Dafydd in the original, since there were many paraphrases, literary references, and translations available to him (*Yorkshire Celtic Studies*, 5 (1945–52), 30). However, Rachel Bromwich points out that no vernacular version of the *Amores* survives from 14th-century Wales, so that parallels between this work and some of Dafydd's poems may indicate that he had access only to the original Latin version (*Tradition and Innovation*, 26–8).

6 *Poetry Wales*, 8 (1973), 54. Dr Bromwich suggests that in this particular example, Dafydd may be quoting from 'Breuddwyd Macsen' (*Ysgrifau Beirniadol*, 12 (1982), 60). The text of *Chwedleu Seith Doethon Rufein* has been edited by Henry Lewis (Gwasg Prifysgol Cymru, Caerdydd, 1967) (2nd edn.).

7 Glenys Goetinck, *Historia Peredur vab Efrawc* (University of Wales Press, Cardiff, 1976), 30–1. See also GDG p.481.

8 Vernam Hull, *Longes mac n-Uislenn* (Oxford University Press, 1949), 45 par.7.

9 See K.H. Jackson, *The International Popular Tale and Early Welsh Tradition* (University of Wales Press, 1961), 114.

10 On the origins and development of the Tristan story see Sigmund Eisner, *The Tristan Legend: A Study in Sources* (Northwestern University Press, Evanston, Illinois, 1969) and R. Bromwich, 'Some remarks on the Celtic sources of *Tristan*', *Transactions of the Honourable Society of Cymmrodorion*, (1953), 32–60.

11 According to Bromwich, the earliest bardic allusion to Esyllt is by Gruffudd ap Maredudd ap Dafydd, a contemporary of Dafydd's. See *Trioedd Ynys Prydein* (University of Wales Press, Cardiff, 1978), 350.

12 On the name Tegau, see Bromwich, ibid., 299, 512, 564.

13 These names are derived from the *Brut* and indicate Dafydd's familiarity with Welsh versions of Geoffrey of Monmouth.

14 This group includes characters such as Fflur, Garwy, Indeg and Ystudfach, and the unknown Eiddilig Gor, Gwaeddan and Ysgolan.

15 See Parry's note on GDG 84.58. This idea of Virgil is also found in the *Chwedleu Seith Doethon Rufein*.

16 Particularly important was *Brut y Brenhinedd*, the Welsh adaptation of Geoffrey of Monmouth's *Historia Regum Britanniae*. With regard to Uthr, for example, R. Bromwich makes a distinction between *gogynfeirdd* and *cywyddwyr* references to the name, as only the latter show clear traces of the *Brut* version of the story (*Trioedd Ynys Prydein*, 522–3).

17 Ibid., 382.

18 In particular a dialogue poem in the *Myvyrian Archaeology* (ed. Owen Pughe *et al.*, Denbigh, 1870), 130, which has been given the heading

'Ymddiddan rhwng Arthur Frenhin a'i ail wraig Gwenhwyfar: Hon oedd y ferch a ddygodd Melwas Tywysog o'r Alban' (Conversation between King Arthur and his second wife Gwenhwyfar: she is the woman whom Melwas Prince of Scotland carried off). The poem is found in a number of variant versions, suggesting a long oral history.

19   *Trioedd Ynys Prydein*, lxxxi–ii.

20   The extracts of poetry used as examples of different metres in the Grammar of Einion Offeiriad provide a glimpse of part of this lost verse. Rachel Bromwich argues convincingly that the Grammar provides a unique insight into the nature of the early Welsh oral tradition and folk love–song, and draws attention to significant parallels between the poetry quoted in the Grammar and Dafydd's own work, supporting her assumption that Dafydd owes a substantial debt to a scarcely surviving popular tradition. See 'Gwaith Einion Offeiriad a Barddoniaeth Dafydd ap Gwilym', *Ysgrifau Beirniadol*, 10 (1977), 157–80.

21   With the increasing tendency of the English burgesses to invest in and lease agricultural lands for the sake of profits (R.R. Davies, *Lordship and Society in the March of Wales 1282–1400* (Clarendon Press, Oxford, 1978), 329), Dafydd had even more reason to construct a rural landscape which was recognizably and specifically 'courtly'. The idealization of land in his poems is not only an affirmation of *uchelwyr* status through ownership of hereditary lands, but also a way of distinguishing between this noble landownership and the materialistic encroachments of the burgesses.

22   From Peter Dronke, *Medieval Latin and the Rise of European Love-Lyric* (Clarendon Press, Oxford, 1965–6), vol.1, 178. The Codex Salmasianus is dated to the seventh or eighth century, and though it contains quotations from Virgil and Ovid, most of the poems are from the fifth and sixth centuries.

23   Rachel Bromwich discusses this *cywydd* and its link with the dream-vision genre in *Tradition and Innovation*, op. cit., 33.

24   On the White Hind in Celtic folk-tale, see R. Bromwich, 'Celtic Dynastic Themes and the Breton Lays', *Etudes Celtiques*, 9 (1960–1), 439–74. The motif of hunting with a pack of hounds is a common prelude to an entry to the Otherworld, as in the tale of *Pwyll* the first branch of the *Mabinogi*, and in the Middle English poem, *Sir Orfeo*. The mythological significance of hunting in early Celtic society has been discussed by Graham Webster, *The British Celts and their Gods under Rome* (B.T. Batsford, London, 1986), 43–51.

25   On Dafydd's use of birds, see Bromwich, *Tradition and Innovation*, 34ff.

26   It seems clear that Eiddig represents the type of wealthy burgess (mostly English but also Welsh) who invested money in land, in the absence of any other opportunities for investment, but who lacked the 'instinctive'

love of land which the *uchelwyr* liked to imagine was their own distinctive characteristic. Dafydd's constant satire of urban figures with no appreciation of the countryside works to contrast materialistic acquisition of land with the 'genuine' love of land which is supposedly the prerogative of the hereditary nobility. This is yet another way in which Dafydd tries to keep a clear distance between the *uchelwyr* and the wealthy bourgeoisie.

27 Dafydd's references to florins, which occur in GDG 44 as well as in GDG 23, have been discussed by D.S. Jones, ' "Fflwring aur" Dafydd ap Gwilym', *Bulletin of the Board of Celtic Studies*, 19 (1960–2), 29–33.

28 Parry has a note explaining some of the legal terms in this poem. See GDG p.508.

29 The same description of the man in the moon is found in the Middle English poem 'The Man in the Moon', G.L. Brook, *The Harley Lyrics* (Manchester University Press, 1968), no.30.

30 Joseph Bédier, *Les Chansons de Colin Muset* (Champion, Paris, 1912), no. 10.

31 Helen Waddell, *Medieval Latin Lyrics* (Constable & Co, London, 1933), 144.

32 Paul Zumthor, *Langue et technique poétiques à l'époque romane* (Klincksieck, Paris, 1963), 156.

33 Brook, op. cit., no.25.

34 'The New Love Poetry', in B. Ó Cuív (ed.), *Seven Centuries of Irish Learning* (Dublin, 1961), 109–11.

35 'Serch Cwrtais mewn Llenyddiaeth Wyddeleg', in J. Rowlands (ed.), *Dafydd ap Gwilym a Chanu Serch yr Oesoedd Canol* (Gwasg Prifysgol Cymru, Caerdydd, 1975), 18–42.

36 The poems have been edited by T.F. O'Rahilly, *Dánta Grádha* (Cork University Press, Dublin, Cork, 1926).

37 The old man laments his lack of love in 'Cân yr Henwr' in Ifor Williams (ed.), *Canu Llywarch Hen* (Gwasg Prifysgol Cymru, Caerdydd, 1970) (reprint), 8ff.

38 On this folk-poetry see Sean Ó Tuama, *An Grá in Amhráin na nDaoine* (Dublin, 1960).

CHAPTER 7

1 The duties of the *clerwr* are defined in the Bardic Grammar as 'to entreat, to satirize, and to put to shame'. See G.J. Williams and E.J. Jones, *Gramadegau'r Penceirddiaid* (Gwasg Prifysgol Cymru, Caerdydd, 1934), 17. On Dafydd's use of the word *clêr* see Rachel Bromwich, *Dafydd ap Gwilym* (Writers of Wales, University of Wales Press, Cardiff, 1974), 27–8.

2 For the social and historical background, see William Rees, *South Wales and the March 1284–1415* (Oxford University Press, 1924); R.R. Davies, *Lordship and Society in the March of Wales 1282–1400* (Clarendon Press, Oxford, 1978) and *Conquest, Co-existence and Change* (University of Wales Press, Cardiff, 1987), especially 412–30.

3 GDG 132, 142, 35, 58, 138, 136, 137, 113, 99, 94, 48, 105.

4 GDG 68, 26, 22, 130, 61, 65, 91, 127, 145, 70, 89, 64, 66, 125.

5 GDG 36, 63, 115, 33, 47, 41, 129, 77, 141.

6 GDG 134, 135, 80, 126, 128, 124.

7 For example, GDG 72, 75, 143, 54, 40, 93, 85, 73, 81.

8 Ifor Williams argued for the identification of the *clêr* with the *clerici vagantes*, or wandering scholars, and claimed that Dafydd was a member of the *clêr*, that is, a secular cleric ('Dafydd ap Gwilym a'r Glêr', *Transactions of the Honourable Society of Cymmrodorion*, (1913–14), 83–204). Theodor Chotzen equated the *clêr* with the native class of low-grade poets, the *clerwyr*, mentioned in the Bardic Grammar (*Recherches sur la poésie de Dafydd ap Gwilym* (H.J., Paris, Amsterdam, 1927), 70ff.). Rachel Bromwich accepts *clêr* as a generic term for popular poets in Wales who supplied much of Dafydd's material, mainly in oral form ('Dafydd ap Gwilym: Y Traddodiad Islenyddol', in J. Rowlands (ed.), *Dafydd ap Gwilym a Chanu Serch yr Oesoedd Canol* (Gwasg Prifysgol Cymru, Caerdydd, 1975), 45). Parry points out that the word *clêr* does not occur at all before the fourteenth century but may have been borrowed from Irish *cléir* at an earlier period (GDG pp.439–41). The low grade attributed to the *clerwyr* and *clêr* in the Bardic Grammar apparently reflects an older situation, since court bards of the fourteenth century, such as Dafydd himself, sometimes refer to themselves non-pejoratively as *clêr*.

9 For some examples, see C.C. Abbott, *Early Medieval French Lyrics* (Constable & Co, London, 1932), 202–9, although at least one of these is a translation from a Latin song. Drinking songs are also preserved in Anglo-Norman; see Dominica Legge, *Anglo-Norman Literature and its Background* (Clarendon Press, Oxford, 1963), 350.

10 The importance of Norman settlements in Wales as a linguistic link between Wales and England is discussed by Marie Surridge, 'Romance Linguistic Influence on Middle Welsh', *Studia Celtica*, 1 (1966), 63–92.

11 The ways in which English words were borrowed into Welsh are described by T.H. Parry-Williams, *The English Element in Welsh* (Honourable Society of Cymmrodorion, London, 1923). Such borrowings are associated with the popular poetry of the *clerwyr* since they appear in the satirical poems of the later *gogynfeirdd*: 'This suggests that English words and expressions were mainly used by the lower order of bards, whose works were restricted, according to the Codes, to lampoon and caricature. It also implies that English words were finding their way to the colloquial language and were being assimilated in considerable numbers' (Parry-Williams, ibid., 5).

12 The role of the friars in England in bringing literature to the people through their miscellanies is discussed by Derek Pearsall, *Old and Middle English Poetry* (Routledge and Kegan Paul, London, 1977), 94ff. See also G.R. Owst, *Literature and Pulpit in Medieval England* (Cambridge University Press, 1933), 7–10, and A. Williams, 'Chaucer and the Friars', *Speculum*, 28 (1953), 499–513. Dafydd's attitude to friars is described by Glanmor Williams, *The Welsh Church from Conquest to Reformation* (University of Wales Press, Cardiff, 1962), 178ff. For a description of the life of wandering clerics, see M.W. Labarge, *Medieval Travellers* (W.W. Norton & Co., New York, 1982).

13 Glyn Roberts describes the role played by the friars, particularly the Dominicans of north Wales, during negotiations between Wales and England before 1282, and their allegiance to the English king as well as their service to Llywelyn ap Gruffydd. He says: 'There can be no doubt, however, that when Edward launched his first campaign against Llywelyn in 1276–7, the Bangor friars were on the English side' (*Aspects of Welsh History* (University of Wales Press, Cardiff, 1969), 221).

14 For a survey of poems on this topic, in French and Latin, see Charles Oulmont, *Les Débats du clerc et du chevalier dans la littérature poétique du moyen-âge* (Slatkine Reprints, Geneva, 1974). Peter Dronke suggests that 'there was presumably always a certain amount of historical truth in this rivalry (even at times when we have no evidence of the kind afforded by the Latin and French debate-poems), as well as a certain amount of keeping the legend alive' (*Medieval Latin and the Rise of European Love-Lyric* (Clarendon Press, Oxford, 1965–6), vol.1, 230 n.2).

15 The Latin poem is discussed by R.S. Haller, 'The "Altercatio Phyllidis et Florae" as an Ovidian Satire', *Medieval Studies*, 30 (1968), 119–33. The Middle English poem *The Owl and the Nightingale* also seems to favour the arguments of the clerical Owl, but the whole poem can be interpreted as a defence of secular love-poetry which coincides with Dafydd's views on the value of love-poetry. See J.W.H. Atkins, *English Literary Criticism—The Medieval Phase* (Peter Smith, Gloucester, Mass., 1961), 143ff.

16   D.J. Bowen sees the poem as a reference to the contemporary political situation, which points to the year 1346 as its date of composition, the year of the Battle of Crécy ('Dafydd ap Gwilym a Datblygiad y Cywydd', *Llên Cymru*, 8 (1964), 27). Rachel Bromwich suggests that the poem provides evidence of the influence of French debate-poems on Dafydd's work ('Dafydd ap Gwilym: Y Traddodiad Islenyddol', 47).

17   GDG 136, 137, 138. On these and others which mock Church ritual, see Glanmor Williams, op. cit., 190ff. The anti-feminist attitude held by the Church is described by G.R. Owst, op. cit., 375ff.

18   This hostility was manifested in ecclesiastical writings which antedate the earliest surviving vernacular secular lyrics of the medieval period. See F.M. Warren, 'The Romance Lyric from the standpoint of Antecedent Latin Documents', *PMLA*, 26 (1911), 280–314.

19   There are precedents in French poetry for this motif of the church as a meeting place. See R. Bromwich, *Tradition and Innovation in the Poetry of Dafydd ap Gwilym* (University of Wales Press, Cardiff, 1972), 26.

20   On the story of Gwyn ap Nudd and Creiddylad, see Alwyn and Brinley Rees, *Celtic Heritage* (Thames and Hudson, London, 1973), 285. This legend also connects Gwyn with forces of darkness and winter struggling to gain control of Creiddylad, pointing to its origins in an ancient fertility myth. See Stephen Knight, *Arthurian Literature and Society* (Macmillan, London, 1983), 18.

21   Elias Owen refers to the popular Welsh belief that the Owl was a sign of ill-luck (*Welsh Folk-Lore* (E.P. Publishing, Wakefield, 1976, reprint), 327). E.G. Stanley comments on a similar tradition underlying *The Owl and the Nightingale*: 'The cry of the owl is a sinister omen, but the nightingale's song brings joy' (*The Owl and the Nightingale* (Nelson, London, 1960), 33).

22   The fox was regarded as a type of vermin, which explains the urge to destroy it. See Elias Owen, op. cit., 193. This *cywydd* contains Dafydd's only reference to *carol*, borrowed directly from the English word, which means he knew of this popular-song form, either in English or French versions.

23   Rachel Bromwich refers to this poem as the most convincing example of Dafydd's use of a generic type borrowed from continental poetry, in this case the *sérénade* ('Dafydd ap Gwilym: Y Traddodiad Islenyddol', 50). If the poem really belongs to that genre, it is clearly a parody rather than an imitation.

24   This scene in the poem is very reminiscent of the story of Pyramus and Thisbe, two lovers who try to kiss through a chink in the wall. This story comes from Ovid's *Metamorphoses*, but is also found in a twelfth-century French version which may have been more accessible to Dafydd. See Edmond Faral, *Recherches sur les sources Latines des contes et romans courtois du moyen-âge* (Champion, Paris, 1913), 5–33.

25 On this poem and a French parallel, see Iorwerth C. Peate, 'Dafydd ap Gwilym a Jean Froissart', *Llên Cymru*, 5 (1958–9), 119–21.

26 On the bird debates and Continental traditions, see R. Bromwich, *Tradition and Innovation*, 36ff.; 'Dafydd ap Gwilym: Y Traddodiad Islenyddol', 46ff; D.J. Bowen, 'Bardd Glyn Teifi', *Y Traethodydd*, 131 (1976), 140–1.

27 The motif of the birds' productivity and the poet's sorrow is common to the *reverdie* genre. Other examples include the Latin poem 'Levis exsurgit zephirus' (H. Waddell, *Medieval Latin Lyrics* (Constable & Co, London, 1933), 156); the Middle English lyric 'Alysoun' (G.L. Brook, *The Harley Lyrics* (Manchester University Press, 1968), 33); and Chaucer's *Parlement of Foules*.

28 Glanmor Williams suggests that the magpie's plumage is reminiscent of a cleric's robes and that Dafydd is mocking the voice of the Church preaching abstinence and virtue (Glanmor Williams, op. cit., 194).

29 Although a simplistic distinction between a land-based Welsh nobility and a town-based bourgeoisie cannot be entirely substantiated, there is every reason to suppose that the *uchelwyr* disliked the English-dominated towns even while depending on them as suppliers of the consumer items which characterized the *uchelwyr* lifestyle (see R.R. Davies, *Conquest, Coexistence and Change* (University of Wales Press, Cardiff, 1987), 417). Dafydd's rejection of materialist values, through satire, actually functions to disguise an embracing of such values by the nobility.

30 It is difficult to read this poem as anything other than a satire, or at least as a piece of conscious irony, since Newborough was one of the English plantation towns under the Edwardian settlement (M. Beresford, *New Towns of the Middle Ages* (Lutterworth Press, London, 1967), 49) and therefore a place where the native Welsh were at best regarded as 'foreigners'. R.R. Davies supplies this quotation: ' "Our town was established", so the burgesses of Newborough (co. Anglesey) reminded the Black Prince rather obsequiously in 1347, "for the habitation of Englishmen" ' (*Lordship and Society in the March of Wales 1282–1400* (Clarendon Press, Oxford, 1978), 325). Even though Welshmen increasingly established themselves in the towns during the fourteenth century (about half the burgesses of Aberystwyth were Welshmen by 1330 according to R.R. Davies, *Conquest, Co-existence and Change* (op. cit.), 421), it is hard to imagine Dafydd paying a sincere tribute—in Welsh— to a town specifically created to entrench the English and displace the Welsh inhabitants of Rhosfyr (Rhosfair), the original settlement.

31 E.J. Kenney (ed.), *P. Ovidi Nasonis: Amores, Ars Amatoria, Remedia Amoris* (Oxford University Press, 1961), *Amores* Book 2, 19, 11. 1–4.

32 The topical references in this poem have helped in its dating, and D.J. Bowen concludes that it was composed either in 1346 or in 1351–2 ('Dafydd ap Gwilym a Datblygiad y Cywydd', 27). See also Bowen's

discussion of the poem in 'Bardd Glyn Teifi', 143–4, where he suggests that this expedition to France could have been a means by which Dafydd received literary influences from the Continent.

33   On this name see Parry, GDG xxviii.

34   Ernest Langlois, *Le Roman de la Rose* (Paris, 1914–24), 11. 9441–54.

35   On the historical evidence for Bwa Bach, see David Jenkins, 'Enwau Personau a Lleoedd yng Nghywyddau Dafydd ap Gwilym', *Bulletin of the Board of Celtic Studies*, 8 (1935–7), 140–5.

36   Eurys Rowlands, 'Iolo Goch', in J. Carney and D. Greene (eds.), *Celtic Studies: Essays in Memory of Angus Matheson* (London, 1968), 133.

37   Ibid., 133–4.

38   Such hostility would not, in any case, be directed towards the English nobility, since it was through them that the *uchelwyr* derived most of their power. R.R. Davies has described how the English overlords readily delegated power to the native squires who were the accepted leaders of their communities (*Conquest, Co-Existence and Change*, 417).

Bibliography

Abbott, C.C.
Early Medieval French Lyrics (Constable & Co., London, 1932).

Allen, P.S.
The Romanesque Lyric (University of North Carolina Press, Chapel Hill, 1928).
Medieval Latin Lyrics (University of Chicago Press, Illinois, 1931).

Alter, Jean V.
Les Origines de la satire anti-bourgeoise en France: moyen-âge-XVIe siècle (Librairie Droz, Geneva, 1966).

Atkins, J.W.H.
English Literary Criticism: The Medieval Phase (Peter Smith, Gloucester, Mass., 1961).

Audiau, Jean
La Pastourelle dans la poésie occitane du moyen-âge (E. de Boccard, Paris, 1923).
Les Troubadours et l'Angleterre (Paris, 1927).

Bakhtin, Mikhail
Rabelais and his world (trans. by Hélène Iswolsky) (M.I.T. Press, Cambridge, 1968).

Bédier, Joseph
Les Fabliaux (Librairie Emile Bouillon, Paris, 1895).
'Les Fêtes de Mai et les commencements de la poésie lyrique au moyen-âge', *Revue des Deux Mondes*, 135 (1896), 146–72.
Les Chansons de Colin Muset, (Champion, Paris, 1912).

Bell, H.I.
The Development of Welsh Poetry (Clarendon Press, Oxford, 1936).

Beresford, Maurice
New Towns of the Middle Ages (Lutterworth Press, London, 1967).

Berry, André — *Florilège des troubadours* (Librairie Firmin-Didot, Paris, 1930).

Bischoff, Bernard — *Carmina Burana, Faksimile-Ausgabe der Handschrift Clm 4660 und Clm 4660a* (Institute of Medieval Music Ltd., New York, 1967).

Bloch, Marc — *La Société Féodale* (2 vols.) (Paris, 1949).

Boase, Roger — *The Origin and Meaning of Courtly Love* (Manchester University Press, 1977).

Bowen, D.J. — 'Dafydd ap Gwilym a Datblygiad y Cywydd', *Llên Cymru*, 8 (1964), 1–32.
'Bardd Glyn Teifi', *Y Traethodydd*, 131 (1976), 133–48.

Brittain, F. — *The Medieval Latin and Romance Lyric* (Cambridge University Press, 1937).

Brody, Saul N. — 'The Comic Rejection of Courtly Love', in Joan M. Ferrante and George D. Economou, (eds.), *In Pursuit of Perfection* (Kennikat Press, New York, 1975), 221–57.

Bromwich, Rachel — 'Some remarks on the Celtic sources of Tristan', *Transactions of the Honourable Society of Cymmrodorion*, (1953), 32–60.
'Celtic Dynastic Themes and the Breton Lays', *Etudes Celtiques*, 9 (1960–1), 439–74.
Tradition and Innovation in the Poetry of Dafydd ap Gwilym (University of Wales Press, Cardiff, 1972).
'Influences upon Dafydd ap Gwilym's Poetry', *Poetry Wales*, 8 no.4 (Spring 1973), 44–55.
Dafydd ap Gwilym, Writers of Wales Series (University of Wales Press, Cardiff, 1974).
'Dafydd ap Gwilym: Y Traddodiad Islenyddol' in John Rowlands (ed.), *Dafydd ap Gwilym a Chanu Serch yr Oesoedd Canol* (Gwasg Prifysgol Cymru, Caerdydd, 1975), 43–57.
'Gwaith Einion Offeiriad a Barddoniaeth Dafydd ap Gwilym', *Ysgrifau Beirniadol*, 10 (1977), 157–80.
Trioedd Ynys Prydein (University of Wales Press, Cardiff, 1978) (2nd edn.).

'Cyfeiriadau Dafydd ap Gwilym at Chwedl a Rhamant', *Ysgrifau Beirniadol*, 12 (1982), 57–76.

Brook, G.L.   *The Harley Lyrics* (Manchester University Press, 1968).

Burke, Peter   *Popular Culture in Early Modern Europe* (Temple Smith, London, 1978).

Cazel, Fred A.   *Feudalism and Liberty: Articles and Addresses of Sidney Painter* (The Johns Hopkins Press, Baltimore, 1961).

Chambers, E.K.   *The Medieval Stage* (2 vols.) (Oxford University Press, 1903).

Chaytor, Henry J.   *The Troubadours and England* (Cambridge University Press, 1923).

Chotzen, T.M.   *Recherches sur la poésie de Dafydd ap Gwilym* (H.J., Paris, Amsterdam, 1927).

Clancy, Joseph P.   *The Earliest Welsh Poetry* (Macmillan, London, 1970).

Conran, Anthony   *The Penguin Book of Welsh Verse* (Penguin Books Ltd., Harmondsworth, 1967).

Contamine, Philippe (ed.),   *La Noblesse au moyen-âge, XIe–Xve siècles* (Presses Universitaires de France, Paris, 1976).
La Vie Quotidienne pendant la Guerre de Cent Ans: France et Angleterre, XIVe siècle (Hachette, Paris, 1976).

Coppin, Joseph   *Amour et mariage dans la littérature française du Nord au moyen-âge* (Librairie d'Argences, Paris, 1961).

Cowell, E.   'Dafydd ap Gwilym', *Y Cymmrodor*, 2 (1878), 101–32.

Curtius, E.   *European Literature and the Latin Middle Ages* (Pantheon, New York, 1953).

Davies, Gareth   'The Poetry of the Welsh *Cywydd*', *Proceedings of the Leeds Philosophical and Literary Society*, 14 (1972), 281–92.

Davies, R.R.   'Cymru yn oes Dafydd ap Gwilym' in John
Rowlands (ed.), *Dafydd ap Gwilym a Chanu
Serch yr Oesoedd Canol* (Gwasg Prifysgol
Cymru, Caerdydd, 1975) 58–75.
*Lordship and Society in the March of Wales
1282–1400* (Clarendon Press, Oxford,
1978).
*Conquest, Co-existence and Change: Wales
1063–1415* (Clarendon Press, Oxford and
University of Wales Press, Cardiff, 1987).

Davies, Wendy   *Wales in the Early Middle Ages* (Leicester
University Press, 1982).

Dejeanne, J.M.L.   *Poésies complètes du troubadour Marcabru*
(Librairie Edouard Privat, Toulouse, 1909).

Dragonetti, Roger   *La Technique poétique des trouvères dans la
chanson courtoise* (De Tempel, Brugge,
1960).

Dronke, Peter   *Medieval Latin and the Rise of European Love-
Lyric* (2 vols.) (Clarendon Press, Oxford,
1965–6).
The Medieval Lyric (Hutchinson, London,
1968).
'Serch *fabliau* a serch *cwrtais*', in John
Rowlands (ed.), *Dafydd ap Gwilym a Chanu
Serch yr Oesoedd Canol* (Gwasg Prifysgol
Cymru, Caerdydd, 1975), 1–17.

Duby, Georges   *The Chivalrous Society* (trans. by Cynthia
Postan) (Edward Arnold, London, 1977).
*The Knight, the Lady and the Priest: The
Making of Modern Marriage in Medieval
France* (trans. by Barbara Bray) (Allen
Lane, London, 1984).

Eisner, Sigmund   *The Tristan Legend: A Study in Sources*
(Northwestern University Press, Evanston,
Illinois, 1969).

Evans, J. Gwenogvryn *The Poetry in the Red Book of Hergest*
(Llanbedrog, 1911).

Evans, K.A.   'Cerddi'r Gogynfeirdd i Rianedd a
Gwragedd', (MA Thesis, University of
Wales, Aberystwyth, 1972).

Faral, Edmond — *Les jongleurs en France au moyen-âge* (Champion, Paris, 1910).
Recherches sur les sources latines des contes et romans courtois du moyen-âge (Champion, Paris, 1913).
'Les Débats du clerc et du chevalier', *Recherches sur les sources Latines des contes et romans courtois du moyen-âge* (Champion, Paris, 1913).
'Le Roman de la Rose', *Revue des Deux Mondes*, 35 (1926), 430–457.

Ferrante, Joan M. and Economou, George D. — *In Pursuit of Perfection: Courtly Love in Medieval Literature* (National University Publications, Kennikat Press, New York, 1975).

Fleming, John V. — *The Roman de la Rose: A Study in Allegory and Iconography* (Princeton University Press, New Jersey, 1969).

Gaselee, Stephen — *The Transition from the Late Latin Lyric to the Medieval Love Poem* (Cambridge, 1931).

Goetinck, Glenys Witchard — *Historia Peredur vab Efrawc* (Gwasg Prifysgol Cymru, Caerdydd, 1976).

Gruffydd, W.J. — 'Rhagarweiniad i Farddoniaeth Cymru cyn Dafydd ap Gwilym', *Transactions of the Honourable Society of Cymmrodorion*, (1937), 257–83.

Greene, R.L. — *The Early English Carols* (Clarendon Press, Oxford, 1935).

Gunn, Alan M.F. — *The Mirror of Love: A Reinterpretation of 'The Romance of the Rose'* (Lubbock, Texas, 1952).

Haller, R.S. — 'The "Altercatio Phyllidis et Florae" as an Ovidian Satire', *Medieval Studies*, 30 (1968), 119–33.

Hanford, J.H. — 'The Progenitors of Golias', *Speculum*, 1 (1926), 38–58.

Hatto, A.T. — *Eos, An Enquiry into the Theme of Lovers' Meetings and Partings at Dawn in Poetry* (Mouton & Co., The Hague, 1965).

Highet, Gilbert   *The Classical Tradition* (Clarendon Press, Oxford, 1936).

Hill, Raymond T. and *Anthology of the Provençal Troubadours* (2 Bergin, Thomas G.   vols.) (Yale University Press, New Haven, 1973) (rev. edn.).

Hilka, Alfons and   *Carmina Burana* (3 vols.) (Carl Winter's Uni-Schumann, Otto   versitatsbuchhandlung, Heidelberg, 1930–41).

Hilton, R.H. (ed.),   *The Transition from Feudalism to Capitalism* (NLB, London, 1976).

Hodgett, Gerald A.   *A Social and Economic History of Medieval Europe* (Methuen & Co. Ltd., London, 1972).

Hoyt, Robert S.   *Europe in the Middle Ages* (Rupert Hart-Davis, London, 1957).

Hull, Vernam   *Longes mac n-Uislenn* (Oxford University Press, 1949).

Jackson, K.H.   *The International Popular Tale and Early Welsh Tradition* (University of Wales Press, Cardiff, 1961).
Early Welsh Gnomic Poems (University of Wales Press, Cardiff, 1961).

Jarman, A.O.H. and   *A Guide to Welsh Literature* (2 vols.) Hughes, G.R.   (Christopher Davies, Swansea, 1976 and 1980).

Jeanroy, Alfred   *Les origines de la poésie lyrique en France au moyen-âge* (Champion, Paris, 1925).

Jenkins, David   'Enwau Personau a Lleoedd yng Nghywyddau Dafydd ap Gwilym', *Bulletin of the Board of Celtic Studies*, 8 (1935–7), 140–5.

Jenkins, D. and   *The Welsh Law of Women* (University of Owen, M.E.   Wales Press, Cardiff, 1980).

Johnston, R.C. and   *Fabliaux* (Basil Blackwell, Oxford, 1965). Owen, D.D.R.

Jones, Dewi Stephen   ' "Fflwring aur" Dafydd ap Gwilym', *Bulletin of the Board of Celtic Studies*, 19 (1960–2), 29–33.

Jones, George F. *Walther von der Wogelweide* (Twayne Publishers Inc., New York, 1968).

Jones, R.M. *Llên Cymru a Chrefydd* (Christopher Davies, Abertawe, 1977).

Jones, T. Gwynn *Rhieingerddi'r Gogynfeirdd* (Dinbych, 1915). 'A "Court of Love" Poem in Welsh', *Aberystwyth Studies*, 4 (1922), 85–96.

Jones, W. Lewis 'The Literary Relationships of Dafydd ap Gwilym', *Transactions of the Honourable Society of Cymmrodorion*, (1907–8), 118–53.

Jones, W.P. *The Pastourelle* (Octagon Books, New York, 1973).

Jusserand, J.J. *English Wayfaring Life in the Middle Ages* (trans. L.T. Smith) (T. Fisher Unwin, London, 1897).

Kenney, E.J. *P. Ovidi Nasonis: Amores, Ars Amatoria, Remedia Amoris* (Oxford, 1961).

Kelly, H.A. *Love and Marriage in the Age of Chaucer* (Cornell University Press, 1975).

Knight, Stephen *Arthurian Literature and Society* (Macmillan, London, 1983).

Koehler, Erich 'Observations historiques et sociologiques sur la poésie des troubadours', *Cahiers de civilisation médiévale*, 7 (1964), 27–51.

Labarge, Margaret Wade *Medieval Travellers* (W.W. Norton & Co., New York, 1982).

Lafitte-Houssat, Jacques *Troubadours et cours d'amour* (Presses Universitaires de France, Paris, 1971).

Langlois, Ernest *Le Roman de la Rose* (5 vols.) (Librairie de Firmin-Didot et Cie, Paris, 1914–24).

Lanly, André *Le Roman de la Rose* (Club de Livre, Paris, 1977).

Lazar, Moshé *Amour courtois et 'fin' amors' dans la littérature du XIÎ siècle* (Klincksieck, Paris, 1964).

Legge, Dominica   *Anglo-Norman Literature and its Background* (Clarendon Press, Oxford, 1963).

Lewis, C.S.   *The Allegory of Love* (Clarendon Press, Oxford, 1936).

Lewis, Henry   *Chwedleu Seith Doethon Rufein* (Gwasg Prifysgol Cymru, Caerdydd, 1967).
Hen Gerddi Crefyddol (Gwasg Prifysgol Cymru, Caerdydd, 1974).

Lindsay, Jack   *Medieval Latin Poets* (Elkin Mathews & Marrot Ltd., London, 1934).

Lloyd-Jones, J.   *The Court Poets of the Welsh Princes*, Sir John Rhŷs Memorial Lecture (British Academy, London, 1948).

Lucas, Angela M.   *Women in the Middle Ages: Religion, Marriage and Letters* (Harvester Press, 1983).

Mann, Jill   'Satiric Subject and Satiric Object in Goliardic Literature', *Mittellateinisches Jahrbuch*, 15 (1980), 63–86.

Meyer, Richard M.   'Alte Deutsche Volksliedchen', *Zeitschrift für Deutsches Alterthum und Deutsche Litteratur* 29 (1885), 121–236.

Moore, Arthur K.   *The Secular Lyric in Middle English* (Greenwood Press, Connecticut, 1970).

Moret, André   *Les Débuts du lyrisme en Allemagne* (Bibliothèque Universitaire, Lille, 1951).

Morris-Jones, J. and Parry-Williams, T.H.   *Llawysgrif Hendregadredd* (Gwasg Prifysgol Cymru, Caerdydd, 1971).

Moser, H. and Tervooren, H.   *Des Minnesangs Frühling* (2 vols.) (S. Hirzel, Stuttgart, 1977).

Muir, Lynette   *Literature and Society in Medieval France: The Mirror and the Image, 1100-1500* (New Studies in Medieval History, Macmillan, 1985).

Murphy, Gerard   *Early Irish Lyrics* (Clarendon Press, Oxford, 1970).

Muscatine, Charles — *Chaucer and the French Tradition* (University of California Press, 1957).

Neilson, W.A. — *The Origins and Sources of the 'Court of Love'* (Russell and Russell, New York, 1967) (first published 1899).

Nykrog, Per — *Les Fabliaux* (Ejnar Munksgaard, Copenhagen, 1957).

Ó Cuív, Brian (ed.) — *Seven Centuries of Irish Learning* (Stationery Office, Dublin, 1961).

O'Rahilly, T.F. — *Dánta Grádha* (Cork University Press, Dublin and Cork, 1926).

Ó Tuama, Sean — *An Grá in Amhráin na nDaoine* (Dublin, 1960). 'The New Love Poetry' in Brian Ó Cuiv (ed.), *Seven Centuries of Irish Learning*, 102–20. 'Serch Cwrtais mewn Llenyddiaeth Wyddeleg' in John Rowlands (ed.), *Dafydd ap Gwilym a Chanu Serch yr Oesoedd Canol*, (Gwasg Prifysgol Cymru, Caerdydd, 1975), 18–42.

Oulmont, Charles — *Les Débats du clerc et du chevalier dans la littérature poétique du moyen-âge* (Slatkine Reprints, Geneva, 1974) (first published 1911).

Owen, Elias — *Welsh Folk-Lore* (E.P. Publishing Ltd., Wakefield, 1976).

Owst, G.R. — *Literature and Pulpit in Medieval England* (Cambridge University Press, 1933).

Paris, Gaston — 'Lancelot du Lac: Le Conte de la Charrette', *Romania*, 12 (1883), 459–534. *Mélanges de littérature Française du moyen-âge* (Champion, Paris, 1912).

Parry, Thomas — 'Dafydd ap Gwilym', *Yorkshire Celtic Studies*, 5 (1949–52), 19–31. *A History of Welsh Literature* (trans. H.I. Bell) (Clarendon Press, 1955). *The Oxford Book of Welsh Verse* (Oxford University Press, 1962). *Gwaith Dafydd ap Gwilym* (Gwasg Prifysgol Cymru, Caerdydd, 1963).

Parry-Williams, T.H.   *The English Element in Welsh* (Honourable Society of Cymmrodorion, London, 1923).

Pearsall, Derek   *Old English and Middle English Poetry* (Routledge and Kegan Paul, London, 1977).

Peate, Iorwerth C.   'Dafydd ap Gwilym a Jean Froissart', *Llên Cymru*, 5 (1958–9), 119–21.

Pfaff, Fridrich   *Der Minnesang des 12. bis 14. Jahrhunderts: vol.2, Walther von der Wogelweide* (Union Deutsche Verlagsgesellschaft, Stuttgart, 1894).

Piguet, Edgar   *L'Evolution de la pastourelle du XIÎ siècle à nos jours* (Société Suisse des traditions populaires, Basle, 1927).

Postan, M.M.   *The Medieval Economy and Society* (Weidenfeld and Nicolson, 1972).

Pounds, N.J.G.   *An Economic History of Medieval Europe* (London, 1976).

Power, Eileen   *Medieval Women* (Cambridge University Press, 1975).

Press, Alan R.   'The Adulterous Nature of *Fin' Amors*: a Re-Examination of the Theory', *Forum for Modern Language Studies*, 6 (1970), 327–41.
    Anthology of Troubadour Lyric Poetry (Edinburgh University Press, 1971).

Pughe, Owen W.(ed.)   *The Myvyrian Archaeology of Wales* (Denbigh, 1870).

Raby, F.J.E.   *A History of Secular Latin Poetry in the Middle Ages* (2 vols.) (Clarendon Press, Oxford, 1957).

Rand, E.K.   'The Classics in the Thirteenth Century', *Speculum*, 4 (1929), 249–69.

Rees, Alwyn and Brinley   *Celtic Heritage* (Thames and Hudson, London, 1973).

Rees, William   *South Wales and the March 1284–1415* (Oxford University Press, 1924).

Reiss, Edmund	'Chaucer's Courtly Love' in Larry D. Benson (ed.), *The Learned and the Lewed* (Harvard University Press, 1974), 95–112.
Reuter, Timothy (ed. and trans.)	*The Medieval Nobility: Studies on the Ruling Classes of France and Germany from the 6th to the 12th century* (North-Holland Publishing Co., Amsterdam, New York, Oxford, 1979).
Richey, M.F.	*Medieval German Lyrics* (Oliver and Boyd, London, 1958).
Robbins, Harry W.	*The Romance of the Rose* (Dutton, New York, 1962).
Robbins, R.H.	'The Middle English Court Love Lyric', in W.T.M. Jackson (ed.), *The Interpretation of Medieval Lyric Poetry* (Macmillan, London, 1980), 205–32.
Roberts, Glyn	'Nodiadau ar y Traddodiad Moliant a'r Cywydd', *Llên Cymru*, 7 (1962), 217–43.
	Aspects of Welsh History (University of Wales Press, Cardiff, 1969).
	'The Dominican Friary of Bangor', in *Aspects of Welsh History*, 215–39.
	'Wales and England: Antipathy and Sympathy 1282–1485', in *Aspects of Welsh History*, 295–318.
Rowlands, Eurys	'Iolo Goch', J. Carney and D. Greene (eds.), *Celtic Studies: Essays in Memory of Angus Matheson* (London, 1968), 124–46.
	Poems of the Cywyddwyr (Dublin Institute for Advanced Studies, 1976).
Rowlands, John	'Delweddau Serch Dafydd ap Gwilym', *Ysgrifau Beirniadol*, 2 (1966), 58–76.
	'Morfudd fel yr Haul', *Ysgrifau Beirniadol*, 6 (1966), 16–44.
	(ed.) *Dafydd ap Gwilym a Chanu Serch yr Oesoedd Canol* (Gwasg Prifysgol Cymru, Caerdydd, 1975).
Rychner, Jean	*Contribution à l'étude des fabliaux*, II (Université de Neuchatel, Librairie E. Droz, Geneva, 1960).

Sayce, Olive — *Poets of the Minnesang* (Clarendon Press, Oxford, 1967).

Scheludko, Dmitri — 'Zur Geschichte des Natureingang bei den Trobadors', *Zeitschrift für Französische Sprache und Litteratur*, 60 (1936–7), 257–334.

Shahar, Shulamith — *The Fourth Estate: A History of Women in the Middle Ages* (trans. by Chaya Galai) (Methuen, London and New York, 1983).

Sidgwick, Frank and Chambers, E.K. — *Early English Lyrics* (Sidgwick & Jackson, London, 1966) (first published 1907).

Southern, R.W. — *The Making of the Middle Ages* (Hutchinson University Library, London, 1953).

Spearing, A.C. — *Medieval Dream-Poetry* (Cambridge University Press, 1976).

Speirs, John — *Medieval English Poetry: The Non-Chaucerian Tradition* (Faber & Faber, London, 1957).

Stanley, E.G. — *The Owl and the Nightingale* (Nelson, London, 1960).

Strecker, Karl — *Die Cambridger Lieder* (Monumenta Germaniae Historica, Weidmann, Berlin, 1966).

Surridge, Marie — 'Romance Linguistic Influence on Middle Welsh', *Studia Celtica*, 1 (1966), 63–92.

Symonds, J.A. — *Wine, Women and Song* (Chatto & Windus, London, 1884) (reprinted by King's Classics 1907).

Thomas, Gwyn — *Y Traddodiad Barddol* (Gwasg Prifysgol Cymru, Caerdydd, 1976).

Tilley, Arthur — *Medieval France* (Cambridge University Press, 1922).

Topsfield, L.T. — *Troubadours and Love* (Cambridge University Press, 1975).

Valency, Maurice — *In Praise of Love* (Macmillan, New York, 1958).

Waddell, Helen	*The Wandering Scholars* (Constable & Co. Ltd, London, 1927). *Medieval Latin Lyrics* (Constable & Co. Ltd, London, 1933).
Walsh, P.G.	*Thirty Poems from the Carmina Burana* (Reading University Medieval and Renaissance Latin Texts, 1976).
Warren, F.M.	'The Romance Lyric from the standpoint of antecedent Latin Documents', *Proceedings of the Modern Language Association of America*, 26 (1911), 280–314.
Webster, Graham	*The British Celts and their Gods under Rome* (B.T. Batsford Ltd, London, 1986).
West, C.B.	*Courtoisie in Anglo-Norman Literature* (Haskell House, New York, 1966).
Whicher, George F.	*The Goliard Poets* (New Directions, New York, 1965).
Wilhelm, James J.	*The Cruelest Month* (Yale University Press, New Haven, 1965). *Seven Troubadours* (Pennsylvania State University Press, 1970).
Wilkinson, L.P.	*Ovid Recalled* (Cambridge University Press, 1955).
Williams, A.	'Chaucer and the Friars', *Speculum*, 28 (1953), 499–513.
Williams, Glanmor	*The Welsh Church from Conquest to Reformation* (University of Wales Press, Cardiff, 1962).
Williams, Gwyn	'Dafydd ap Gwilym: Poet of love', *Poetry Wales*, 8 (1973), 18–27.
Williams, G.J. and Jones, E.J.	*Gramadegau'r Penceirddiaid* (Gwasg Prifysgol Cymru, Caerdydd, 1934).
Williams, Ifor	'Dafydd ap Gwilym a'r Glêr', *Transactions of the Honourable Society of Cymmrodorion*, (1913–14), 83–204. *Canu Llywarch Hen* (Gwasg Prifysgol Cymru, Caerdydd, 1953).

Williams, Ifor and Roberts, Thomas — *Cywyddau Dafydd ap Gwilym a'i Gyfoeswyr* (Gwasg Prifysgol Cymru, Caerdydd, 1935) (2nd edn.).

Williams, J.E. Caerwyn — 'Beirdd y Tywysogion: Arolwg', *Llên Cymru*, 11 (1970), 3–94.
'Cerddi'r Gogynfeirdd i Wragedd a Merched, a'u Cefndir yng Nghymru a'r Cyfandir', *Llên Cymru*, 13 (1974–9), 3–112.
The Poets of the Welsh Princes, Writers of Wales Series (University of Wales Press, Cardiff, 1978).

Wimsatt, James — *Chaucer and the French Love Poets* (University of North Carolina Press, Chapel Hill, 1968).

Wright, F.A. and Sinclair, T.A. — *A History of Later Latin Literature* (Routledge, London, 1931).

Zeydel, Edwin H. — *Vagabond Verse, Secular Latin Poems of the Middle Ages* (Wayne State University Press, Detroit, 1966).

Zink, Michael — *La Pastourelle, Poésie et Folklore au Moyen Age* (Bordas, Paris, 1972).

Zumthor, Paul — *Langue et technique poétiques à l'époque romane, XIe–XIIIe siècles* (Klincksieck, Paris, 1963).
Essai de poétique médiévale (Editions du Seuil, Paris, 1972).

Index

from popular poetry, 28, 30, 31, 38, 50, 52, 62, 72, 80, 86–8
bourgeoisie, xii, 48–9, 62, 63, 66–70, 73, 106, 107, 187, 189, 190, 209, 211, 213–14, 221, 224–5, 228, 230, 246 n.26, 251 n.29
'Breichiau Morfudd' (GDG 53), 149, 155–6, 179, 218
'Breuddwyd Macsen', 245 n.6
Bromwich, Rachel, x–xi, 112, 147, 151, 152, 242 n.21, 243 n.28, 244 n.5, 245 n.6, 246 n.20, 248 n.8, 250 n.23
Bwa Bach, 119, 124, 167, 220, 224, 227

'Cae Bedw Madog' (GDG 31), 174
'Caer Rhag Cenfigen' (GDG 140), 143–4
Cambridge Songs, 30–1, 179
'Campau Bun' (GDG 56), 126, 149
canso, 23, 25, 77, 80, 108, 122
Canterbury Tales, 29, 33, 70
  Franklin's Tale, 188, 224
  Knight's Tale, 70
  Merchant's Tale, 70, 188
  Miller's Tale, 67, 70
  Wife of Bath's Tale, 70
canu rhydd, x, 146, 184
Carmina Burana, 32–40, 49, 51–2, 53, 55, 193, 241 n.16
carol, 48, 250 n.22
'Caru Merch Fonheddig' (GDG 37), 118–19
'Caru yn y Gaeaf' (GDG 145), 200–1
chanson à personnages, 50, 187
chanson de gestes, 3
chanson de mal mariée, 59–60, 63, 65, 187, 208
Chanson de Roland, 3
chanson de toile, 58, 59, 72
Chaucer, Geoffrey (see also Canterbury Tales), 29, 33, 67, 70, 74, 188, 224, 251 n.27
chivalry, 4, 7, 25, 106, 119
Chrétien de Troyes, 3, 149, 150
Church, attitude to itinerant clergy, 32
  attitude to love, 16–17, 18, 30, 64

as audience, 112
corruption of, 19, 33, 34
doctrine of, 18, 20, 33
and popular song, 49–50, 194
as social institution, 33, 34, 171, 187, 188–9, 191–2, 194–7
'Chwarae Cnau i'm Llaw' (GDG 50), 175–6
classical inheritance, 28–30, 38–9, 44, 45, 46, 243 n.32
clêr, xi, 186, 189, 190–2, 248 n.1, n.8
clerici vagantes (see also goliards), 32, 190, 248 n.8
Colin Muset, xi, 48, 54, 55–8, 74, 177–80.
Continental influence, ix–xii, 72, 76, 78, 79, 104–5, 107–9, 112, 114–15, 121, 126, 138–42, 152, 186, 189, 191, 231–2
cortezia, 7, 23, 186, 229
courtly love, 1, 3–5, 7, 16, 18, 20, 23, 25, 26, 44, 61, 62–3, 65, 73, 85, 98, 107, 114, 121, 136–8, 140, 149, 161, 177, 182, 184, 190, 223, 227, 230
  conflict of, 5, 8, 11, 14, 16, 18, 19, 21, 22, 25, 26, 35, 46, 83, 98, 101, 114, 122–3, 165, 229
  dual nature of, 9, 12, 25, 36, 56, 73, 100, 122–3, 129, 159, 223
  extended or 'popularized', xii, xiii, 55, 58, 62, 73–4, 177, 178, 184–5, 229–31
  and knighthood, 33, 106, 109
  and marriage, 29, 62–4, 65, 66–70, 74, 154, 188, 223–4
  and new nobility, 49, 61–3, 66, 73–4, 114–15, 136
  spiritual aspect of, 11, 13, 14, 18, 35, 235 n.27
court of love, 63, 103–4
courtoisie (cortoisie), 4, 7, 28, 62, 73, 119, 142, 180, 229
court-poetry, ix, 27, 39, 53, 54, 63
  European, xi, 1, 50–1, 122, 126, 131, 138–42, 156, 170, 182, 242 n.21
  French, see trouvères